The BOOK OF MORMON *and* The Constitution

H. VERLAN ANDERSEN

COMPILED AND PRESENTED
BY
HANS V. ANDERSEN, JR.

This book is not an official publication of The Church of Jesus Christ of Latter-day Saints. All opinions expressed herein are the author's and are not necessarily those of The Church of Jesus Christ of Latter-day Saints.

Daddy loved the Book of Mormon. He wrote this book to increase our awareness of our dependency on the living prophet as well as the Book of Mormon, a book for our day.

—Hans V. Andersen, Jr.

Order from:
Hans V. Andersen, Jr.
1724 South 165 West
Orem, UT 84058
(801) 224-3368

(Cover photo is of an original Book of Mormon.)

ISBN: 0-96445522-1-8
Library of Congress Catalog Card Number: 95-70298

SunRise Publishing
PO Box 1001
Orem, UT 84059
(800) 748-6766

Table of Contents

INTRODUCTION

Just as a wayward child fills the thoughts of a righteous parent with sorrow, and saps that parent's power, confidence and peace, a member who rejects President Benson by clinging to socialism brings a sapper into his own heart and mind for rejecting a prophet of God. The latter has the greater tragedy because he has control over his own faith, thoughts and beliefs. Rebellion against God's prophet is to reject God with a knowledge of our rejection. This is true of course, only for those who believe he is a prophet.

This lack of unity will break down our strength, our power, our confidence and cohesiveness as members of families, wards and the Church of Jesus Christ. Instead of seeing the rock cut without hands filling the earth we fall back to the prophecies of Nephi, Christ, Mormon and Moroni who saw us, warned us, talked of our individual apostasy from Christ's Church in the latter days and our being swept off. Our armor will turn to rice paper, our resolve will falter, and our apostate enemies will take courage in seeking to undo our prophet.

While the world cheers the apparent faltering of communism we too are tempted to join in, as if peace is about to be ushered in. Daddy realized the communists in Russia were not our greatest enemy, as does the prophet. Righteous nations have always been protected. Read the following words of President Benson who, according to the world, can't see what they see so clearly.

> I testify that wickedness is rapidly expanding in every segment of our society. (See D&C 1:14-16; 84:49-53.) It is more highly organized, more cleverly disguised, and more powerfully promoted than ever before. Secret combinations lusting for power, gain, and glory are flourishing. A secret combination that seeks to overthrow the freedom of all lands, nations, and countries is increasing its evil influence and control over America and the entire world. [See Ether 8:18-25] (*Ensign*, November 1988, p. 87)

Daddy agreed with the prophet. It's clear to all but those who reject the prophet that while many joined the world in celebrating the demise of communism, President Benson was making his strongest statements ever about our sad state of affair and the increasing power of the enemies of Christ. He, like Nephi on his tower (Helaman 8) was accusing us of joining with the Gadianton Robbers. Nobody believed him either, when he said they were ripening for destruction. His detractors talked of their great power as a nation, and pooh pooh'd the idea they had corrupted their laws and in doing so had joined with the Gadianton Robbers.

This was of particular interest to our family because as far back as we can remember, Daddy taught us the Book of Mormon was written for us who have it. In particular, he taught us the period of their history covering Alma, Helaman and the first part of 3rd Nephi are only a foreshadow of our own time leading up to the millennium, just as the Nephites had their shorter millennium. He taught us that their self-rule, their Church, their secret combinations, apostasy, their priestcraft etc. are laid out for all of us to see.

One of the things Daddy pointed out was that the Book of Mormon, between the Nephites and Jaredites covered over 3,000 years. Yet, over 40% of the pages of the Book of Mormon cover the relatively short period of 125 years before Christ came to the Nephites. This period of time, if it truly is a foreshadow of our day, is packed with information we need to study, apply to our own situation, and try to draw the applicable parallels. Where else in recorded history do we read of a people having at the same time: the gospel, self-rule, and a separation of church and state. Daddy has addressed these parallels in this book. He realized this was part of the message President Benson was trying to deliver in his constant reference to the Book of Mormon. One such reference follows.

> The record of the Nephite history just prior to the Savior's visit reveals many parallels to our own day as we anticipate the Savior's second coming. The Nephite civilization had reached great heights. They were prosperous and industrious. They had built many cities with great highways connecting them. They engaged in shipping and trade. They built temples and palaces. But, as so often happens, the people rejected the Lord. Pride became commonplace. Dishonesty and immorality were widespread. Secret combinations flourished because, as Helaman tells us, the Gadianton robbers 'had seduced the more part of the righteous until they had come down to believe in their works and partake of their spoils' (Hel. 6:38) 'The people began to be distinguished by ranks, according to their riches and their chances for learning' (3 Nephi 6:12) And 'Satan had great power, unto the stirring up of the people to do all manner of iniquity, and to the puffing them up with pride, tempting them to seek for power, and authority, and riches and the vain things of the world,' even as today (v. 15).
>
> Mormon noted that the Nephites 'did not sin ignorantly, for they knew the will of God concerning them' (v. 18) (*Ensign*, May 1987, p. 4)

President Benson used the term "parallels." This was a common belief of Daddy and the prophet's that went back many years. One of the letters to Daddy from President Benson illustrating this common belief years ago is at the end of this introduction. No doubt this is one reason President Benson urged Daddy over the years, to finish this book.

Another applicable quote on point, which also throws cold water on those basking in the *all is well* spirit, follows. Is President Benson talking to us, or are we supposed to suppose he's talking to someone else, and hope they hear it? What parallel could be drawn, *even as today,* that ties to Gadianton robbers seducing *the more part of the righteous*?

> Now we have not been using the Book of Mormon as we should. Our homes are not as strong unless we are using it to bring our children to Christ. Our families may be corrupted by worldly trends and teachings unless we know how to use the book to expose and combat falsehoods in socialism, rationalism, etc. . . . The situation in the world will continue to degenerate unless we read and heed the words of God and quit building up and upholding secret combinations, which the Book of Mormon tells us proved the downfall of ancient civilizations. (*Ensign*, January 1988, p. 5)

What is socialism? What are its falsehoods the Book of Mormon will help us combat? How does a person quit building up and upholding secret combinations? Is President Benson just talking to be talking, and saying nothing? If you really want to know, you need to read this book.

As President Benson said time and again back in the 60's, *I am unalterably opposed to socialism, either in whole or in part,...* (The Proper Role of Government). To those who believe in the law of the harvest, that in the next life we will be put with people who believe in allowing others the same amount of free agency we believe others should have, this book will be a confirmation of your resolve to avoid using government to enjoy the benefits of socialism.

Daddy loved the Book of Mormon. I still recall the day he excitedly came into my room to show me what he had just discovered in the Book of Mormon. He read to me 3 Nephi 3:7-10. He then said he had read that over a thousand times, if he had read it once, and had never seen it. It was the clearest proof the Gadianton robbers were communists and Satan's sales pitch hadn't changed over the centuries. He raised his voice as he went on to ask, "If I could miss something that clear, what else am I missing?" He studied the Book of Mormon with a real intensity.

A few years ago a former Church employee came to my office and asked if he could get a copy of the book, "your dad and the prophet were working on." Since this work wasn't public I ask how he knew about it. He said he had worked in the Church office building some years before, and he saw these manuscripts of what he assumed was a book, going back and forth weekly in the mail between Daddy and the prophet. He said the secretary there took calls coming in from President Benson at least once or twice a week to Daddy, and she wanted a copy too, as she too knew they were working on these chapters shuttling back and forth between them for several months.

I had heard enough conversations between Daddy and President Benson to know they had talked often about this book, over the years. In Appendix II is a copy of another letter from President Benson to Daddy back in 1967. No doubt President Benson had many friends who assisted him, but in going through Daddy's papers, many letters and correspondence after he was gone, I was pleased to see Daddy was one of those friends.

We should conclude with the observation that this book was never in its final form. It was written when both Daddy and President Benson were still alive. We considered taking some literary license, and 'fixing it' in some places, but concluded our fixing would detract, not enhance it for the friends and family who will read it, so we left it as is. You'll note some chapters overlap in scriptural references and thoughts. Daddy attempted to whittle it down two or three times, so when we reconstituted it, going through his old chapters and his new, we eliminated only obvious duplications. Where such an elimination could not be accomplished with ease, we left the material in.

Both the first and last chapter have the same title. Daddy spent more time working on these two chapters than any other. He believed that unity behind the prophet was critical to our cohesiveness as a Church. He realized from Jacob 5, that there would be a lot of strange fruit on the tree, but he hoped to reduce the odds of his friends and family being part of that strange fruit by stressing unity with the prophet. Even his last conversation with me shortly before he died was to bear his own testimony of the brethren, and of the need to always be loyal to the prophet. On a few occasions he mentioned people he ran in to, who said they agreed with him, but they disagreed with the Church's lack of action. Daddy felt sorrow for people who lacked total loyalty to the Lord's prophet, whoever that prophet was. In all his writings and in our many conversations over the years, I never once saw a hint, a trace, a doubtful remark about the prophets. The apostate is always miserable. He has no Moses and wishes he were one.

He felt bad he could not be more persuasive in his writings to bring all to such a position. He couldn't settle on whether he could most effectively address this prime concern in the beginning or the end, so he addressed it in the preface and both the first and last chapters. You'll also note the preface is long. We found two prefaces, and didn't know which one he wanted, so we put them together as one.

We also added a fourth appendix on children and pride. Daddy had done a great deal of writing on children, and this seemed like a good place to add this information, since enforced priestcraft targets the destruction of the faith of children in our day.

Daddy had a wonderful experience serving as a General Authority, where he got to work with other Church leaders besides President Benson. Daddy's funeral was held July 20, 1992. President Monson was the concluding speaker. A few of his remarks are given below.

> Of all the individuals I know, who would like to be here today, it would be Ezra Taft Benson, the prophet of the Lord, and the President of the Church. For, he loved Verlan Andersen, and he loves all of us....
>
> As I describe my friend Verlan, I would like to say that he was a man of integrity. When he knew what was right he followed it. There was no dissuasion. There was no temptation....
>
> Verlan Andersen never endorsed that with which he did not agree, for he wanted to be able to defend his position, and his position was always on the side of the Lord. He truly was a man of integrity....

THE CHURCH OF JESUS CHRIST OF LATTER-DAY SAINTS
47 EAST SOUTH TEMPLE STREET
SALT LAKE CITY, UTAH 84150

EZRA TAFT BENSON

July 28, 1976

Dear Verlan,

I acknowledge with appreciation your letter of July 24 regarding the two pieces of legislation which you and your associates are supporting. I am very pleased to note that you feel that what you are proposing is supported strongly by the Book of Mormon. I am a great believer in the Book of Mormon and feel strongly that it was written for our day and time. I have said to many people that a person will come to be better informed regarding what's happening in the world today by reading the Book of Mormon than all the magazines and newspapers combined. My great concern is whether we have time enough through the legislative route and the great lack of support for sound principles to get the job done, because of the rate at which the subversive program is closing in on us.

I have just listened to two tapes of the Alan Stang Report. I don't know if you've heard of these, Verlan. This is a new service of the JBS and I understand some 150 stations are carrying the program now. It runs 5 minutes per day for five days of the week, all of which are on one cassette tape. The program is sponsored and purchased by business firms. KSL is running it on time purchased and the service purchased by Larson Ford and I understand it plays every day at 1:30 p.m., Monday through Friday. You may want to write to Alan Stang, Belmont, Mass., 02178 and ask them to send you a sample copy or their promotion tape. It may be you could get it on a Provo station or it may be that a group of you could join together and get it for your own personal use. I believe Reid Bankhead and some of the others might join with you, including Cleon Skousen, with whom I discussed the matter in the hope that he might find use for it. They are sending a copy to me weekly complimentary. It's really news behind the news and is a job well done and most timely.

With warm regards.

Sincerely,

Ezra Taft Benson

H. Verlan Andersen
1155 East 930 North
Provo, Utah 84601

PREFACE

CHURCH AND STATE, RELIGION AND POLITICS

THE BOOK OF MORMON AND THE CONSTITUTION—A MIXING OF RELIGION AND POLITICS

As the title of this work suggests, it consists of a discussion of the Book of Mormon and the United States Constitution. This involves a mixing of the subjects of religion and politics which to some may seem novel enough to require an explanation. Therefore, we are devoting this preface to a consideration of our reasons for doing so.

THE MAGNITUDE OF THE PROBLEM OF GOVERNMENT

For as long as man has been on earth, government has been one of his most difficult and serious problems. Both secular and religious history show that governments have caused more death, more destruction and more suffering than all other agencies combined. Even if we consider the losses caused by international wars alone, this is so. But when we add to this ghastly toll the millions upon millions who have been tortured, murdered, plundered, and enslaved by their own political masters, the problem of government looms above all others.

As serious as are the physical problems caused by government, it is submitted that those of a moral nature are infinitely worse. Of course, it is impossible to completely separate the two. But the adverse affect which governments are having on moral and religious values may be the most serious problem of mankind.

THE GOSPEL HAS THE SOLUTION TO ALL PROBLEMS

It would be unreasonable to believe that the Lord has failed to provide the proper solution to the problem of government. To assume that He has not given us the correct answers would be to doubt or deny His love and concern for us. His gospel contains the knowledge necessary to solve every problem whether it be religious, political, financial, or moral. As Nephi said:

> Feast upon the words of Christ; for behold, the words of Christ will tell you all things what ye should do. (2 Ne. 31:3)

If the gospel has the solution to the problem of government, then we as Church members would appear to have an awesome responsibility to use our best efforts to implement its principles in the communities, the states, and the nation. We can most effectively do this by first coming to a unity among ourselves.

WHY IS THE GOSPEL NOT UTILIZED MORE TO SOLVE POLITICAL PROBLEMS?

It will be conceded by all that little attempt is being made today to use the principles of Christianity to solve the problem of government. Seldom do we hear the Lord and His teachings mentioned in connection with politics. Today the test of the propriety of a proposed law or political platform seems to be how it will affect the economy. The politics of virtually everyone appears to have become largely materialistic. The effect of government action on morals, justice, and freedom seems to be ignored. Why is this so?

Perhaps some see no connection between religion and politics. Even members of the Church who have complete faith that the gospel has the answers, may fail to go to it for political guidance. A variety of excuses are offered for this neglect. Let us examine a few of them.

Is It Constitutional For Religionists To Become Politically Involved?

In the minds of some, the doctrine of "separation of church and state" forbids religionists from becoming involved in political matters. The constitutional provision upon which this doctrine is usually based reads as follows:

> Congress shall make no law respecting an establishment of religion or prohibiting the free exercise thereof; (1st Amendment)

The restraint or prohibition is against government, not the individual. Congress is forbidden to pass laws respecting religion. Instead of prohibiting religious leaders and organizations becoming involved in politics, it guarantees it.

Should There Be A Separation Of Religion And Politics?

The answer is obvious when it is recognized that government is an agency of force. It exists for the exclusive purpose of adopting laws and compelling people to obey them. Every law either commands or forbids certain conduct and carries a penalty for disobedience.

The problem of determining when it is right or wrong to deprive a human of life, liberty or property, is a moral issue of the most serious nature. In fact, there is no question of greater moral significance. Since this is the problem which must be answered with respect to every law, every decree, every rule, and indeed every act of government, it is impossible to avoid the conclusion that everything government does is either good or evil.

Governments are necessary, and laws must be enforced which punish crime according to the nature of the offense. Scriptures such as the Ten Commandments with their related statutes and judgments justify and command that crimes such as murder, robbery and theft be severely punished.

If innocent conduct is punished, those befriending such laws must regard themselves as thieves, enslaver's or murderers, whether it is an individual or a government. It is immoral to fine, imprison, and execute without justification.

There are no members of society who should be more concerned about politics than those whose duty it is to care for the moral and religious needs of the people. As was stated by Lincoln, ours is a government of the people, by the people and for the people. Every citizen has not only the right but the sacred duty to uphold, support and defend the Constitution.

Do The Scriptures Prohibit Political Involvement By Religionists?

The following two scriptures might be interpreted by some to have this effect:

> We believe in being subject to kings, presidents, rulers, and magistrates, in obeying, honoring, and sustaining the law. (Articles of Faith, #12)
>
> Let no man break the laws of the land, for he that keepeth the laws of God hath no need to break the laws of the land.
>
> Wherefore, be subject to the powers that be, until he reigns whose right it is to reign, and subdues all enemies under his feet. (D&C 58:21, 22)

The scriptures require Church members to be law abiding. Befriending that law which punishes innocent conduct is another issue which should be examined. In this connection let us consider the following scripture:

> And that law of the land which is constitutional, supporting that principle of freedom in maintaining rights and privileges, belongs to all mankind, and is justifiable before me.
>
> Therefore, I, the Lord, justify you, and your brethren of my church in befriending that law which is the constitutional law of the land;
>
> And as pertaining to law of man, whatsoever is more or less than this cometh of evil. (D&C 98:5-7)

Church members as citizens, have the constitutional right to speak and write against unconstitutional laws. They have a religious duty to do so as well.

When we encounter laws which contravene our principles, we might recall what the Lord did in a similar situation. The scribes and Pharisees along with their predecessors, had corrupted the code of laws He had given the children of Israel. For this He severely condemned them. Nevertheless, He submitted to their unjust laws and even permitted Himself to be crucified under one of them. He told His followers:

> The scribes and the Pharisees sit in Moses' seat:
> All therefore whatsoever they bid you observe, that observe and do; but do not ye after their works: for they say, and do not. (Matt. 23:2, 3)

CAN POLITICAL BELIEFS AFFECT PERSONAL SALVATION?

Some may remain aloof from politics because they believe it has nothing to do with salvation or exaltation. With this thought in mind let us look at this scripture:

> We believe that governments were instituted of God for the benefit of man, and that he holds men accountable for their acts in relation to them, both in making laws and administering them for the good and safety of society. (D&C 134:1)

In a nation of self-governing people like the United States, all citizens have a moral responsibility to the Lord for their political conduct. With the privilege of self-rule comes the obligation to exercise that privilege in accordance with the Lord's commandments. Moral principle is as applicable in group action as in individual action.

When one decides to befriend or oppose a law, he exercises moral judgment. This judgment is also his personal political philosophy and code of justice. His judgment indicates whether he is just.

One's political philosophy also contains his views on human freedom. Every act he would allow others their freedom to do is allowed by the laws he favors. Conduct which he wants to use force and the fear thereof to prohibit is forbidden by those laws. Thus, one's political philosophy is an expression of his beliefs on free agency. When we recall what the scriptures have to say regarding the fate of those who made the wrong decision on this matter in the pre-existence, we may want to be certain we do not use force to deny a rightful freedom here. This is the question at issue with respect to every law and every government action upon which we pass judgment.

It seems that one can jeopardize his eternal welfare through group action as well as through individual conduct. Even though one acts in concert with others, and even though there may be thousands or millions who join with him in punishing the innocent, in judging unjustly and in opposing freedom, he is not thereby absolved from personal accountability.

If Ye Are Not One Ye Are Not Mine

There is probably no subject about which there is more dispute, disagreement, and contention than that of politics. Because of this, some may abstain from political activity. Others may desist for fear they might offend. Recognizing that this is a highly controversial subject, and that they might lose friends, business patronage, or social standing by becoming involved, they remain aloof.

Of course we should avoid contention both in the Church and without. Many scriptures affirm this and declare that the penalty therefore is exclusion from the Kingdom of God. Where the Lord dwells there will be harmony, as this statement regarding the City of Enoch indicates:

> And the Lord called his people Zion, because they were of one heart and one mind. . . (Moses 7:18)

But do we become one by keeping our differences to ourselves? Can we achieve unity by remaining silent? Obviously we cannot. To become of one heart and one mind, demands a free exchange of ideas and views in an atmosphere of love and harmony. Furthermore, we must recognize the impossibility of finding the correct answers to the problems of government anywhere except in the scriptures. Until we cast away the misleading precepts of men and recognize the Lord as our King and Lawgiver, we shall neither find the truth nor come to a unity. We can become united only on the basis of truth, and a knowledge thereof comes only from God. Our Lawgiver has given us a simple scripture on this. It is one universal standard applicable to individual action as well as political laws. Our Savior called it . . . "the law and the prophets."

Having agreed upon these two fundamental truths, the next step should not be beyond our reach. It should not be difficult to come to a unity of belief in determining which laws are in conformity with the Golden Rule. That is the one universal standard for distinguishing good from evil which all men of every nationality and in every age know and can apply. The Savior in His infinite wisdom has provided us with a short, simple, easily applied rule of conduct with respect to laws and government which will enable us to obey His commandment to be one. President McKay has said:

> Next to being one in worshipping God, there is nothing in this world upon which this Church should be more united than in upholding and defending the Constitution of the United States. (CR, Oct, 1939, p. 105)

Another observation regarding political unity is this by Brigham Young:

> Let the Latter-day Saints be agreed upon their temporal and financial interests. I will ask the question: do you think the Father and the Son are agreed in their political views and their financial operations? Why every Christian in the world says yes, and we say yes; and we cannot be one, in the sense Jesus prayed for us to be, without this. (JD 11:278)

It is fervently hoped that what is contained herein will help Church members as well as others come to a unity of understanding regarding the laws and Constitution which the Lord has caused to be established. Our failure to do this soon may bring us down into destruction both temporally and spiritually.

One of the worst evils of which men are capable is to disobey the Lord's commandments when acting through the agency of government. The punishments decreed for those who do so are among the most severe known. The reasons are easy to see.

When a government is prostituted from its God-ordained purposes so that instead of prohibiting evil, punishing the wicked, and protecting the work of the Lord, it does just the opposite; when, through its evil example it corrupts the hearts of all the people by teaching that good is evil and evil is good, it becomes the agent of Satan and causes abominations to reign. The Lord will not tolerate such a government. He will destroy it along with those who built it up because, as He has decreed, abominations shall not reign. This choice land has a special blessing for the righteous and a cursing for the wicked which only readers of the Book of Mormon are aware of. (Ether 2)

When the Lord establishes the government of a nation and grants unto its voting citizens the political opportunity to alter the laws He has commanded them to obey, He thereby gives them the power to preserve liberty on the one hand, or to commit the awful wickedness described above on the other. He makes it possible for them to choose between His plan of freedom and Satan's plan of slavery. In essence, those living under such a government are once more faced with the same issue which confronted us in the pre-earth life. However, since in this life we are walking by faith and without a full understanding of the issue, the penalties for choosing wrong will not be nearly as severe as before. Nonetheless, they are so painful that no one will want to suffer them.

The Lord has brought two groups of people to the Americas, established His Church among them and given them a government subject to the voice of the people. The first group to receive these blessings were the Nephites. They came here about six hundred years B.C. and lived under a monarchy for about five hundred years before the Lord gave them the privilege of self-rule. They governed themselves for about one hundred and twenty five years before they so completely corrupted their laws and prostituted the political power they possessed that the Lord found it necessary to destroy those who supported such wickedness.

The second group, who are called Gentiles by the Book of Mormon prophets, began arriving in the Americas about 1500 A.D. They lived under foreign monarchies for about three hundred years before the Lord saw fit to establish a constitutional system of self-government among them. While this system has already lasted about seventy years longer than did the Nephite government called the reign of the judges, there is much evidence that the Gentiles are using their power of self-rule to corrupt God's laws, as did the Nephites. In this book we shall undertake to point out in what manner we are repeating their mistakes and what we must do to avoid their tragic fate.

The Nephites corrupted their laws twice. The record indicates that the first time the corruption occurred, it was due to the fact that many of the righteous people were seduced and deceived into doing so. It is concluded herein that the abandonment of the Lord's laws in the United States is happening for somewhat the same reason.

It is entirely possible that the most pervasive and dangerous deception of this age is the belief that the laws of God do not apply to our political conduct. The only place the great majority of us use force to affect the freedom of others is through the agency of government, and so our political decisions are, in reality, decisions about human freedom.

It is suspected that, generally speaking, people do not realize that these are the issues they are deciding when they exercise their God-given powers of self-government. After life itself, freedom is the greatest gift God has to give. But with full political freedom comes the opportunity to choose Satan's plan of slavery.

Herein we shall discuss these three basic truths concerning our political responsibilities: (1) With respect to those members of the Church who live under the Constitution of the United States, the Lord has commanded us to obey His will concerning the laws of the land. (2) This same group has been instructed to distinguish between the Lord's laws which are constitutional and those which are not, for, as He has said, and as pertaining to law of man whatsoever is more or less than this cometh of evil. (3) The penalties we will suffer for failing to obey the Lord's political commandments are most severe and include a loss of the power of the priesthood.

In discussing these truths we shall compare the features of the Nephite government called the reign of the judges with those of the Constitution of the United States. We shall develop a standard by which voting citizens may distinguish between those laws which are constitutional and those which are not. We shall contrast the political sins of the Nephites with those of the people living under the United States Constitution and point out that our living prophets are calling upon us to heed the warnings of the Book of Mormon in order to avoid the scourge and judgment which otherwise will come upon us.

There is only one Church on the earth today which was established by the Lord and has His approval. There is only one government and one set of laws which were divinely established in these latter days and had the Lord's approval. Those were the laws of the Constitution of the United States of America.

Gentiles belonging to the Lord's Church and living under the government He established are as much obligated to obey His commandments respecting the one organization as the other. Our failure to obey God's will concerning the laws of the land will bring to pass our destruction as it did in the case of the Nephites. Only by coming to a unity of belief regarding our political responsibilities and then fulfilling them can we hope to avoid the fate of the Jaredite and Nephite nations which preceded us on this chosen land.

Those who would live in a Zion Society, must be of one heart and of one mind,

And the Lord called his people ZION, because they were of one heart and one mind, and dwelt in righteousness; and there was no poor among them.

And it came to pass in the thirty and sixth year, the people were all converted unto the Lord, upon all the face of the land, both Nephites and Lamanites, and there were no contentions and disputations among them, and every man did deal justly one with another.

And it came to pass that there was no contention in the land, because of the love of God which did dwell in the hearts of the people.

And there were no envyings, nor strifes, nor tulmults, nor whoredoms, nor lyings, nor murders, nor any manner of lasciviousness; and surely there could not be a happier people among all the people who had been created by the hand of God.

There were no robbers, nor murderers, neither were there Lamanites, nor any manner of -ites; but they were in one, the children of Christ, and heirs to the kingdom of God.

And how blessed were they! For the Lord did bless them in all their doings. . . (Moses 7:18, 4 Ne. 1:2, 15-18)

I

IF YE ARE NOT ONE YE ARE NOT MINE

FREE AGENCY IS THE STANDARD BY WHICH ACTIONS MAY BE JUDGED

The late President David O. McKay once stated:

> A fundamental principle of the Gospel is free agency, and references in the scriptures show that this principle is (1) essential to man's salvation; and, (2) may become a measuring rod by which the actions of men, of organizations, of nations may be judged. (CR Oct. 1, 1965)

The scriptures verify that we were judged by our attitude toward free agency in the pre-earth life. Those who opposed it are even now suffering the worst punishment known. If it be true as President McKay has indicated, that free agency may become the measuring rod by which we will be judged here in mortality, it is of transcendent importance that we know and do those things which provide freedom and that we identify and avoid those which injure or destroy it. The attempt to destroy freedom in the pre-earth life was probably undertaken mainly by teaching false doctrines concerning it. This appears to be one of the main ways of destroying it here on earth also. But in addition to this, we can use our mortal bodies to injure and destroy the freedom of others by forcibly depriving them of one of those physical possessions they must have to exercise it—life, liberty and property. The great majority of us do not use our own physical powers to directly destroy one another's freedom. Since we all love freedom and consider it evil when others take from us any of those possessions necessary for its exercise, we know it is wrong to do such things to others. All moral people know it is evil to steal, enslave, commit murder and teach falsehood. Furthermore even if we are tempted to commit crimes, our fear of being punished and excluded from polite society deters us from doing so. But these truths which are so clear when we act alone, ofttimes become obscure when we act through the agency of government. Also when we use government to destroy freedom on our behalf, we do not run the risk of being punished. Under these conditions government becomes the perpetrator rather than the punisher of evil. And finally when we use government to destroy free agency, we can keep our sins hidden by voting in secret.

Freedom Is Destroyed Most Often By The Agency Of Government

The Lord establishes governments to protect freedom. They accomplish this purpose by punishing those who undertake to destroy it. If a criminal wrongfully takes from another one of the freedom elements, it is the function of government to take from him one of the elements of his own freedom—either his life, his liberty, or his property. By so doing it enforces the principles of the Golden Rule and the Ten Commandments. Both of these codes require that government do to the wrongdoer that which he did unto another. Only by adequately punishing those who intentionally undertake to destroy freedom, can government protect it.

But voters and officers of government ofttimes use its powers to destroy freedom rather than protect it. Sometimes they do so knowingly, but it is suspected that it is more common for them to do so because they have been deceived. The most common method used by governments to destroy freedom is to take life, liberty and property from those who have neither intended evil nor caused harm. This, of course is contrary to the moral principles of the Golden Rule and invariably has the effect of destroying freedom.

All conduct may be divided into two categories: (1) That which is motivated by an intent to destroy freedom, and (2) That which is not. All man-made laws which provide for a penalty may be divided into two categories: (1) Those which punish conduct of the first type, and (2) Those which punish that of the second. Laws of the first type are good and have the effect of preserving freedom if the penalty is just. Laws of the second type are evil and have the opposite effect. In spite of this, there are many times more laws of the second type being enforced today than there are of the first. Generally people support these freedom-destroying laws because they are deceived regarding their nature and purpose.

This deception and its awful consequences could be avoided merely by heeding the Lord's commandments regarding government. The extent to which men are deceived regarding the precise line between good and evil laws today, is evident from the fact that freedom is being destroyed by governments all over the earth. Further evidence of deception is found in the fact that there is massive disagreement regarding which laws preserve, and which destroy freedom. This confusion and disagreement need not exist because the Lord has revealed His will concerning man-made laws.

In forming their beliefs about governments, the Christian world seems to have forgotten that the Lord has prescribed His laws of freedom in the Ten Commandments and the Golden Rule. And how many members of the Lord's Restored Church go to their scriptures for help in distinguishing between those laws which preserve and those which destroy free agency?

Every Law Has The Effect Of Either Destroying Freedom Or Preserving It. Everyone Can Be Judged According To Their Attitude Toward Free Agency

The Lord allows wicked governments to exist so that we can see evil and the destruction of free agency and choose to accept or reject it. We came to distinguish between good and evil.

In these latter days relatively few people know about the restored Gospel and it would seem unjust to punish them for not accepting it. Perhaps they will be given a chance to hear the message hereafter. However everyone knows that part of the Lord's Gospel known as the Golden Rule. We will be judged according to how closely we follow it. Especially is this true with respect to the use of force. We are all acutely aware that we do not want others taking or injuring our life, our liberty or our property. We know that when we unjustly destroy these possessions in others, we are violating the Golden Rule. Thus when it comes to the use of force, if we follow the Golden Rule, we will all have the same code of behavior. With respect to the use of force and the destruction of the freedom elements, we all should have the same measuring rod as

President McKay has indicated. Since all of us live under a government of some type and since force is the means used by governments to carry out their purposes, everyone is in a position to see force used and to judge between that which is just and that which is unjust. Everyone can apply the principles of the Golden Rule to judge the actions of government. By so doing, we make decisions regarding the all-important principle of free agency. Furthermore we can do so without inconvenience and without cost. We are judged by the desires of our hearts. The Lord permits wicked governments to exist on earth so that we may see them in operation and make decisions between what they do and what the Golden Rule would dictate. The amount of freedom we shall have in the next life will depend upon the political choices we make here in mortality just as the amount of freedom we have in mortality was determined by the decisions we made about free agency in the pre-earth life. Since men have joy or misery depending upon the amount of freedom they have, the political decisions we make are probably the most important ones of all.

THE BOOK OF MORMON AND THE CONSTITUTION MAKE POLITICAL UNITY POSSIBLE

Inasmuch as the Lord has established the laws and Constitution, That every man may act ". . . according to the moral agency which I have given unto him . . .," those who oppose the laws He has established for this purpose, may be justly accused of taking the wrong side in the battle over free agency. The consequences of doing so may be far more severe than most imagine.

While the Constitution of the United States is generally not regarded as scripture, the commandments the Lord has given regarding it place Church members under the obligation to treat it as if it were. (D&C 98:4-11; 101:77-80) Furthermore those who want to obey the Lord in this matter are given no latitude for error in deciding which laws they should befriend and oppose. Anything which is either more or less than those He approves, cometh of evil. (D&C 98:7)

This book is written in the hopes that it will aid Church members to distinguish those laws which are constitutional from those which are not. By so doing we can come to a unity in our political beliefs and practices.

It will be impossible to follow President McKay's admonition to unitedly uphold and support the Constitution unless we do this. In undertaking to achieve this goal, we shall go not only to the Constitution itself, but also to the political laws given by the Lord in prior dispensations. We will find that His laws regarding freedom are always in harmony regardless of when given.

That scripture however which we will rely on most heavily in making the distinction between those laws which preserve and those which destroy freedom, is the Book of Mormon. That book is filled with accounts of wars, contention and strife in which the issue of freedom was at stake. The lessons taught by those accounts provide a complete understanding of the freedom issue and it is believed that one of the main reasons they were written was to give us guidance in our struggle for freedom today.

Since harmony brings joy while contention brings misery, self-interest demands that we come to a unity, and by so doing escape the misery of the contentious. The Lord who desires that we become as He and His Father, has commanded us to be one, and has decreed that if we are not, we are not His. (John 17:11, 21, 22; D&C 38:27) He has also commanded that there be no contention among us. (3 Ne. 19:28-30) Those who would live in a Zion Society, must be of one heart and one mind. (Moses 7:18; 4 Ne. 1:2, 13, 15-18)

The enormous amount of contention, strife and disagreement in the field of politics indicates that very few understand the Lord's commandments on government sufficiently to become united on them. However President McKay has indicated in the following quote that there is a greater need to come to a unity on this issue than on any other except that of worshipping God:

> Next to being one in worshipping God, there is nothing in this world upon which this Church should be more united than in upholding and defending the Constitution of the United States. (CR Oct. 8, 1939)

In Case Of Dispute We Can Achieve Unity By Following The Prophet

But suppose that after studying both those laws which are constitutional and those which the scriptures indicate are opposed thereto, we still have differences in our political views. What course should then be followed? President McKay has given some explicit advice on this point. Let us consider it.

Following his statement on the position of the Church on Communism given in April, 1966, (See Appendix I) there was considerable discussion and debate in the press and among the people over this issue. Apparently in the hopes of helping to resolve this conflict, President McKay delivered a discourse entitled A PLEA FOR UNITY, in the semi-annual general conference in 1967. In this talk, he urged Church members to become united in rejecting communism with its divisiveness.

This discourse is of the greatest importance to Church members because it presents with unmistakable clarity how unity should be achieved when contentions arise. Among other things President McKay said:

> The greatest safeguard we have for unity and strength in the Church is found in the priesthood, by honoring and respecting it. Oh, my brethren—presidents of stakes, bishops of wards, and all who hold the priesthood—God bless you in your leadership, in your responsibility to guide, to bless, to comfort the people over whom you have been appointed to preside and to visit. Guide them to go to the Lord and seek inspiration so to live that they may rise above the low and the mean, and live in the spiritual realm. Recognize those who preside over you and, when necessary, seek their advice.

After illustrating the foregoing principle with a story from the Bible, President McKay continued thus:

> Here is a lesson for all of us in this Church. Let us, too, recognize the local authority. The bishop may be a humble man. Some of you may think you are superior to him, and you may be, but he is given authority direct from our Father in heaven. You recognize it. Seek his advice and the advice of your stake president. If they cannot answer your difficulties or your problems, they will write to the General Authorities and get the advice needed. Recognition of authority is an important principle. (CR Sept. 29, 1967)

Priesthood members who believe that the Lord directs His Church, will not question the method outlined by President McKay for settling differences which arise over free agency or other matters. It is not an imperfect man which governs the Church, but the Lord Himself and He will never allow a prophet to lead Church members astray.

According to a revelation received in the early days of the Church, the living prophet is the only one entitled to receive commandments and revelations in this Church. (D&C 28:2, 6, 7) If we really believe this, we will sustain him in his decisions as long as the Lord sees fit to keep him in that position.

At various times the Lord has seen fit to test the faith of Church members by permitting prophets to remain in office through an advanced age, and even when their mental faculties were not always at their highest level. No one needs concern himself about such a situation because the Lord always makes them equal to the tasks He places upon them regardless of their age or condition. On any issue, we can feel perfectly secure in following the prophet. It is impossible to achieve unity and the joy which comes therefrom otherwise. Only contention and misery can be expected if we deviate from this divine mandate.

First: The prophet is the only man who speaks for the Lord in everything. . . .

Second: The living prophet is more vital to us than the standard works.

President Wilford Woodruff tells of an interesting incident that occurred in the days of the Prophet Joseph Smith:

> . . . Brother Brigham took the stand, and he took the Bible, and laid it down; he took the Book of Mormon, and laid it down; and he took the Book of Doctrine and Covenants, and laid it down before him and said: 'There is the written word of God to us, concerning the work of God from the beginning of the world, almost, to our day. And now,' said he, 'when compared with the living oracles those books are nothing to me; those books do not convey the word of God direct to us now, as do the words of a Prophet or a man bearing the Holy Priesthood in our day and generation. I would rather have the living oracles than all the writing in the books.' That was the course he pursued. When he was through, Brother Joseph said to the congregation: 'Brother Brigham has told you the word of the Lord, and he has told you the truth.' [In Conference Report, October 1897, pp. 18-19]

Third: The living prophet is more important to us than a dead prophet.

The living prophet has the power of TNT. By that I mean "Today's News Today." God's revelations to Adam did not instruct Noah how to build the ark. Noah needed his own revelation. Therefore, the most important prophet, so far as you and I are concerned, is the one living in our day and age to whom the Lord is currently revealing His will for us. Therefore, the most important reading we can do is any of the words of the prophet contained each week in the Church Section of the *Deseret News* and any words of the prophet contained each month in our Church magazines. Our marching orders for each six months are found in the general conference addresses, which are printed in the *Ensign* magazine. (Ezra Taft Benson, *Fourteen Fundamentals in Following the Prophet,* BYU Devotional, 26 Feb. 1980)

II

Our Living Prophet Has Issued A Warning

Our Living Prophet Says Church Still Under Condemnation

On April 5, 1986, Ezra Taft Benson, Prophet, Seer and Revelator cited D&C 84:58-59 and said the Church is still under condemnation for failing to heed the Lord's message to do as the Book of Mormon says. He called attention to the scourge and judgment which hangs over us and urged us to study that book with care. He told us to make it the center of our personal study, family teaching, preaching and missionary work. He quoted the words of the prophet Joseph Smith that it is the keystone of our religion, and that a man could get nearer to God by abiding by its precepts, than by any other book. (*Ensign*, May, 1986, pp. 4-7)

The Prophet's Warning Against Pride

In his message, President Benson devoted much attention to the sin of pride. He called it the great sin noting that according to the Book of Mormon those who seem to have the most difficulty with it are the learned, and the rich. He referred to scriptures which state that when the earth is cleansed by burning in the last days, the proud shall be as stubble. He quoted prophecies from the Book of Mormon which tell us that the humble followers of Christ are few.

But the scriptures he cited to which we call special attention, are those which tell us that pride destroyed the Nephites, (Moro. 8:27) and that the Lord has warned us to "beware of pride, lest ye become as the Nephites of old." (D&C 38:39)

In this work we shall undertake to show the manner in which pride destroyed the Nephites and how our own nation is being destroyed because of the same sin. In doing so we shall reconcile those statements in the Book of Mormon which attribute the destruction of the Nephites to pride, with those which attribute it to secret combinations, (Ether 8) and the corruption of our laws. (Mosiah 20; Hela. 4, 5, 8; 3 Ne. 7) We shall show that pride led to a corruption of their laws which in turn resulted in a takeover and destruction of their government by secret combinations.

The Book Of Mormon Contains A Special Message Regarding Freedom

It is submitted that one of the most important messages the Book of Mormon has for the Gentiles is found in the detailed history it gives of a people who governed themselves under a political system similar to our own. Except for the Nephites who lived under the reign of the judges, and the Gentiles who live under the United States Constitution, history furnishes no other examples of nations having simultaneously, (1) the gospel, (2) the power of self-rule, and (3) a separation between church and state.

The Book of Mormon repeatedly illustrates how essential it is to our eternal welfare that we obey the Lord's commandments pertaining to government. Under a government of self-rule, it is in the political area where we vote for the Lord's plan of freedom or Satan's plan of slavery. Here is where we indicate whether we belong with the just or the unjust, and whether we are able to overcome the disposition to abuse authority.

The Lord has given us the Ten Commandments, the Golden Rule and the laws and Constitution of the people, all of which pertain to our political conduct. According to the Book of Mormon our failure to obey these commandments when we act through government, will result in our destruction as it resulted in the destruction of the Nephites.

The detailed description it gives of the events of that period are most fascinating when read with this thought in mind. The political issues, the wars, the continuing attempts by dissident factions to alter the God-given laws and overthrow the Nephite government, can be of immense value to us if we utilize that information as we exercise our own constitutional voting rights.

It cannot be by mere chance that the authors of the Book of Mormon devoted almost one half of it to that brief one hundred and twenty five year period during which the Nephites governed themselves by majority vote. Nor can it be other than by design that Nephite history occupies nearly all of the space, while the Jaredites who lived under monarchies, but were the greater nation (Ether 1:43) receive relatively little attention. Of course there may be other reasons for slighting the Jaredite history.

Prior Warnings By Our Living Prophet

Has there been any prophet of modern times who has dwelt more often and more forcibly on the topics of the Book of Mormon and government than President Benson?

Let anyone who really accepts him as a prophet and desires to know how he feels about secret combinations and the threat they pose to our constitutional system of government, search the record. Over a period of many years he has given speeches and authored a large number of books and articles in which he pointed out the mortal danger this nation faces from this source. In his utterances he quoted Book of Mormon prophets extensively.

But did we listen, or did we treat him, President McKay and others who spoke on these matters, as the people treated Noah? The threat of extermination by nuclear war hangs over us today like the threat of extermination over the world at the time of the deluge. But with this difference: While the people of Noah's day probably could not see a cloud in the sky, the threat of our extinction is so obvious that there is hardly a person in the civilized world who is unaware of it.

Furthermore everyone should be able to recognize the totally evil nature of the source of the danger. Who is there in the free world who cannot now identify the ultimate wickedness on earth? What member of the Church is still unable to recognize that group which twenty years ago, President McKay called the greatest satanical threat on the face of the earth.

And still, like the people of Noah's day, we tend to ignore the prophets, both ancient and modern. We seem to be so caught up in gratifying our pride and indulging our carnal and sensual appetites, that we refuse to believe that the earth will be cleansed by fire as President Benson reminds us will happen.

Statements by President Benson

I have noted within the Church a difference in discernment, insight, conviction, and spirit between those who know and love the Book of Mormon and those who do not. That Book is a great sifter. (*Ensign*, December 1988, p. 4)

The Book of Mormon brings men to Christ through two basic means. First, it tells in a plain manner of Christ and His gospel. It testifies of His divinity and of the necessity for a Redeemer and the need of our putting trust in Him. . . . Second, the Book of Mormon exposes the enemies of Christ. It confounds false doctrines and lays down contention. (see 2 Ne. 3:12) It fortifies the humble followers of Christ against the evil designs, strategies and doctrines of the devil in our day. The type of apostates in the Book of Mormon are similar to the type we have today. God, with his infinite foreknowledge, so molded the Book of Mormon that we might see the error and know how to combat false educational, political, religious, and philosophical concepts of our time. (*Ensign*, January 1988, p. 3)

Two great American Christian civilizations—the Jaredites and the Nephites—were swept off this land because they did not 'serve the God of the land, who is Jesus Christ' (Ether 2:12) What will become of our civilization? (*Ensign*, November 1987, p. 7)

III

The Lord's Book Of Mormon Commandments To The Gentiles

The Gentiles Must "Do" As The Lord Has Commanded Or Be Scourged

In a revelation given through the prophet Joseph Smith in the year 1832, the Lord placed the whole Church under condemnation and said that it would remain thereunder until the members did certain things He had commanded them to do in the Book of Mormon. He stated that a consequence of a failure to do as He had directed, would be that a scourge and a judgment would be poured out upon the children of Zion. (D&C 84:54-59)

In His condemnation the Lord accused Church members of these sins: (1) you have treated lightly the things you have received; (2) vanity and unbelief; (3) failing to remember the new covenant, even the Book of Mormon and the former commandments which I have given them, not only to say, but to do according to that which I have written; (4) the pollution of His holy land by the children of the kingdom.

President Ezra Taft Benson in a keynote address delivered in the General Conference of April, 1986, referred to the aforementioned revelation and indicated that the Church was still under condemnation. He urged Church members to cleanse the inner vessel by repenting of immorality and pride. He placed great emphasis upon the need to study the Book of Mormon. In utterances since that date, he has not ceased to urge Church members to study that book.

DOES THE BOOK OF MORMON CONTAIN COMMANDMENTS NOT FOUND ELSEWHERE?

After considering the revelation referred to above, one is led to wonder why the Lord singled out the Book of Mormon for special attention. What commandments has He given therein which are not found in other scriptures? The revelation mentions vanity and unbelief and says Church members have treated lightly that which they have received. These sins, together with the sin of immorality, were also mentioned by President Benson in his keynote address. But admonitions on these topics are not peculiar to the Book of Mormon. Let us consider what else the Lord might have had in mind.

The decree that the children of the kingdom shall not pollute my holy land, may help us identify the special message the Book of Mormon has for us. We know that it contains an account of two other nations which polluted this holy land and were exterminated because they polluted it. Is the Lord instructing us to study the specific cause of their destruction and take heed that we do not commit the same errors? The following scripture seems to justify this conclusion:

> And now, we can behold the decrees of God concerning this land, that it is a land of promise; and whatsoever nation shall possess it shall serve God, or they shall be swept off when the fulness of his wrath shall come upon them. And the fulness of his wrath cometh upon them when they are ripened in iniquity. (Ether 2:9)

The above statement was repeated four different times in essentially these same words in this same chapter. One of these verses is directed specifically to the Gentiles. (The Gentiles here referred to are the non-Lamanite, non-Jewish readers of the Book of Mormon.) It says this:

> And this cometh unto you, O ye Gentiles, that ye may know the decrees of God—that ye may repent, and not continue in your iniquities until the fulness come, that ye may not bring down the fulness of the wrath of God upon you as the inhabitants of the land have hitherto done. (Ether 2:11)

Since these admonitions are found only in the Book of Mormon they, together with similar scriptures, may be the commandments the Lord was referring to in D&C 84.

Let us observe that the foregoing scripture is not only a decree, but also a prophecy. The prophecy is that the Gentiles will become so wicked that unless we repent and discontinue our iniquities, we will bring down the fulness of the wrath of God upon us as did the Jaredites and the Nephites. This appears to be the "scourge and judgment" spoken of in D&C 84.

What Must The Gentiles Do To Avoid The Fulness Of The Lord's Wrath?

What specific iniquities must the Gentiles repent of to avoid the fate of the Jaredites and the Nephites? Perhaps we can answer this question by noting the specific cause of their destruction. The Book of Mormon states it in these words:

> And they (secret combinations) have caused the destruction of this people of whom I am now speaking, (the Jaredites) and also the destruction of the people of Nephi. (Ether 8:21)

Following the above statement, the Lord issued this commandment to the Gentiles through Moroni:

> Wherefore, O ye Gentiles, it is wisdom in God that these things should be shown unto you, that thereby ye may repent of your sins, and suffer not that these murderous combinations shall get above you, which are built up to get power and gain—and the work, yea, even the work of destruction come upon you, yea, even the sword of the justice of the Eternal God shall fall upon you, to your overthrow and destruction if ye shall suffer these things to be.
>
> Wherefore, the Lord commandeth you, when ye shall see these things come among you that ye shall awake to a sense of your awful situation, because of this secret combination which shall be among you; or wo be unto it, because of the blood of them who have been slain; for they cry from the dust for vengeance upon it, and also upon those who built it up. (Ether 8:23, 24)

This is another commandment to the Gentiles found only in the Book of Mormon. More accurately speaking, it is the same commandment as that contained in Ether 2, but it more explicitly states the nature of the wickedness of which the Gentiles must repent. From it we know the following: (1) Secret combinations will be among the Gentiles; (2)

When such occurs, the Gentiles must repent or be destroyed; (3) The Lord has commanded that when these secret combinations come among us, we shall awake to a sense of our awful situation.

ARE SECRET COMBINATIONS AMONG THE GENTILES TODAY?

In his book, *The Millennial Messiah,* the late Bruce R. McConkie says this with reference to secret combinations:

> Next Moroni turns the key so that all who have ears to hear can understand what the secret combination is and can identify those who build it up. 'For it cometh to pass,' he says, 'that whoso buildeth it up seeketh to overthrow the freedom of all lands, nations, and countries.' This is a worldwide conspiracy. It is now entrenched in many nations, and it seeks dominion over all nations. It is Godless, atheistic, and operates by compulsion. It is communism. (McConkie, *The Millennial Messiah,* p. 66)

The Book of Mormon confirms the fact that the secret combinations among the Nephites had the same philosophy and engaged in the same practices as the communists of today. They denied the existence of God, advocated state ownership of all property, and sought control over free governments by murder, intrigue and aggressive warfare. (3 Ne. 3:1-10; Ether 8:25-26; Hela. 2:8; 6:21-24)

With the foregoing in mind, let us note just two of the many statements which have been made by modern prophets during recent years regarding Communism. In the year 1936, The First Presidency of the Church consisting of Heber J. Grant, J. Reuben Clark, Jr., and David O. McKay, issued a statement on this subject which reads in part as follows:

> With great regret we learn from credible sources, governmental and others, that a few Church members are joining, directly or indirectly the Communists and are taking part in their activities. . .
>
> Communism is not a political party nor a political plan under the Constitution; it is a system of government that is the opposite of our Constitutional government . . .
>
> Communism being thus hostile to loyal American citizenship and incompatible with true Church membership, of necessity no loyal American citizen and no faithful Church member can be a Communist.
>
> We call upon all Church members completely to eschew Communism. . . (*Improvement Era*, July 1936)

Contained in *A Statement by President David O. McKay Concerning the Position of the Church of Jesus Christ of Latter-day Saints on Communism,* given to the Priesthood of the Church in the General Conference of April, 1966, is the following:

> The position of this Church on the subject of Communism has never changed. We consider it the greatest satanical threat to peace, prosperity, and the spread of God's work among men that exists on the face of the earth.
>
> In this connection, we are continually being asked to give our opinion concerning various patriotic groups or individuals who are fighting Communism and speaking up for freedom. Our immediate concern, however, is not with parties, groups, or persons, but with principles.
>
> We therefore commend and encourage every person and every group who is sincerely seeking to study Constitutional principles and awaken a sleeping and apathetic people to the alarming conditions that are rapidly advancing about us. .
>
> The entire concept and philosophy of Communism is diametrically opposed to everything for which the Church stands . . .
>
> Communism destroys man's God-given free agency. No member of this Church can be true to his faith, nor can any American be loyal to his trust, while lending aid, encouragement, or sympathy to any of these false philosophies; for if he does, they will prove snares to his feet. (The full text of this statement appears as Appendix I herein.)

Those who believe in the foregoing pronouncements know that the Lord's prophecy in the Book of Mormon that secret combinations would come among the Gentiles during these latter days was fulfilled at least fifty years ago. Their presence here in the United States at that time was publicly announced by the prophets. We also know that the time for the Gentiles to heed the Lord's commandment to awake to a sense of your awful situation came at least twenty years ago when President McKay told the Priesthood of the Church to awaken a sleeping and apathetic people to the alarming conditions which are rapidly advancing about us.

A third fact disclosed by the prophets' words quoted above is that any Church member who lends aid, encouragement, or sympathy to any of the false philosophies of communism is a traitor to both Church and country. According to scriptures which will be discussed in subsequent chapters, almost all men may be guilty of such disloyalty. A person may tentatively judge the extent to which he accepts Communist philosophy by comparing his political beliefs with the Ten Points of the Communist Manifesto found in Appendix III. The penalty which the Lord imposes upon those who help build up the secret combinations by giving aid, encouragement or sympathy to their false philosophies, will be discussed hereafter.

Words of President Benson

The second great reason why we must make the Book of Mormon a center focus of study is that it was written for our day. The Nephites never had the book; neither did the Lamanites of ancient times. It was meant for us. Mormon wrote near the end of the Nephite civilization. Under the inspiration of God, who sees all things from the beginning, he abridged centuries of records, choosing the stories, speeches, and events that would be most helpful to us.

"Behold, I speak unto you as if ye were present, and yet ye are not. But behold Jesus Christ hath shown you unto me, and I know your doing" (Mormon 8:34-35).

If they saw our day, and chose those things which would be of greatest worth to us, is not that how we should study the Book of Mormon? We should constantly ask ourselves, "Why did the Lord inspire Mormon (or Moroni or Alma) to include that in his record? What lesson can I learn from that to help me live in this day and age?"

And there is example after example of how that question will be answered. For example, in the Book of Mormon we find a pattern for preparing for the Second Coming. A major portion of the book centers on the few decades just prior to Christ's coming to America. By careful study of that time period, we can determine why some were destroyed in the terrible judgments that preceded His coming and what brought others to stand at the temple in the land of Bountiful and thrust their hands into the wounds of His hands and feet.

From the Book of Mormon we learn how disciples of Christ live in times of war. From the Book of Mormon we see the evils of secret combinations portrayed in graphic and chilling reality. In the Book of Mormon we find lessons for dealing with persecution and apostasy. We learn much about how to do missionary work. And more than anywhere else, we see in the Book of Mormon the dangers of materialism and setting our hearts on the things of the world. Can anyone doubt that this book was meant for us and that in it we find great power, great comfort, and great protection? (Ezra Taft Benson, *Ensign,* Nov. 1986, p. 6-7)

IV

THE BOOK OF MORMON WARNS THE GENTILES

WHEN NEPHITE PROPHETS USED THE TERM "GENTILE," TO WHOM DID THEY REFER?

In prior chapters we concluded that the Book of Mormon contains a special message for those who have the gospel and also the privilege of self government. In this chapter we shall attempt to point out some of those warnings, but to do so, we must be able to determine when a warning is directed to that group, and who that group is. It is submitted that when the Nephite prophets used the term Gentile, they were referring mainly to Church members who live under the United States constitutional system of government. Let us determine if this is so. The title page of the Book of Mormon indicates that it is,

> written to the Lamanites, . . . and also to Jew and Gentile.

We have no difficulty identifying Lamanites and Jews, but who are the Gentiles? Obviously they must be all those to whom the Book of Mormon is written who are neither Lamanite nor Jew. The title page further helps us to identify Gentiles by noting that the Book of Mormon is,

> . . . to come forth in due time by way of the Gentile—

Thus the prophet Joseph Smith and all others from Gentile nations who have been instrumental in bringing the Book of Mormon forth, are characterized as Gentiles by Book of Mormon prophets. Of course the term is also used in a broader sense to mean all members of Gentile nations from whence such Church members come. See for example Nephi's account of his vision of the settling of America by those who came forth out of captivity from the Gentile Nations. (1 Ne. Chap. 13)

From this we can conclude that any Book of Mormon warnings, commandments and prophecies concerning Gentiles are applicable to Church members from Gentile nations who read that book, or who know or should know that it is the word of God. When Joseph Smith dedicated the Kirtland Temple in 1836 he said:

> Now these words, O Lord, we have spoken before thee, concerning the revelations and commandments which thou hast given unto us, who are identified with the Gentiles. (D&C 109:60)

Unless The Gentiles Repent They Will Be Destroyed

Of special interest to us should be those prophecies which state that the Gentiles would become so wicked that unless we repent, we will suffer a destruction similar to that of the Nephites and Jaredites. Perhaps some Church members will want to apply such predictions exclusively to non-member Gentiles. Neither logic nor the wording of the scriptures justify this.

Reason says that those scriptures would serve little purpose if they applied only to those who never become aware of them. But aside from this, the prophets have in many instances made it very clear that the sins and punishments predicted, pertain to those who belong to the restored Church of Jesus Christ.

Those prophets who spoke most extensively to the Gentiles are the Lord, Nephi and Moroni. Jacob and Mormon also had some things to say to us. However in interpreting the meaning of the Lord's warning contained in D&C 84:54-59, wherein He speaks of "the Book of Mormon and the former commandments which I have given," we must assume that He meant to include not only what He said personally, but what His inspired prophets said as well. They are all the words of the Lord.

Warnings referred to in more detail later include 3 Ne. 16:10, 13, 15 and D&C 101:39, 40. Apparently to make certain that Gentile readers of the Book of Mormon fully realize the fate which awaits us unless we repent, the Lord repeats Himself in much the same language in two other places. (See 3 Ne. 20:15, 16; 21:11-14) Mormon uses similar words yet a third time. (Morm. 5:22-24) And finally the Lord instructs Mormon to list for the fourth time, essentially the same sins He mentions in the scripture quoted above. (Compare 3 Ne. 30:1, 2 with 3 Ne. 16:10)

NEPHI'S WARNING TO THE GENTILES

In the far reaching vision given to Nephi regarding this promised land, only a part of which he was permitted to record, he saw many things pertaining to the Gentiles. He saw that the Spirit of God worked upon Columbus and others and brought them here out of captivity; that they were white, and exceedingly fair and beautiful, like unto his people before they were slain; that they humbled themselves before the Lord and were delivered by His power out of the hands of all other nations; that they became a mighty Gentile nation; that they had the Bible and brought forth the Book of Mormon which they took to the Lamanites. (1 Ne. Ch. 13, Ch. 22) But then Nephi foresaw that this mighty Gentile nation along with all others, would become so proud and wicked that unless they repented they would be destroyed. (2 Ne. 27:1, 2) As did the Lord, Nephi accused the Gentiles of the sin of pride:

> Because of pride, and because of false teachers, and false doctrines, their churches have become corrupted, and their churches are lifted up; because of pride they are puffed up. (2 Ne. 28:12)

That he meant to include Church members in his condemnation seems apparent from his reference to those in Zion who are at ease, and lulled away into carnal security; who cry Zion prospereth, all is well; who hearken unto the precepts of men and become angry at the truth. (See 2 Ne. Ch. 28)

So sweeping are his predictions regarding our destruction that he feels called upon to warn the reader against assuming that "the Gentiles are utterly destroyed;" (2 Ne. 30:1) for says he:

> . . . as many of the Gentiles as will repent are the covenant people of the Lord. (2 Ne. 30:2)

Nephi prophesied, as did the Lord, that a great day of decision would come for the Gentiles when they would either repent and be granted peace and everlasting life, or be brought down into captivity, and also into destruction, both temporally and spiritually. (1 Ne. 14:6, 7)

MORONI'S WARNINGS TO THE GENTILES

While Mormon is the principal author of the Book of Mormon, it was his son, Moroni who has served as the connecting link between his civilization and our own. He it was who personally delivered the plates to the prophet Joseph Smith for translation. He it was who alone, and under the most dangerous and difficult circumstances, protected and completed the precious record that we might have it. Can we imagine his loneliness and suffering during those long years when he was hiding from his enemies and, without help, painstakingly translated, abridged and engraved on the plates the Jaredite history? We Gentiles owe that man a great debt and it is important that we hear what he has to tell us. While he was yet in the flesh, the Lord permitted him to see our day. He recorded what he saw.

> Behold, the Lord hath shown unto me great and marvelous things concerning that which must shortly come, at that day when these things shall come forth among you.
>
> I speak unto you as if ye were present, and yet ye are not. . . . why have ye polluted the holy church of God? . . . (Read Mormon 8:34-38)

Who but Church members can pollute the holy church of God? Let us mention two other warnings issued to the Gentiles by Moroni. The first is found in Ether 2:8-12 where he states four different times in as many verses that those who occupy this chosen land of promise must either serve God or be swept off. In doing so he singles out the Gentiles. The other warning we mention is Ether 8:23-24, dealing with secret combinations. While assuring us that they will be among us, we can prevent them from overthrowing and destroying us, provided of course we act in time.

EACH OF US WILL BE CONFRONTED BEFORE THE BAR OF GOD BY NEPHI AND MORONI

Every person who knows the Book of Mormon to be the word of God should be aware that eventually he will face a heavenly tribunal which will demand an accounting of what he did about the knowledge contained therein. Both Nephi and Moroni warn us of this confrontation.

We quote Nephi first.

> And now, my beloved brethren, and also Jew, and all ye ends of the earth, hearken unto these words and believe in Christ . . .
>
> And if they are not the words of Christ, judge ye—for Christ will show unto you, with power and great glory, that they are his words, at the last day; and you and I shall stand face to face before his bar; and ye shall know that I have been commanded of him to write these things, . .
>
> And you that will not partake of the goodness of God, and respect the words of the Jews, and also my words, and the words which shall proceed forth out of the mouth of the Lamb of God, behold, I bid you an everlasting farewell, for these words shall condemn you at the last day. (2 Ne. 33:10, 11, 14)

Moroni's valediction and warning is equally specific.

> And I exhort you to remember these things; for the time speedily cometh that ye shall know that I lie not, for ye shall see me at the bar of God; and the Lord God will say unto you: Did I not declare my words unto you, which were written by this man, like as one crying from the dead, yea, even as one speaking out of the dust? (Moro. 10:27)

With the Lord and the other Book of Mormon prophets calling from the dust for us to repent, and with the Lord and our living prophet now reminding us of that message, the time to determine what that repentance must consist of is now upon us.

WORDS OF EZRA TAFT BENSON

An important test I use in passing judgment upon an act of government is this: If it were up to me as an individual to punish my neighbor for violating a given law, would it offend my conscience to do so? Since my conscience will never permit me to physically punish my fellow man unless he has done something evil, or unless he has failed to do something which I have a moral right to require of him to do, I will never knowingly authorize my agent, the government, to do this on my behalf.

I realize that when I give my consent to the adoption of a law, I specifically instruct the police—the government—to take either the life, liberty, or property of anyone who disobeys that law. Furthermore, I tell them that if anyone resists the enforcement of the law, they are to use any means necessary—yes, even putting the lawbreaker to death or putting him in jail—to overcome such resistance. These are extreme measures but unless laws are inforced, anarchy results. (Ezra Taft Benson, *An Enemy Hath Done This*, p. 132)

V

Governments May Be Used To Preserve Or Destroy Freedom

The Lord Uses Government To Provide Free Agency

We shall now discuss the fact that it is the Lord's purpose to provide us with freedom and that He establishes governments for this purpose. The scriptures relate that the Lord gave men their agency in the pre-existence and that a war was fought in the pre-mortal state over that issue. (Rev. 12:7-9; D&C 29:36, 37; Moses 4:2-4)

That pre-earth war continues here on earth and government is the agency the Lord and Satan use to carry on the conflict. Note this statement regarding the Lord's reasons for establishing the laws and Constitution of the United States:

> According to the laws and constitution of the people, which I have suffered to be established, and should be maintained for the rights and protection of all flesh, according to just and holy principles; That every man may act . . . according to the moral agency which I have given unto him, that every man may be accountable for his own sins in the day of judgment.
>
> Therefore, it is not right that any man should be in bondage one to another.
>
> And for this purpose have I established the Constitution of this land, by the hands of wise men whom I raised up unto this very purpose, and redeemed the land by the shedding of blood. (D&C 101:77-80)

A government subject to the voice of the people was established among the Nephites for this same purpose. (Mosiah 29:30, 32, 38)

IT IS SATAN'S PURPOSE TO USE GOVERNMENT TO DESTROY FREE AGENCY

Since Satan's purposes are always diametrically opposed to those of the Lord, we know that it is his goal to destroy human freedom. When he was cast out of heaven and into the earth,

> . . . he became Satan, yea, even the devil, the father of all lies, to deceive and to blind men, and to lead them captive at his will, even as many as would not hearken unto my (the Lord's) voice. (Moses 4:4)

As might be supposed, since the Lord uses government to preserve freedom, Satan uses the same agency to destroy it. These two contending forces are constantly battling for political supremacy. President McKay warned us of this battle for political supremacy, where it started, and who's on whose side when he said:

> . . . Even in man's pre-existent state, Satan sought power to compel the human family to do his will by suggesting that the free agency of man be inoperative. If his plan had been accepted, human beings would have become mere puppets in the hands of a dictator, and the purpose of man's coming to earth would have been frustrated. Satan's proposed system of government, therefore, was rejected, and the principle of free agency established in its place. (CR April 1950, pp. 33-35)

One of the greatest values of the Book of Mormon is that it explains and illustrates the lies, false philosophies and methods Satan uses to deceive people into aiding him in his efforts to capture control of government. Since all men desire freedom, they must be deceived before they will aid him in his plan to destroy it. Much of this book is devoted to discussing such deceptions.

The Lord caused a government subject to the voice of the people to be established among the Nephites. Because of pride and abominations, the Nephite voters were seduced into allowing their government to come under the control of the secret combinations. The Book of Mormon provides a rather detailed account of how this occurred. Doubtless these details were included in the record for the special benefit of the Gentiles living under the Constitution of the United States. Let us note some of the principle facts surrounding the takeover.

The Takeover Of The Nephite Government By The Gadianton Robbers

The Nephite government called the reign of the judges was established in the year 92 B.C. At the time of its institution, the people were told that since this government was subject to the voice of the people, the Lord would hold them accountable if they corrupted their laws. They were told this:

> And if the time comes that the voice of the people doth choose iniquity, then is the time that the judgments of God will come upon you; yea, then is the time he will visit you with great destruction even as he has hitherto visited this land. (Mosiah 29:27)

The voters were able to maintain the Lord's laws in force in the central government fairly well for almost sixty years. During this period, some of the local governments like those in the city of Ammonihah and in the land of Antionum were thoroughly corrupted by the people. As a consequence, those responsible were either destroyed or defected away to the Lamanites. Also during this period, there were other apostate Nephite groups who rebelled against the central government and attempted to seize control of it. However the righteous Nephites successfully resisted all of these attempts.

Even though the Nephites were able to prevent the corruption of their laws by external forces, finally in about the sixtieth year of the reign of the judges, they fell victim to a diabolical internal movement which gradually seduced them to corrupt their laws. This satanic group known as the Gadianton Robbers, was organized in the fortieth year of the reign of the judges for the specific purpose of seizing control of the government.

At the outset the members of the group were regarded as traitors, robbers and murderers. All those who were detected were put to death. (Hela. 1:12; 2:12) As time went on however, the Nephites became proud and wicked. The majority of the people began to believe in the philosophy of the Gadianton Band, and incorporated their philosophy into their laws. The following passages indicate the manner in which the corruption and takeover occurred:

> For as their laws and their governments were established by the voice

> of the people, and they who chose evil were more numerous than they who chose good, therefore they were ripening for destruction, for the laws had become corrupted. (Hela. 5:2)
>
> And it came to pass on the other hand, that the Nephites did build them (The Gadianton Band) up and support them, beginning at the more wicked part of them, until they had overspread all the land of the Nephites, and had seduced the more part of the righteous until they had come down to believe in their works and partake of their spoils, and to join with them in their secret murders and combinations.
>
> And thus they did obtain the sole management of the government . . . (Hela. 6:38, 39)

A Description Of The Activities Of A Fully Corrupted Government

The Book of Mormon enables us to recognize when a government has fallen under the control of Satan's secret combinations by giving us the following graphic description of the Nephite government while it was being operated by the Gadianton Band:

> And seeing the people in a state of such awful wickedness, and those Gadianton robbers filling the judgment-seats—having usurped the power and authority of the land; laying aside the commandments of God, and not in the least aright before him; doing no justice unto the children of men;
>
> Condemning the righteous because of their righteousness; letting the guilty and the wicked go unpunished because of their money; and moreover to be held in office at the head of government, to rule and do according to their wills, that they might get gain and glory of the world, and, moreover, that they might the more easily commit adultery, and steal, and kill, and do according to their own wills—(Hela. 7:4, 5)

The Nephites Ignored The Call To Repentance By Their Prophet

Nephi, the son of Helaman II, was the principal prophet among the Nephites at the time they corrupted their laws. He had once been chief judge and governor of the entire nation. But when the Nephites became wicked, he resigned his position to spend full time preaching. He preached repentance in the land northward for several years, but had little success. Upon returning and finding the people in a state of such awful wickedness, he climbed upon the tower in his garden and began to pour out his soul unto God.

His mourning caused passers-by to stop and wonder at so much grief. Observing that a crowd had gathered, Nephi took the opportunity to preach a sermon in which among other things, he said:

> O, how could you have forgotten your God . . . But behold, it is to get gain, to be praised of men, yea, and that ye might get gold and silver. And ye have set your hearts upon the riches and the vain things of this world, for the which ye do murder, and plunder, and steal, and bear false witness against your neighbor, and do all manner of iniquity.
>
> Yea, wo be unto you because of that great abomination which has come among you; and ye have united yourselves unto it, yea, to that secret band which was established by Gadianton. (Hela. 7:20, 21, 25)

After Nephi had accused his hearers of corrupting their laws and uniting themselves to the secret combination, many of them were so angry that they wanted to kill him. His life was spared however and, after being visited by the Lord, he continued to cry repentance and to warn the people of great destruction if they did not repent.

His warnings went unheeded and the promised destruction came. First there was a civil war and then a famine. This last calamity brought repentance and a cleansing of their government. (Hela. 11)

The Book Of Mormon Warns Gentiles Living Under The Constitution

It seems most likely that the Lord inspired Mormon to include the details of this Nephite experience with self-government in his record as a warning to the Gentiles living under the United States Constitution. Like the Nephites, we also have been given a divinely established government subject to the voice of the people. And like them, we once regarded the members of the secret combinations as traitors and criminals. But during the last sixty or seventy years, we also have come down to believe in their works and partake of their spoils and join with them in their evil combinations.

In subsequent chapters we shall discuss in some detail the extent to which we have corrupted our God-given laws and adopted those proposed by secret combinations. We shall also undertake to point out what we must do to avoid the scourge and judgment the Lord has promised unless we heed His Book of Mormon warnings. However our first interest is to understand how the Nephite voters could have been deceived and seduced into accepting communism.

VI

Almost All Men Are Inclined To Destroy Free Agency

Many Are Called But Few Are Chosen

Having shown that the Lord uses government to provide freedom while Satan uses it for the opposite purpose, we will now discuss the tragic truth that almost all men have a tendency to join Satan in his plan.

There are a substantial number of scriptures which warn that the number who will qualify to inherit the Lord's Kingdom will be small indeed. In the Tree of Life vision shown to Lehi and Nephi, they saw that the people of the world divided themselves into four groups, only one of which partook of the fruit of the tree and remained faithful. (1 Ne. 8:11) In the vision given to Joseph Smith and Sidney Rigdon regarding the three degrees of glory, they were shown that while there are three main glories, an enormous number of people will inherit the Telestial kingdom which is the lowest of the three:

> But behold, and lo, we saw the glory and the inhabitants of the telestial world, that they were as innumerable as the stars in the firmament of heaven, or as the sand of the seashore. (D&C 76:109)

Even those who belong to the Lord's Church and have the advantage of knowing the laws which must be obeyed to gain eternal life are warned that the possibility of failure is great. The Lord admonished His disciples in the Holy Land and in the Americas with these words:

> Enter ye in at the strait gate: for wide is the gate, and broad is the way, that leadeth to destruction, and many there be which go in thereat:
>
> Because strait is the gate, and narrow is the way, which leadeth unto life, and few there be that find it.
>
> Many will say to me in that day, Lord, Lord, have we not prophesied in thy name? and in thy name have cast out devils? and in thy name done many wonderful works?

> And then will I profess unto them, I never knew you: depart from me, ye that work iniquity. (Matt. 7:13, 14, 22, 23; 3 Ne. 14:13, 14, 22, 23; see also 3 Ne. 27:33)

Essentially this same admonition is found in a revelation given to the Gentiles in these latter days. In the following scripture, Church members who enter into the covenant of celestial marriage and seek celestial glory are told this:

> Verily, verily, I say unto you, except ye abide my law ye cannot attain to this glory.
>
> For strait is the gate, and narrow the way that leadeth unto the exaltation and continuation of the lives, and few there be that find it, because ye receive me not in the world neither do ye know me.
>
> Broad is the gate, and wide the way that leadeth to the deaths; and many there are that go in thereat, because they receive me not, neither do they abide in my law. (D&C 132:21, 22, 25)

The statement that many are called but few are chosen, is found a number of places in the scriptures. (Matt. 20:16; 22:14; D&C 95:5; 121:34, 40) However it is in the revelation known as Doctrine and Covenants Section 121 that a rather complete explanation is provided as to why the many are not chosen.

WILL ALMOST ALL MEN BE UNFIT TO WIELD THE LORD'S POWER?

The statement that many are called but few are chosen is repeated twice in Doctrine and Covenants Section 121. Verses 35 and 36 give this as the reason for the failure of the many:

> Because their hearts are set so much upon the things of this world, and aspire to the honors of men, that they do not learn this one lesson—
>
> That the rights of the priesthood are inseparably connected with the powers of heaven, and that the powers of heaven cannot be controlled nor handled only upon the principles of righteousness.

On the other hand verses 39 and 40 explain that the reason almost all men are not chosen, is this:

> We have learned by sad experience that it is the nature and disposition

> of almost all men, as soon as they get a little authority, as they suppose, they will immediately begin to exercise unrighteous dominion.
>
> Hence many are called, but few are chosen.

Let us undertake to understand why the Lord has given two different explanations for the failure of the many. We know that these two reasons must be consistent and directly related. What we will do is try to understand what that relationship is. We will defer until the next chapter a discussion of the fact that the many are not chosen because they set their hearts upon the things of this world and aspire to the honors of men. In this chapter we will consider the disposition of men to abuse authority. Before doing so however, let us determine what it means not to be chosen.

The Lord is obviously talking to holders of the Priesthood in this revelation. In verse 36 quoted above He states that the reason the many are not chosen is that they fail to learn a lesson regarding how the rights of the priesthood must be controlled or handled. In verse 37 He goes on to warn priesthood holders that even though the rights of the priesthood may be conferred upon us, we may forfeit them by improper conduct. His exact words are:

> That they may be conferred upon us, it is true; but when we undertake to cover our sins, or to gratify our pride, our vain ambition, or to exercise control or dominion or compulsion upon the souls of the children of men, in any degree of unrighteousness, behold, the heavens withdraw themselves; the Spirit of the Lord is grieved; and when it is withdrawn, Amen to the priesthood or the authority of that man. (v. 37)

In still another verse in this same section, He states these to be the qualifications for wielding His power:

> No power or influence can or ought to be maintained by virtue of the priesthood, only by persuasion, by long-suffering, by gentleness and meekness, and by love unfeigned; (v. 41)

These scriptures appear to compel the conclusion that of the many called to hold the priesthood> in this life, only a few will be able to continue to do so in the next. The reason given in these verses is that almost all of us are inclined to use compulsion unrighteously. Let us observe in what manner we may be gratifying this tendency.

How Do We Manifest A Disposition To Exercise Unrighteous Dominion?

The scripture quoted above forbids the unrighteous use of control or dominion or compulsion in our relationships with others. But in what manner do we use force or compulsion on one another either righteously or unrighteously?

Since almost all of us are unable, afraid, or ashamed to use unrighteous force on one another directly, it is difficult to believe we manifest the disposition to do so in this manner. But when the reins of government are placed in our hands, most of those considerations which deter us are removed. The lack of ability is no longer a problem because the power of government is now at our disposal.

We no longer are restrained by fear because we now have the police power on our side. And since we can usually quiet the voice of conscience by deceiving ourselves into believing that the Golden Rule does not apply to the actions of government, we can quite easily suppress this restraint. And finally we can undertake to exercise unrighteous dominion by doing nothing more inconvenient than voting or arguing for a bad law.

From this we can conclude that the disposition to exercise compulsion is more likely to be manifested in our political beliefs and practices than in any other manner. It would also appear that the very reason the Lord establishes governments by the voice of the people is so that the voters have the opportunity to exercise unrighteous dominion without fear, shame, or inconvenience. The choice to preserve or destroy free agency is thus unimpeded by any consideration except that of conscience. Satan is given the same opportunity to entice us to accept his plan of slavery, as the Lord has to entice us to choose freedom.

The Scriptures teach:

> Wherefore, man could not act for himself save it should be that he was enticed by the one or the other. (2 Ne. 2:16)

> And it must needs be that the devil should tempt the children of men, or they could not be agents unto themselves; for if they never should have the bitter they could not know the sweet—(D&C 29:39)

In order for man to exercise free agency, he must have a choice between alternatives. The only alternative to freedom is bondage, and the only alternative to truth is falsehood. Thus Satan must have the opportunity to tempt us to choose slavery and to believe falsehoods. A government subject to the voice of the people provides us with these choices.

Satan has been extremely successful in deceiving men into believing that the use of force to destroy freedom is justified when done in concert with others and through the power of the state. Or to state the matter otherwise, Satan has deceived virtually all people into believing that the Golden Rule and the principles of private morality do not apply to the actions of governments. In so doing he has seduced the people in every nation to use the police power and the armed forces to destroy freedom on a massive scale. The almost universal disposition to exercise unrighteous dominion has contributed enormously to his success.

In subsequent chapters we shall examine in some detail a wide assortment of laws by means of which we violate the Golden Rule. Also we will show that almost all men befriend at least some of them. One has great difficulty in finding any other means except through government, wherein virtually all of us exercise unrighteous dominion on one another. Let us then in the next chapter, consider the other character defect which the Lord stated would cause the many to forfeit the Priesthood. This is the sin of pride or, setting our hearts upon the things of this world and the honors of men.

Behold, my son, I will write unto you again if I go not out soon against the Lamanites. *Behold, the pride of this nation*, or the pride of the Nephites, *hath proven their destruction* except they should repent.

Pray for them, my son, that repentance may come unto them. But behold, I fear lest the Spirit hath ceased striving with them; and in this part of the land they are also seeking to put down all power and authority which cometh from God; and they are denying the Holy Ghost.

And after rejecting so great a knowledge, my son, they must perish soon, unto the fulfilling of the prophecies which were spoken by the prophets, as well as the words of our Savior himself. (Moroni 8: 27-29 *Emphasis Added*)

VII

The Consequences Of Pride

How Common Is The Sin Of Pride?

In the preceding chapter we observed that the Lord gave two separate reasons for the conclusion that, Many Are Called But Few Are Chosen. One of these reasons—that almost all men are disposed to exercise unrighteous dominion—was discussed in the prior chapter. The other reason we will discuss herein.

It was the Lord who said that the reason the many are not chosen is "because their hearts are set so much upon the things of this world, and aspire to the honors of men . . ." (D&C 121:35) If we accept His statement as true, we must face the fact that almost all of us have a problem with the sin of pride. The Lord also stated that because of this sin, the many do not learn those lessons which must be learned in order to wield the powers of heaven. The consequence of this failure is that the many are not chosen and Amen to their priesthood.

Do other scriptures confirm the conclusion that the sin of pride is almost universal today? Nephi who saw our day, recorded that "because of pride, and wickedness, and abominations, and whoredoms, they have all gone astray save it be a few who are the humble followers of Christ..." (2 Ne. 28:14) Moroni used similar words to describe our condition. Said he:

> . . . there are none save a few only who do not lift themselves up in the pride of their hearts. . . (Mormon 8:36)

The Lord was even more sweeping in condemning the Gentiles who would sin against His gospel in these latter days. Here are some of His words:

> At that day when the Gentiles shall sin against my gospel, and shall reject the fulness of my gospel, and shall be lifted up in the pride of their hearts above all nations, and above all the people of the whole earth . . . I

will bring the fulness of my gospel from among them. (3 Ne. 16:10)

The Lord recognized the possibility of our repentance, but said if we did not do so, we should be trodden under foot as salt that hath lost its savor. (v. 15) The salt of the earth are those who have made covenants with the Lord. (D&C 101:39, 40)

In a modern day revelation the Lord has placed the whole Church under condemnation because of pride. He has threatened that a scourge and a judgment will be poured out upon the children of Zion unless they repent of vanity and unbelief, and do as He has instructed in the Book of Mormon. (D&C 84:54-59)

These and many other scriptures which might be cited, fully confirm the fact that today the many have set their hearts upon the things of this world and they aspire to the honors of men.

Pride Is A Sin Which Should Concern All Men

A sin which is as widespread and dangerous to our eternal welfare as is pride, deserves to be studied with meticulous care. Since it afflicts almost all men, wisdom dictates that every person should be able to recognize it in his own life if he is afflicted, understand its consequences, and learn ways to overcome it.

The worst consequence of pride is that it causes misery both to the one afflicted and also to his associates. It invariably produces contention with its resulting misery. It leads to envy, hate and anger.

It causes one to have an insatiable desire to be honored or worshipped. It produces spiritual blindness and subjects one to the influence of the deceiver. If pride were a disease it would be the worst disease a man could have because the victim of pride is blinded to an awareness of the symptoms of the disease of pride to exactly the same degree he is afflicted with the disease. The scriptures provide instructive examples of these consequences in the lives of various individuals. Let us first consider the effect of pride on Lucifer.

Lucifer Exemplified Pride In Its Most Extreme Form

Although at one time Satan was "an angel of God who was in authority in the presence of God," (D&C 76:25) he fell from his exalted position and is now suffering indescribable misery. The scriptures indicate that the cause of his horrible fate was his pride. Some indication of the extent of his fault is given in the following words of Isaiah:

> How art thou fallen from heaven, O Lucifer, son of the morning! how art thou cut down to the ground, which didst weaken the nations!
>
> For thou hast said in thine heart, I will ascend into heaven, I will exalt my throne above the stars of God: . . .
>
> I will ascend above the heights of the clouds; I will be like the most high. (Isa. 14:12-14)

Satan's fall occurred when his offer to be God's only begotten Son was rejected and the offer of Christ was accepted. At this point he became angry and rebellious and sought to destroy man's free agency:

> And I, the Lord God, spake unto Moses, saying: That Satan, whom thou hast commanded in the name of mine Only Begotten, is the same which was from the beginning, and he came before me, saying—Behold, here am I, send me, I will be thy son, and I will redeem all mankind, that one soul shall not be lost, and surely I will do it; wherefore give me thine honor.
>
> But, behold, my Beloved Son, which was my Beloved and Chosen from the beginning, said unto me—Father, thy will be done, and the glory be thine forever.
>
> Wherefore, because that Satan rebelled against me, and sought to destroy the agency of man, which I, the Lord God, had given him, and also, that I should give unto him mine own power; by the power of mine Only Begotten, I caused that he should be cast down; (Moses 4:1-3)

This scripture teaches a lesson of transcendent importance. It sets forth the stark contrast between the humility, submissiveness and obedience of the Savior on the one hand, and the pride, lust for power and honor, and rebelliousness of Satan on the other. The joy and misery which humility and pride brought into the lives of these two individuals, and can bring into the lives of all others, is a matter for serious reflection.

Other Scriptural Examples Of The Consequence Of Pride

The theme that pride causes a person to be envious, angry and hateful when some honor or possession he wrongfully seeks is bestowed on his brother, is repeated frequently in the scriptures. We find it in the life of Cain who, when the Lord rejected his offering and accepted that of Abel, murdered his brother and appropriated his flocks.

Esau also became murderously jealous and hateful when the birthright he had sold, and the blessing he coveted, were given to his brother Jacob. To his credit let it be noted that these evil feelings later changed to love and friendship. The brothers of Joseph became so envious at the favoritism shown him by their father Jacob, that they were ready to put him to death. They were restrained from doing so only when the opportunity to sell him into slavery presented itself.

The envy and hate which the pride of Laman and Lemuel caused them to have toward their younger brother Nephi, is repeatedly mentioned in the Book of Mormon. Unfortunately they never repented of these feelings, but transmitted them to their posterity thus causing a series of wars which lasted for hundreds of years. Pride, envy and a lust for power and the possessions of others have been the primary cause of international war and bloodshed throughout the history of the world.

Pride Leads To Envy, Hate, Anger And Misery

The one consequence of pride which should be feared above all others is the misery which it produces in the life of its victim. Men are that they might have joy. But pride is wickedness, and wickedness never was happiness. To the extent pride exists, joy is made impossible and misery inevitable. A proud person is envious. Like Satan he seeks that which he does not deserve and cannot rightfully possess. He wants the possessions, honor and glory which belong to others. Rather than recognizing that the earth and all honor and glory belong to God, he wants such things for himself.

Envy leads to anger and hate against the object of the envy. But feelings of envy, anger and hate are the very essence of misery. Indeed Satan and his followers are called "vessels of wrath." (D&C 76:33) The torment they suffer is so horrible that it is known only by those who experience it. (D&C 76:45) The danger of disobeying that commandment which decrees: Thou shalt not covet, is most obvious.

The most important characteristic possessed by man is his capacity to experience joy on the one hand and misery on the other. The whole object of existence should be to obtain the one and avoid the other. But the extent to which we will experience the one feeling or the other throughout the eternities, appears to depend largely upon whether we are humble or proud; whether we set our hearts upon the things of this world and the honors of men, or have an eye single to the glory of God. One horrible aspect of pride which seems to exist is that it can never be completely satiated. No matter how extensively it may be gratified, as long as it persists the desire for more is never extinguished. Thus eternal misery is assured each person who fails to repent of it.

PRIDE LEADS TO SPIRITUAL BLINDNESS, SELF-DECEPTION AND FALSEHOOD

Satan is the father of lies and it is his mission here on earth:

> . . . to deceive and to blind men, and to lead them captive at his will, even as many as would not hearken unto my voice. (Moses 4:4)

To be influenced by the prompting of the Spirit of the Lord requires that we humbly approach Him seeking the truth. As the Lord stated in the Sermon on the Mount:

> Ask, and it shall be given unto you; seek, and ye shall find; knock, and it shall be opened unto you. (Matt. 7:7)

On the other hand as the following scripture says, the proud are beyond the influence of the Lord's Spirit:

> And whoso knocketh, to him will he open; and the wise, and the learned, and they that are rich, who are puffed up because of their learning, and their wisdom, and their riches—yea, they are they whom he despiseth; and save they shall cast these things away, and consider themselves fools before God, and come down in the depths of humility, he will not open unto them. (2 Ne. 9:42)

The inability of the proud to know and understand spiritual truths includes the inability to exercise faith, as the following scripture states:

> And again, behold I say unto you that he (a man) cannot have faith and hope, save he shall be meek, and lowly of heart. (Moro. 7:43)

To the extent we forget God and lavish on ourselves the praise which belongs to Him, to that extent we lose touch with spiritual reality. That lie which is spiritually fatal above all others is that there is no God. This false belief which has its foundation in pride, brings us under the influence of the Deceiver and we lose the ability to think logically about spiritual matters.

What Is The Relationship Between Pride And The Disposition To Exercise Unrighteous Dominion?

We have noted herein that the Lord has given two reasons for the failure of the many: (a) the disposition to exercise unrighteous dominion and, (b) pride. It is of interest to note that these are the two reasons assigned for the destruction of the Nephite nation. The scriptures state that both the Jaredites and the Nephites were exterminated because of secret combinations. Those evil organizations used the power of government to exercise unrighteous dominion and destroy freedom. (Ether 8:21, 25; Hela. 2:13, 14) But the following scripture attributes the destruction of the Nephites to pride:

> . . . Behold, the pride of this nation, or the people of the Nephites, hath proven their destruction except they should repent. (Moro. 8:27)

We have also observed how Satan's pride led him to attempt to destroy free agency in the pre-existence. He it is who forms secret combinations here on earth for this purpose. His organizations are among us today and they pose the same threat to us as they did to the Nephites. The Lord has warned us of our fate if we become proud as did the Nephites: . . . "but beware of pride, lest ye become as the Nephites of old." (D&C 38:39)

It appears from all of this that there is an inseparable connection between the sin of pride and the disposition to exercise unrighteous dominion. The proud find it impossible to obey the Golden Rule because one who considers himself above others, cannot treat them as he wants to be treated. These feelings of superiority dispose him to dictate the lives of those he considers inferior in knowledge, wisdom and judgment.

Believing himself more important, he wants others to believe the same thing. He desires to be honored, praised and looked up to. This leads him to seek for things which others do not have—things which set him apart from the common herd. To obtain these trappings which he believes will distinguish him, he seeks for the things of this world and the honors of men and will resort to devious and dishonest methods to obtain them. He will resort to compulsion when the opportunity presents itself.

Government is that agency which affords the greatest opportunity of all to gratify pride and exercise unrighteous dominion. One in control of this agency of force can use it to gain the things of this world, and also the honors of men. Governments have been used to commit more plunder and to confer more titles, honors, distinctions, licenses, privileges, degrees, etc., than all other agencies combined. In doing these things they exercise unrighteous dominion and destroy free agency.

In what follows in this book we will demonstrate first that it was always the proud among the Nephites who were constantly attempting to gain control of government so that they could use it to obtain the things of this world and the honors of men. After doing this, we shall undertake to show that it is pride which has led us to corrupt our laws, and that we must remove those corruptions or suffer destruction.

The Lord could, I suppose, have avoided the war in Heaven over free agency. All He needed to have done was to have compromised with the Devil—but had he done so he would have ceased to be God.

While it is more difficult to live the truth, such as standing for free agency, some of us may in the not too distant future be required to die for the truth. But the best preparation for eternal life is to be prepared at all times to die—fully prepared by a valiant fight for the right.

Let us act like men, men who are sons of God, men with a sure knowledge that there will be a resurrection—and a final judgment. (Ezra Taft Benson, Conference Report, April, 1964)

Now, we may rest assured of this: If there is no devil, there is no God. But there is a God and there is a devil, and the bringing of peace requires the eliminiation of Satan's influence. Where he is, peace can never be. Further, peaceful co-existence with him is impossible. He cannot be brought to co-operate in the maintenance of peace and harmony. He promotes nothing but the works of the flesh. . . .

As a prelude to peace, then, the influence of Satan must be conpletely subjugated. Even in heaven there could be no peace with him after his rebellion. There, in the world of spirits, the Father and the Son could find no ground upon which they could co-operate with him. He had to be cast out—not compromised with, but cast out. (Marion G. Romney, First Presidency Message, *Ensign,* Octobe 1983, p. 5)

VIII

THE SIN OF PRIDE

IS THE GRAVITY OF THE SIN OF PRIDE RECOGNIZED?

In prior chapters we noted our living prophet's warning to repent of the sin of pride, and the Lord's admonition to beware of pride, lest ye become as the Nephites of old. We also quoted a number of Book of Mormon scriptures wherein the Lord, Nephi and Moroni prophesied that pride would be almost universal among the Gentile members of the Church during these last days. (see Appendix IV)

It is suspected that usually people pay little attention to admonitions against the sin of pride because its gravity and the severity of the penalty is not understood. Furthermore, the victims of the disease seem incapable of recognizing that they are afflicted. In this chapter we desire to discuss the nature of this sin and the eternally fatal consequences which result therefrom. In order to do so properly, it seems necessary to consider the relationship between pride and the desire to exercise unrighteous dominion.

HUMILITY, FREEDOM AND JOY, VERSUS PRIDE, SLAVERY AND MISERY

The Book of Mormon states the whole purpose of existence in this simple sentence: "Men are that they might have joy." (2 Ne. 2:25) But this supreme goal is possible only to those who enjoy freedom; hence the primary object of life should be to know and do those things necessary to obtain that liberty without which joy is impossible. We obtain liberty for ourselves by seeking the freedom of others. We do this only if we are humble enough to love our neighbor and seek to help him.

On the other hand, one who is proud cannot be free because his pride causes him to exercise unrighteous dominion which, according to the law of the harvest, causes him to forfeit his freedom. This in turn causes misery. Let us consider these truths more fully.

Why Is Free Agency Necessary?

It is submitted that one of the most profound philosophical concepts one will ever understand is that, "it must needs be that there is an opposition in all things." (2 Ne. 2:11) Unless there is a possibility of choosing eternal torment, one cannot choose eternal joy. Thus the whole purpose of life depends upon freedom of choice.

Satan And His Followers Chose To Destroy Freedom Of Choice

The first exercise of agency of which we have record is that of Christ and Satan in the pre-earth life. It seems strange that the alternatives they were choosing between was whether or not freedom of choice should even exist. In light of the conclusions drawn above, that there can be no joy without misery, and that neither is possible without freedom to choose, it seems incredible that anyone would propose a plan which would destroy the whole purpose of existence. No one has ever accused Satan of being stupid. Why then did he choose misery?

It also seems strange that in choosing to destroy free agency, Satan and his followers deliberately elected to forfeit their own. Surely they knew of the eternal law of the harvest: that as we do unto others, so shall it be done unto us. The fate they chose for themselves is horrible beyond description.

> They shall go away into everlasting punishment, which is endless punishment, to reign with the devil and his angels in eternity, where their worm dieth not, and the fire is not quenched, which is their torment—
>
> And the end thereof, neither the place thereof, nor their torment, no man knows;
>
> Wherefore, the end, the width, the height, the depth, and the misery thereof, they understand not, neither any man except those who are ordained unto this condemnation. (D&C 76:44, 45, 48)

If the consequences described above were known to Satan's followers, how was it possible that:

> . . . a third part of the hosts of heaven turned he (Satan) away from me (the Lord) because of their agency. (D&C 29:36)

Perhaps we lack a full explanation of the reason for their decision. Nevertheless the information given by the scriptures regarding Satan's basic character, and also the knowledge we have of the character of those who choose to follow his plan in this life, may give us the information we seek.

WHY SATAN AND HIS FOLLOWERS SOUGHT TO DESTROY FREE AGENCY

We obtain some understanding of Satan's character from the account found in the fourth chapter of the Book of Moses wherein we are told that he sought to destroy the agency of man and to obtain God's power. (Moses 4:3) His lust for honor and power is also mentioned by the Lord in D&C 29:36.

But that scripture which most clearly reveals his insensate lust for power, honor, and glory, is the one which describes his attempts to induce Moses to worship him. It so fully reveals his true nature that he inspired wicked men to remove it from the records so he could keep his insane desire to be worshipped hidden from the world. The Lord however made the deleted information available again through the prophet Joseph Smith:

> . . . Satan came tempting him, saying: Moses, son of man, worship me. And it came to pass that Moses looked upon Satan and said: . . . get thee hence, Satan; deceive me not . . . I will not cease to call upon God, I have other things to inquire of him; for his glory has been upon me, wherefore I can judge between him and thee. Depart hence, Satan.
>
> And now, when Moses had said these words, Satan cried with a loud voice, and ranted upon the earth, and commanded, saying: I am the Only Begotten, worship me.
>
> And it came to pass that Moses began to fear exceedingly; and as he began to fear, he saw the bitterness of hell. Nevertheless, calling upon God, he received strength, and he commanded, saying: Depart from me, Satan, for this one God only will I worship, which is the God of glory.
>
> And now Satan began to tremble, and the earth shook; and Moses received strength, and called upon God, saying: In the name of the Only Begotten, depart hence, Satan.
>
> And it came to pass that Satan cried with a loud voice, with weeping,

> and wailing, and gnashing of teeth; and he departed hence, even from the presence of Moses, that he beheld him not. (Moses 1:12-22)

This scripture is quoted this extensively so that it will be seen that Satan's pride, his desire to be worshipped, completely consumes him. So filled is he with envy and a lust for power and glory, that he is utterly incapable of contemplating any other goal or worrying about the terrible consequences to himself. He completely loses control of himself when his demand to be worshipped is refused.

He and his followers are what the scriptures call "vessels of wrath." (D&C 76:33) They are so filled with hate that there is no room for anything else. In one sense of the word they are insane because the only thought processes of which they are capable are those directed toward gratifying their pride and inducing others to worship them.

This loss of ability to utilize one's intelligence to consider and act upon laws which must be obeyed to obtain freedom and joy, is perhaps the most fearful of all the consequences of pride. It is the penalty imposed upon those possessed of a lying spirit. Satan has been called a liar from the beginning. Not only does he deceive others, but himself as well. He is a pitiful victim of his own insensate desire to pervert the truth.

If this analysis of Satan's character is correct, then it is understandable why he would try to destroy free agency. By so doing he magnifies himself in his own eyes. He enlarges his kingdom and increases his power. He brings into captivity more followers and compels them to worship him, thus gratifying his all-consuming lust for glory and dominion.

In so doing, Satan provides that opposition to good which is necessary in all things. Just as God cannot lie, Satan cannot promote the truth. Just as God is love, Satan is hate. Just as the Lord seeks to make men free, Satan seeks to make them slaves.

The Choices We Made In The Pre-Mortal Sphere

God, the Father, being in control, made it possible for His spirit children to choose between these two opposing leaders and philosophies in the pre-existence. Even though the consequence was that a full one-third part chose evil, the necessity of making the choice available was unavoidable. Nothing either good or evil could have happened otherwise. (2 Ne. 2)

A second very large group whose exact size is impossible for us to determine, so conducted themselves in the pre-earth life that they were entitled to come to earth, obtain bodies, and then go to the Celestial Kingdom without being further tempted by Satan. This fact was revealed to the prophet Joseph, and he described it thus:

> And I also beheld that all children who die before they arrive at the years of accountability are saved in the celestial kingdom of heaven. (D&C 137:10)

Now let us consider more closely the character of those of us who come to earth, obtain bodies, and must once again be subject to the temptations of Satan. Even though we chose Christ and rejected Satan in the pre-existence, almost all of us are afflicted with pride and a disposition to follow Satan's plan. Here is the scripture which declares this to be so and describes the consequences we suffer as a result thereof:

> Behold, there are many called, but few are chosen. And why are they not chosen?
>
> Because their hearts are set so much upon the things of this world and aspire to the honors of men that they do not learn this one lesson—
>
> That the rights of the priesthood are inseparably connected with the powers of heaven, and that the powers of heaven cannot be controlled nor handled only upon the principles of righteousness;
>
> That they may be conferred upon us it is true; but when we undertake to cover our sins, or to gratify our pride, our vain ambition, or to exercise control or dominion or compulsion upon the souls of the children of men, in any degree of unrighteousness, . . . Amen to the priesthood or the authority of that man. (D&C 121:34-37)

Our Pride May Be Costing Us That Which We Value Above All Else

It is most apparent that the tendency to be proud and to destroy free agency varies from person to person. But if we accept the foregoing scriptures as true, we are compelled to admit that these Satanic dispositions are so strong and difficult to overcome in almost all of us, that of the many called, only a few of us will be chosen. Or to state the matter otherwise, when given the chance to choose between Christ and Satan here on earth, our weaknesses are such that we will choose Satan to such an extent that we unfit ourselves to exercise the power of the priesthood in the next life.

Like Satan, our pride blinds us to our own self-interest. Our hearts are set so much upon the things of this world and the honors of men that we either are incapable of recognizing, or refuse to recognize, that in seeking for them, we are losing the right to exercise the power of the priesthood. Also like Satan, we will stoop to the exercise of unrighteous dominion to obtain them.

Pride is a disease which causes spiritual blindness. It prevents its victim from even recognizing he is ill. Because of the very nature of the malady, recovery is impossible as long as one is afflicted because repentance requires humility.

There are some vitally important truths regarding the acquisition and retention of knowledge which are involved here. The Lord God Almighty in His infinite wisdom, love and mercy dispenses justice to each of His children with an even hand. Although we may not be able to recognize this fact now, the time will come when we will. (Mosiah 16:1) Through the workings of the spirit He grants each that portion of the truth we are able to understand and live. (Alma 29:8) If one receives and obeys such truths, the Lord increases his understanding with each advance toward the light. As Alma explains the matter:

> . . . and he that will not harden his heart, to him is given the greater portion of the word, until it is given unto him to know the mysteries of God until he know them in full. (Alma 12:10)

On the other hand,

> . . . they that will harden their hearts, to them is given the lesser portion of the word until they know nothing concerning his mysteries; and they are taken captive by the devil, and led by his will down to destruction. Now this is what is meant by the chains of hell. (Alma 12:11)

If we understand that by the words "they will harden their hearts," Alma was referring to the proud, then the terrible consequences of this sin become apparent.

The results which flow from the operation of this basic law regarding the acquisition and retention of knowledge are the only ones which are either possible or beneficial. The things of God are understood only by the spirit of God, which spirit can influence only those who are humble and obedient. Also, since he who sins against the greater light receives the greater condemnation, the operation of the law mercifully spares us punishment to which we would otherwise be subject.

Some may have difficulty recognizing the operation of this law either in their own lives or in the lives of their associates, and may thus doubt the justice of God. In pondering this matter it is well to remember that in dispensing justice the Lord does not immediately punish every sin and reward every virtue. To do this would largely destroy free agency, eliminate the need for faith, and prevent the development of character. Rewards and punishments are postponed so that we can make choices under circumstances which permit us to be enticed to do good or evil without an absolute knowledge of the consequences of the choice. Lehi provides this insight:

> Wherefore, the Lord God gave unto man that he should act for himself. Wherefore, man could not act for himself save it should be that he was enticed by the one or the other.
>
> . . . (men) have become free forever, knowing good from evil; to act for themselves and not to be acted upon, save it be by the punishment of the law at the great and last day, according to the commandments which God hath given. (2 Ne. 2:16, 26)

It should also be observed that this delay in inflicting punishment also permits a probationary period for repentance.

Pride—The Worst Of All Sins?

If it is pride which leads one to become a son of perdition, then it must be considered as the worst of all possible sins. Also, as we shall note as we study Nephite history, time after time it led to enforced priestcraft which in turn caused those who practiced it to commit the unpardonable sin of shedding innocent blood. And finally, if it is causing almost all bearers of the priesthood to lose the priesthood, it should be regarded as one of the most common and fearful of the sins we are able to commit.

Pride leads to many other sins. It causes us to be idolatrous and to spend our time seeking for the things of this world and the honors of men. Because of the feelings of superiority it engenders, we find it impossible to love our neighbor as ourself. Rather than wanting to serve others, we believe it their duty to serve, praise, and honor us. We find it difficult to share our means except possibly for the purpose of being praised for having done so. Because of pride we deny ourselves the guidance of the Holy Ghost.

Pride has many sources. It can arise from one's feelings about his wealth, education, status, position, birth, appearance or achievements. Accomplishments in any field of endeavor such as music, science, sports, academics, writing, speaking or acting may produce feelings of superiority. It also seems to be a disease which is highly contagious because today, according to the prophets and the scriptures, it afflicts almost everyone.

WHAT MUST WE DO TO REPENT?

Of course humility is the only possible cure for the sin of pride and, according to the prophet Jacob, here is the manner in which the remedy must be applied:

> And whoso knocketh, to him will he open; and the wise, and the learned, and they that are rich, who are puffed up because of their learning, and their wisdom, and their riches—yea, they are they whom he despiseth; and save they shall cast these things away, and consider themselves fools before God, and come down in the depths of humility, he will not open unto them. (2 Ne. 9:42)

How many are willing to voluntarily cast away their honors and their riches, come down in the depths of humility, and consider themselves fools before God? Jacob says the Lord will not open unto us until we do. Must calamity come before repentance is possible? Mormon states it to be a general rule that the only thing which will bring repentance and humility is great tragedy. (Hela. 12:1-3)

IX

The Influence Of Prior Governments On Reign Of The Judges

Influence Of Brass Plates

In this work we are primarily concerned with the Nephite experience with self government. However, since our understanding of this experience can be materially aided if we have in mind the religious and political beliefs handed down by their ancestors, we will devote this chapter to a discussion of those governments under which they and their forefathers had lived.

The Brass Plates brought to America by the Nephites contained a detailed record of the laws and governments of the Israelites down to the year 600 B.C., and were regarded by them as the word of God. These plates were to them both the law and the prophets. They contained the will of the Lord on matters both religious and political and their influence on Nephite governments in any period can hardly be overestimated.

The Nephites were led by living prophets to whom they looked for new revelations. But the Brass Plates contained the Ten Commandments and these were the rock foundation of their religious-political code of justice.

The Concept That The Lord Is King And Lawgiver

There is probably no truth contained in the Brass Plates which had a greater impact on Nephite history than this: The Lord is political ruler and lawgiver, and the people can look to Him for guidance and protection when they are obedient to His commandments. The Book of Mormon, like the Old Testament, is filled with accounts of divine intervention on behalf of those who serve and place their trust in the Lord. Throughout their entire history the Nephites were continually finding themselves in such desperate circumstances that they were compelled to go to Him for help.

THERE WAS ONLY ONE SET OF LAWS AND THEY CAME FROM GOD

Those who accept the Lord as king and lawgiver should consider themselves as rebels against His wishes and authority if they enact laws contrary to His laws. To adopt and enforce laws which punish conduct which He has not condemned, is in and of itself a sin of the most serious nature. It would be a forcible taking of life, liberty or property without justification and thus a violation of His commandments. No one has a right to alter the laws of God. Moses told his people:

> Ye shall not add unto the word which I command you, neither shall ye diminish ought from it, that ye may keep the commandments of the Lord your God which I command you. (Deut. 4:2)

In the days of the Israelites the Ten Commandments applied as much to those who enforced them as they did to those against whom they were enforced. Furthermore, not only was it a sin in the eyes of the Lord to punish the innocent, but it was a sin to fail to punish the guilty. (Deut. 19:18-21)

The Israelites entered into a blood covenant to obey the laws, statutes and judgments; (Ex. 24:7, 8) they were to be binding upon them and their posterity forever; (Deut. 29:29) the people were commanded to teach them diligently unto their children; (Deut. 6:7-10) and as a nation they were to be blessed or cursed depending upon the extent to which the laws were obeyed. (Deut. 11:26-28)

ONLY THE PROPHETS AND THE RIGHTEOUS SHOULD HOLD PUBLIC OFFICE

It is illogical to choose men to judge and enforce laws who fail to obey the laws themselves. Such a person is dishonest and cannot be trusted. Unless he believes in a law firmly enough to obey it, he will not be respected and would be a hypocrite if he enforced it.

Since the Israelites and the Nephites believed that they were enforcing the laws of God, the only acceptable candidates for the position of judges were prophets and righteous men. These of course were their religious leaders, priests and teachers. When the political system was established among the Israelites, this is the instruction given concerning the selection of judges or rulers:

> Moreover thou shalt provide out of all the people able men, such as fear God; men of truth, hating covetousness; and place such over them, to be rulers of thousands, and rulers of hundreds, rulers of fifties, and rulers of tens; (Ex 18:21; see also Deut. 1:15)

From the following scripture it appears that after the Levites were separated from the other tribes to serve as priests and do the service of the tabernacle, they also served in the capacity of appellate judges:

> If there arise a matter too hard for thee in judgment . . . thou shalt come unto the priests the Levites, and unto the judge that shall be in those days, and enquire; and they shall shew thee the sentence of judgment. (Deut. 17:8-9; see also Ex. 28:30)

Israelite history provides examples of judges such as Samson and Eli whose personal lives were not entirely above reproach. However as a general rule, the judges were the most righteous and God-fearing men who could be found.

When the Israelites rejected the Lord as their king and demanded a king like other nations, (1 Sam. 8:6, 7) the Lord had His prophets choose their rulers and anoint them to their positions as kings. In so doing the people continued to recognize the Lord as the governing hand in their political affairs.

Union Of Church And State Among The Israelites

Inasmuch as the commandments, statutes and judgments of God were enforced by the Israelites as the laws of the land, and inasmuch as those who taught and enforced them were prophets, priests and other religious leaders, there appeared to be no necessity for a separate state organization. Indeed what functions would remain for a civil government to perform under such circumstances? The religious and political affairs were almost completely integrated and the people could see no need for forming a separate government organization which would only laden them with taxes.

Insofar as we can determine, the united church and state organization had little need to impose taxes. Apparently the people forged their own weapons of war, and when contributions were needed for the building of such things as the ark of the covenant and the tabernacle, the people stepped forward and made sufficient voluntary contributions. The tithes collected seemed to provide all which was needed to carry on united activities. (Lev. 27:26-34)

The Levites who spent their time in serving in religious and judicial capacities, were supported by the tithes of the people. (Num. 18:21) Of course when the people chose to have a king as other nations, their monarchs did not hesitate to impose heavy taxes just as the Lord warned would be the case. (1 Sam. 8:10-18)

Influence Of Nephite Monarchies On The Reign Of The Judges

Since the monarchial form of government which existed among the Nephites appeared to be a continuation of the system of king-rule among the Israelites, we seem justified in assuming that it served to strengthen and perpetuate the customs and influence of the Israelite political system. There are however, some facts related in the Book of Mormon which deserve special mention.

Nephite Kings Were Outstanding Examples Of Personal Righteousness

The Book of Mormon indicates that in most instances, the Nephite kings were inspired prophets of God. The record states that Nephi, Mosiah I, Benjamin and Mosiah II were all exceptional men and great leaders in every sense of the word. Not only were they mighty kings and prophets, but skilled military leaders as well. Mormon is especially lavish in his praise of King Benjamin. (Words of Mormon) He does him the well deserved honor of copying into the record a part of his final discourse.

No Imposition Of Taxes

One crowning evidence of the superiority of the Nephite kings over many of the Israelite monarchs, was that they labored with their own hands for their support rather than burdening the people with taxes. (Mos. 2:14; 29:40) Of course the wicked King Noah imposed a twenty percent tax on his people, (Mosiah 11:3) and the Lamanite kings went even farther and exacted a fifty percent tax from the same group. (Mosiah 19:26)

It also might be noted that after a great many of his men had been killed in trying to throw off Lamanite bondage, King Limhi,

> . . . commanded that every man should impart to the support of the widows and children, that they might not perish with hunger; and this they did because of the greatness of their number that had been slain. (Mosiah 21:17)

We must recognize however that this edict by King Limhi was for the purpose of more equitably apportioning the cost of war rather than to enrich the king or any of his subjects.

The Law Of Moses Enforced By The Nephite Kings

As was true of the Israelites during their periods of righteousness, the Nephite kings enforced the Ten Commandments with their related statutes and judgments. (1 Ne. 4:15; 2 Ne. 5:10; Jarom 1:5) In his great discourse King Benjamin reminded his people;

> Neither have I suffered that ye should be confined in dungeons, nor that ye should make slaves one of another, nor that ye should murder, or plunder, or steal, or commit adultery; nor even have I suffered that ye should commit any manner of wickedness, and have taught you that ye should keep the commandments of the Lord, in all things which he hath commanded you— (Mosiah 2:13;, for a similar statement by King Mosiah II, see Mosiah 29:14, 15)

Union Of Church And State During The Reign Of Nephite Kings

Because the Nephite kings were, in most instances, also prophets of God, they did not need the guidance of other prophets as did so many of the Israelite kings. Thus there was an even greater unity of church and state within the Nephite monarchies than within those of the Israelites.

The Nephite kings appointed the priests and teachers who assisted them in teaching and enforcing the laws of God throughout their realm. (Mosiah 6:3; 11:5)

The Law Of Primogeniture

One common practice among both the Israelites and the Nephites which had an enormous influence on the Nephite government called the reign of the judges, was that of handing down religious and political offices from father to eldest son. It will be remembered that the right to officiate in the Aaronic Priesthood among the Israelites was restricted to the descendants of Levi and that the right to reign as king usually descended from father to son.

The insistence of Laman and Lemuel on their right to rule because they were the elder brethren, caused an enormous amount of bloodshed. (Mosiah 10:11-17) The practice among the Nephites of appointing the eldest son of the previous leader as his successor influenced the people in their voting during the reign of the judges.

The foregoing should help us understand more clearly the reasons and objectives of certain leaders who undertook to alter the laws and form of the Nephite government. Especially should it help explain why such leaders were able to obtain such large followings. The people who lived under the reign of the judges still remembered and studied the political systems of their ancestors and often sought to return to them.

X

Reasons For Changing From Monarchy To Self-Government

The Change In Form Of Government Caused Continual Civil War

When it is remembered that the Nephites had lived under a monarchial form of government for five hundred years and had been ruled over by righteous kings who had dispensed justice and effectively taught and enforced the commandments of the Lord, one is constrained to ask why a change was made.

The Lord who knows the end from the beginning knew that within one hundred and twenty five years He would come among the Nephites, destroy the wicked, and inaugurate a period of perfect happiness, peace and prosperity which would last for almost two hundred years. Why then did He establish for this relatively short period, a government of self-rule which He knew would cause almost continual civil war, and result in the deaths of hundreds of thousands of Lamanites and Nephites?

As we shall note in succeeding chapters, right from the time the new government was established until the coming of Christ, there were continual attempts made by rebellious factions to overthrow this government and substitute something different. Many thousands died in these attempts. The Book of Mormon provides some reasons for the change made in the Nephite government. Let us examine them.

Dangers And Problems Of A Monarchial System Of Government

When King Mosiah proposed to the Nephite people a change in their form of government, they resisted the idea. Their kings had been just, had not imposed taxes, and the people were content to continue as they were. In order to convince them that a change should be made, Mosiah found it necessary to circulate among them a document explaining his reasons therefor.

A portion of that writing has been copied into the record and one of the reasons given therein is that a nation cannot always count on having righteous men for kings. Mosiah pointed out the terrible consequences which befell the people of King Noah when he became wicked. (Mosiah 29:18) He reminded them that,

> . . . ye cannot dethrone an iniquitous king save it be through much contention and the shedding of much blood. (Mosiah 29:21)

Mosiah admitted that a monarchial system was better, but went on to explain that,

> . . . because all men are not just it is not expedient that ye should have a king or kings to rule over you.
>
> For behold, how much iniquity doth one wicked king cause to be committed, yea, and what great destruction! (Mosiah 29:16, 17)

The prophet Alma, in explaining his reasons for refusing to serve as king, gives this further argument against monarchies:

> . . . Behold, it is not expedient that we should have a king; for thus saith the Lord; ye shall not esteem one flesh above another, or one man shall not think himself above another; therefore I say unto you it is not expedient that ye should have a king. (Mosiah 23:7)

THE MOST IMPORTANT REASON: SELF-RULE PROVIDES GREATER FREEDOM

The scriptures explain that it is the purpose of the Lord to provide free agency for His children. A government subject to the voice of the people promotes this purpose more than any other type and it seems reasonable to conclude that this is the primary reason for establishing this system of government. In the following quote, Mosiah stated this to be one of his purposes:

> And now I desire that this inequality should be no more in this land, especially among this my people; but I desire that this land be a land of liberty, and every man may enjoy his rights and privileges alike, so long as the Lord sees fit that we may live and inherit the land, . . . (Mosiah 29:32)

Let us note the nature of those rights and privileges which the Nephite voters acquired under their new government.

1. In the past, the kings had proclaimed the law of Moses to be the law of the land and had enforced it against their subjects. Under the new arrangement the people, by majority vote, could repeal or amend those laws, or adopt new ones in their stead. Not only could such changes be made nationally, but on a local basis as well. The majority even had the right to change their form of government back to a monarchy.
2. In the past the king inherited the right to reign, subject to the law of common consent which was nearly always granted. He also had the power to appoint priests, teachers, judges, and other functionaries of government. Under the new government the people had the right to choose their judges and administrators by ballot.
3. Each person had a right to run for public office and, if elected, to be paid for his services out of public funds.
4. The people had the power to adopt laws providing for the collection of taxes. This was perhaps the most fearsome power they possessed, and the one which caused the most temptation and trouble.

Responsibilities Accompanying Increased Rights And Privileges

When the Lord grants people increased freedom, invariably He also gives them increased duties. In this scripture Mosiah reminds the Nephite voters of this fact:

> And I command you to do these things in the fear of the Lord; and I command you to do these things, and that ye have no king; that if these people commit sins and iniquities they shall be answered upon their own heads. (Mosiah 29:30)

Mosiah also told the people of the punishments they must expect if they committed sins and iniquities:

> Now it is not common that the voice of the people desireth anything contrary to that which is right; but it is common for the lesser part of the

> people to desire that which is not right; therefore this shall ye observe and make it your law—to do your business by the voice of the people.
>
> And if the time comes that the voice of the people doth choose iniquity, then is the time that the judgments of God will come upon you; yea, then is the time he will visit you with great destruction even as he has hitherto visited this land. (Mosiah 29:26, 27)

Why Would The Lord Destroy A People For Voting Wrong?

In the foregoing scripture the Lord promises destruction if the people chose iniquity by corrupting their laws. The Nephite people appeared to realize that it would be sinful for them to do so because the record tells us that when they accepted the new form of government:

> . . . they relinquished their desires for a king, and became exceedingly anxious that every man should have an equal chance throughout all the land; yea, and every man expressed a willingness to answer for his own sins. (Mosiah 29:38)

What sins could they commit under the new system which they could not commit theretofore? What sins can any people commit under a government subject to the voice of the people? It seems that today, we do not exercise our power of self-government in the fear of the Lord as Mosiah advised his people to do in the quote above. Neither do most of us suspect that we might be visited with great destruction for voting wrong. Probably we do not sense the nature of the duties and responsibilities which come with the rights and privileges of self-rule as did the Nephites. Let us try to understand their attitude and also why the Lord would destroy them for voting wrong.

The Power Of Self-Rule Is The Power To Alter God's Commandments

The Nephites were aware that from the very beginning the Israelite governments, as well as their own, had enforced the Ten Commandments and imposed the penalties provided for violation. Is it not likely that they would consider it a sin to alter those laws?

Under king-rule they had their freedom to violate the laws of God but only at the risk of being punished for doing so. Now they have the power to repeal those laws so they can violate them without being punished. They also have the power to reduce or even eliminate the penalties.

Is it surprising that the Lord would destroy them for perverting His laws in this manner? Ponder the effect such changes would have upon the morals of the youth if the laws which punished evil were repealed, and a new set which punished good were adopted. Government being one of the most effective influences in society would then be teaching that good is evil and evil is good. It can hardly be expected that the Lord would tolerate this for long.

The Power To Tax Is The Power To Commit Plunder Through Government

It will be recalled that the righteous Nephite kings had not imposed taxes on the people but had performed their heavy duties free of charge. The new government however was endowed with the power to collect taxes with which to pay judges and other officers who would administer the affairs of state.

When it is remembered that Nephite voters had the power to make laws creating new public offices and compel the payment of public salaries, the opportunity for corruption becomes apparent. Any Nephite voter who was thinking would realize that this new political system opened up enormous opportunities for committing sins. If he could get enough people to go along with him, he could commit plunder on a grand scale and do so without fear of punishment. Perhaps the Nephites were thinking about these possibilities when they agreed to answer for the sins of their government.

To abuse the power to tax in this manner would of course be a violation of the Lord's commandment, "Thou shalt not steal." If the Nephites converted their government into an instrument of plunder, and if no human agency was available to punish the sin, then it would only be expected that the Lord would step in and visit them with great destruction just as He promised.

As we shall see as we discuss the activities of the new government, the power to tax, along with the power to create new government jobs, proved to be a temptation which hundreds of thousands of Nephites could not resist. Many attempts were made by various groups to seize control of the government and use it for these purposes.

The Power Of Self-Government Is The Power To Destroy Freedom

By granting people the freedom of self-government, the Lord at the same time gives them the power to destroy that freedom. The amount of freedom in any nation depends upon the laws of that nation and how they are enforced. God's laws protect freedom by punishing evil and protecting good. Satan's laws destroy freedom by punishing good and protecting and committing evil. If the Nephites were to corrupt the purpose of their government in this manner, they would realize they were doing evil and again, since there is no human agency to punish them, it can only be expected that the Lord will punish them.

Separation Of Church And State Does Nothing To Alter The Lord's Commandments Concerning Government

When the Church is set up as a separate organization, it seems easy to forget that the Lord's commandments and laws concerning government still apply. The following reminds us of our political accountability:

> We believe that governments were instituted of God for the benefit of men; and that he holds men accountable for their acts in relation to them, both in making laws and administering them, for the good and safety of society. (D&C 134:1)

In a nation of self-governing people, every citizen can expect to be held accountable for obeying the Lord's commandments concerning government. The separation of Church and state does nothing to alter this fact. In the following chapters we shall note how well the Nephites remembered and obeyed the Lord's commandments regarding government during that period when their Church was set up as a separate organization.

XI

The Nephite Experience With Enforced Priestcraft

Much Of The Book Of Mormon Is Devoted To The Subject Of Priestcraft

We shall now discuss some of the most disturbing, yet valuable information contained in the Book of Mormon. It is the knowledge provided regarding the plan of Satan to use government to deceive and enslave mankind. The detailed description of this plan, and the many examples of its implementation, are found in the history of that relatively brief period from about 160 B.C. to the time of Christ's advent in 34 A.D. There are very few details given of Nephite political history either prior or subsequent to this period. But during this 204-year span, there is a wealth of information about governments, wars and political issues, virtually all of which relates to Satan's attempts to capture control of the Nephite government and use it to teach false doctrines and enslave the people.

Most of Nephite political history is concerned with the attempts of various apostate groups to implement the diabolical plan of enforced priestcraft. The Nephites, having been given their political freedom to do so, were continually voting with both pen and sword on this political issue.

One of the most frightening pieces of information contained in the history of this period is the description of the fate it gives of those who, once having known the truth, allowed their pride to lead them to fight and die for the plan of enforced priestcraft. They committed some of the most horrible crimes imaginable because they acted under the influence of the evil one. The importance this information has for us today cannot be overestimated because the doctrine of enforced priestcraft is now almost universally accepted.

WHAT IS "ENFORCED PRIESTCRAFT?"

The Book of Mormon defines priestcraft as follows:

> He commandeth that there shall be no priestcrafts; for, behold, priestcrafts are that men preach and set themselves up for a light unto the world, that they may get gain and praise of the world; but they seek not the welfare of Zion.
>
> Behold, the Lord hath forbidden this thing. . . (2 Ne. 26:29, 30)

A definition of "enforced priestcraft" is also contained in the Book of Mormon. It is contained in the following quote which describes the philosophy of a man named Nehor who first tried to incorporate it into the Nephite laws during the reign of the judges:

> And he had gone about among the people, preaching to them that which he termed to be the word of God, bearing down against the church; declaring unto the people that every priest and teacher ought to become popular; and they ought not to labor with their own hands, but that they ought to be supported by the people. (Alma 1:3)

Thus there are two types of priestcraft: That which is enforced and that which is not. The enforced type advocated by Nehor is imposed by the police power. Laws are passed which create public jobs for priests, teachers and any others who may be engaged in the project of state education. The taxing power is used to compel the payment of their salaries. This topic will be discussed more fully later.

One of the most abominable aspects of enforced priestcraft is not mentioned in the above quote, but was an essential part of Nehor's scheme. This is that government uses its powers to give itself an exclusive monopoly on the business of education. This means that all competing institutions are abolished. This is the usual aim of all who favor enforced priestcraft and was an integral part of Nehor's plan. (Alma 2:4) From these facts we observe that there are two essential aspects of enforced priestcraft: (1) The compulsory teaching of false doctrines, the most pernicious of which is that of enforced priestcraft. (2) The prohibition of the teaching of the Lord's plan of freedom. Let us consider some of the accounts given of the practice of enforced priestcraft in the Book of Mormon.

Enforced Priestcraft Was Practiced Under King Noah

The first case of enforced priestcraft described by the Book of Mormon was that practiced by the people of King Noah. He imposed a twenty per cent income tax to support himself, his corp of paid teachers and their wives and concubines. Rather than teaching and enforcing the Ten Commandments, they violated nearly every one of them in carrying on their evil scheme.

They became idle, engaged in adultery, used the power of government to steal and taught lies. Then when Abinadi and Alma tried to teach the Gospel of Freedom, they martyred the one and tried to kill the other. The wickedness and suffering which enforced priestcraft caused this people is incalculable. The underlying fault which brought this calamity on the people was pride. This fact is indicated by the following passage which describes how Noah chose his priests:

> For he put down all the priests that had been consecrated by his father, and consecrated new ones in their stead, such as were lifted up in the pride of their hearts. (Mosiah 11:5)

The Amulonites Practiced Enforced Priestcraft

As the martyred Abinadi had prophesied as he was being burned to death at the stake, king Noah was also put to death by fire. However his wicked priests who barely escaped with their lives, kidnapped some Lamanite maidens, took them to wife and started a community of their own in the wilderness. A short time later however, a Lamanite army found them and took them captive. This state of bondage did not last long. Remembering the soft life they had led as professional teachers, they induced the Lamanite king to hire them to teach the Nephite language and certain business skills to his people. Thus, once again they commenced to practice enforced priestcraft.

Their evil profession once again subjected them to the influence of Satan. When a group of Lamanites who had been converted by the sons of Mosiah refused to take up arms against an army of Lamanites who came against them, it was mainly these Amulonites and another group of apostate Nephites who practiced enforced priestcraft, who slew a thousand of those saints while they were kneeling defenseless on the ground. The record tells us:

> Now the greatest number of those of the Lamanites who slew so many of their brethren were Amalekites and Amulonites, the greatest number of whom were after the order of the Nehors. (Alma 24:28; See also Alma 25:5-7)

There is a very important fact pointed out about the type of priestcraft practiced by the Amulonites which is that they taught no religion, but only secular subjects. The following passage carefully explains this:

> And they (the Lamanites) were a people friendly one with another; nevertheless they knew not God; neither did the brethren of Amulon teach them anything concerning the Lord their God, neither the law of Moses; nor did they teach them the words of Abinadi;
>
> But they taught them that they should keep their record, and that they might write one to another.
>
> And thus the Lamanites began to increase in riches, and began to trade one with another and wax great, and began to be a cunning and a wise people as to the wisdom of the world, yea, a very cunning people, delighting in all manner of wickedness and plunder . . . (Mosiah 24:5-7)

Here then is a case of enforced priestcraft without religion because these Amulonites were after the order of Nehor. (Alma 24:28, 29) This being so, every government supported educational system, whether it teaches religion or not, falls under the Book of Mormon definition of enforced priestcraft. To the extent that a government controls education, the individual members of society cannot; and it matters not the nature of the subjects being taught. In every case freedom to exchange knowledge is restricted by force. Not only is tax money forcibly taken and used to teach that which the government decrees, but students are ofttimes compelled to spend their time under the supervision of government teachers. Thus they are denied their right to use that time in a different learning environment.

THE AMLICITES PRACTICED ENFORCED PRIESTCRAFT

In the fifth year of the reign of the judges, a man named Amlici who was very cunning and wise as to the wisdom of the world, came among the Nephites preaching enforced priestcraft. So successful was he, that he thought he had won a majority to accept the doctrine. Therefore he successfully induced the government to submit the issue to the vote of the people. Under his proposal the government of freedom would be abolished, a monarchy established with himself as king, and the practice of enforced priestcraft would be adopted.

Fortunately Amlici lost the election. When this occurred he and his followers became so angry that they formed an army and undertook to overthrow the Nephite government by force. In this they also failed, but only after more than eighteen thousand had been slain. They then induced a huge Lamanite army to join them in a second attempt which also ended in their defeat. In this battle so many were killed that they were not counted. Those Amlicites who did not perish, joined with and became part of the Lamanites.

It seems incredible that almost half of the Nephites would rebel against their own government merely for the sake of supporting the practice of enforced priestcraft. What could have induced them to do so? The following scripture which, after describing the execution of Nehor for murdering Gideon, states that the doctrine was popular because of pride and a love for the things of the world:

> Nevertheless, this (the execution of Nehor) did not put an end to the spreading of priestcraft through the land; for there were many who loved the vain things of the world, and they went forth preaching false doctrines; and this they did for the sake of riches and honor. (Alma 1:16)

This experience teaches that when a group of people who have known the Gospel, become so proud that they accept the doctrine of enforced priestcraft, they so subject themselves to the influence of Satan that they rebel against God, commit murder, and risk their lives in support of their profession. Not only may their pride cost them everything they prize here on earth, but in the eternities as well. Mormon explains the eternal consequences of the decision made by those who did and those who did not accept the doctrine of enforced priestcraft in these words:

> And in one year were thousands and tens of thousands of souls sent to the eternal world, that they might reap their rewards according to their works, whether they were good or whether they were bad, to reap eternal

> happiness or eternal misery, according to the spirit which they listed to obey, whether it be a good spirit or a bad one. For every man receiveth wages of him whom he listeth to obey, . . . (Alma 3:26, 27)

THE AMMONIHAHITES PRACTICED ENFORCED PRIESTCRAFT

The people of the city of Ammonihah, having the political autonomy which enabled them to do so, corrupted their laws and established enforced priestcraft in their city. In the tenth year of the reign of the judges, Alma went there to call them to repentance. However the majority refused to listen. The record says that "Satan had gotten great hold upon the hearts of the people of the city." (Alma 8:9)

And indeed he had for when Alma and Amulek made some converts in the city, the lawyers, priests and judges, all of whom were after the order of Nehor, became so violently angry, that they first cast the male converts out of the city and then burned their wives and children to death. And so once again we see the practice of enforced priestcraft leading its practitioners to commit murder. For this terrible crime, the Lord slew every living inhabitant of the city.

THE ZORAMITES PRACTICED ENFORCED PRIESTCRAFT

Like the people of Ammonihah, the Zoramites living in the land of Antionum had also corrupted their laws and adopted the practice of enforced priestcraft. The record states that their pride was so great that they forcibly excluded the poor from their places of worship and refused to associate with them. Alma and his missionary companions went among them to call them to repentance and had much success among the poor.

However the rulers of the city became so angry at the converts that they ejected them from the land. Then when these outcasts found refuge among the converted Lamanites in the land of Jershon, this so enraged the haughty Zoramites that they joined the Lamanites and waged war against the entire Nephite nation. Their purpose, like that of the Amlicites, was to overthrow that government which permitted religious freedom.

Even though the Lamanite-Zoramite-Amulonite-Amalekite armies which combined together to destroy the Nephite government was more than twice the size of the Nephite army opposing them, the Lord intervened once again to protect His government of freedom. The valiant Nephite troops were so strengthened that they slaughtered an enormous number of their enemies and drove the remainder from their lands. And so once again the Book of Mormon provides a graphic description of the terrible consequences of enforced priestcraft.

THE KING-MEN UNDERTOOK TO PRACTICE ENFORCED PRIESTCRAFT

The war with the Zoramites had cost the lives of so many Nephites, and there were so many other dissensions among them, that it became necessary for Helaman and the other religious leaders to regulate the affairs of the Church. The record says that in doing this, "They did appoint priests and teachers throughout all the land over all the churches." (Alma 45:22)

These appointments caused a mortal hatred among certain people in the church. Apparently it arose either because Helaman and his brethren had removed some priests and teachers who had previously held office, or because they failed to appoint some who, because of high birth, felt they had a right to office. It also appears that it was not only positions in the church which were affected by these appointments, but government positions as well. It is likely that in most if not all cases, those who failed to secure an appointment in the church, were also effectively denied the office of judge which was a paid position.

These conclusions seem justified since it was the custom of the Nephites to elect to the position of judge, those who were appointed as church leaders. Being selected as a priest in the church seemed to be tantamount to being elected as judge. In any event the greater part of those who became angry at Helaman and his brethren were "the lower judges of the land, and they were seeking for power." (Alma 46:4) They united behind a man named Amalickiah who sought to overthrow the government and make himself king. He promised his followers,

> . . . that if they would support him and establish him to be their king that he would make them rulers over the people. (Alma 46:5)

Once again we find a very large number of Nephites who, because of their insensate desires for the things of this world and the honors of men, chose enforced priestcraft. In doing so they supported Amalickiah in his traitorous undertaking to overthrow the government.

However Amalickiah found that he did not have enough followers to win an election and so he, like so many other power-hungry apostate Nephites before him, tried to lead his people to the land of Nephi, join the Lamanites, and then return and seize control of the Nephite government by bloody warfare.

The Nephite armies were able to head the army of Amalickiah in its flight and return it to the land of Zarahemla. But Amalickiah and a few of his men were able to escape and join the Lamanites. This proved to be extremely unfortunate because Amalickiah, through murder and intrigue was able to make himself king over the Lamanites. He then commenced a terrible two-front war against the Nephites which lasted some eleven years. This war caused an immense amount of death and destruction.

The only events of this war which we will mention here are the two attempts of a group called kingmen to take over control of the Nephite government and make it a monarchy. Apparently those involved in these attempts were those who had supported Amalickiah's bid for power. The record describes them thus:

> Now those who were in favor of kings were those of high birth, and they sought to be kings; and they were supported by those who sought power and authority over the people. (Alma 51:8)

These kingmen first tried to establish a monarchy through the ballot box. Failing this, they waited until the war with the Lamanites reached a critical state, and then revolted against the government. They drove the chief judge from his seat and established a king over the land of Zarahemla. The reign of this monarchy was very short. Moroni returned from the battle front with an army and put the king and many of his followers to death, thus reestablishing a government of freedom.

Professional Teachers Should Study The Accounts Of Enforced Priestcraft Given In The Book Of Mormon

There were a number of other attempts made by apostate Nephites to overthrow the Nephite government, but the foregoing should be adequate to teach us what we should know about enforced priestcraft. It is difficult to avoid the conclusion that the many descriptions of this abominable practice and its horrible consequences contained in the Book of Mormon were placed there to warn us against allowing our own government to practice it.

Any person who engages in the teaching profession might do well to learn about the risks he runs in doing so by studying the accounts given of such men as Sherem, Korihor, Amlici, Amalickiah, Antionah and Zoram. There is also a record of two men, Alma and Zeezrom, who experienced eternal torment for opposing the Lord's work, but then repented. The graphic account given of the terrible sufferings of these men before they were forgiven, might also be of interest. (Alma 15, 36)

We are not given the step-by-step backsliding of this Jareditic civilization till it reached the social and governmental chaos the record sets out, but those steps seem wholly clear from the results. Put into modern terms, we can understand them. First there was a forsaking of the righteous life, and the working of wickedness; then must have come the extortion and oppression of the poor by the rich; then retaliation and reprisal by the poor against the rich; then would come a cry to share the wealth which should belong to all; then the easy belief that society owed every man a living whether he worked or not; then the keeping of a great body of idlers; then when community revenues failed to do this, as they have always failed and always will fail, a self-helping by one to the goods of his neighbor; and finally when the neighbor resisted, as resist he must, or starve with his family, then death to the neighbor and all that belonged to him. This was the decreed "fulness of iniquity."

Lehi, with Ishmael, and their families, came to this "a choice land above all other lands, a chosen land of the Lord," with the same promisd blessings and the same overhanging judgments that were made to Jared and his brother.

The recounting of the history of this people is unnecessary, because you know it. Beginning with mere disputes, there grew bickerings, then quarrelings, then ruptures, then two peoples, then one cursed for its iniquities, then wars and counterwars, while this people marched steadily towards their "fulness of iniquity." (J. Reuben Clark, *Stand Fast By Our Constitution*, pp. 177-179.)

XII

The Nephite Experience With Secret Combinations

A Review Of The Second Sixty Years Of Self-Government

In the prior chapter we surveyed the major political events of the first sixty years of the reign of the judges among the Nephites. In that period, many wars were fought and hundreds of thousands were killed. Insofar as can be determined, in every case the aggressors were led, urged on, and incited by apostate Nephites seeking to overthrow the Nephite government and impose a system of enforced priestcraft.

We will now consider the second sixty years of self-rule and we will find that during this period, the efforts to capture political control continued with the aggressors being secret combinations. Furthermore the attempts made by this group were as unceasing and frequent as were those of the proponents of priestcraft. Since a great many Lamanites had been converted to the Gospel at this time and the race wars between them and the Nephites had ceased, we find Lamanites and Nephites joining together on both sides. Regardless of this change, the purpose of the aggressors was still the same as theretofore—to capture control of the Nephite government and abolish freedom. The government was overthrown twice during this second period. In the first instance, the Gadianton Band obtained control through secret murders, intrigue and the teaching of false political doctrines. The Nephite voters were seduced into abolishing the laws of God and substituting therefore the laws proposed by the secret combinations.

The second overthrow occurred just three or four years before the coming of Christ. In this case the Robbers through murder and corruption brought about a dissolution of the government but were unable to seize control. In this instance the Nephites knowingly and intentionally corrupted the Lord's laws. Then when the prophets tried to preach repentance, they were slain. When there was an attempt made to bring the judges responsible for these murders to justice, they formed a secret combination, murdered the chief judge, and caused the Nephite government to break up into tribes. Unpunished prophet-murder is the one crime the Lord will not tolerate and so He virtually exterminated the Nephite nation when He came among them in the year 34 A.D. Let us note the methods used by the Gadianton Band in their surreptitious takeover of the Nephite government. To provide a better understanding of why so many Nephites and Lamanites elected to join, fight, and die for the secret combinations, let us note what the record says about their purpose and philosophy.

What Is The Purpose Of Secret Combinations?

We have no record of secret combinations among the Nephites prior to the fortieth year of the reign of the judges. But in that year a group formed under the leadership of a man named Gadianton, and these groups bore his name among the Nephites from that time forward. They were called robbers and murderers because, as the record states:

> It was the object of all those who belonged to his band to murder, and to rob, and to gain power, (and this was their secret plan, and their combination) . . . (Hela. 2:8)

The power these organizations always seek is political. They want to control the armies and the police because these are the greatest physical forces in society and when they control them, they can steal, kill and commit other wickedness with impunity. Without power over government, they must act in secret through their combinations: hence the name, secret combinations. If those in political power are using government as the Lord intends, and are punishing evil which comes to their attention, then the only way these organizations can operate is in secret.

Moroni describes their insatiable lust for power in these words:

> For it cometh to pass that whoso buildeth it up seeketh to overthrow the freedom of all lands, nations, and countries; and it bringeth to pass the destruction of all people, for it is built up by the devil, who is the father of all lies; . . . (Ether 8:25)

What Is The Philosophy Of The Secret Combinations?

We noted that the purpose of those advocating enforced priestcraft was to seize control of government so that they might use it for the main purposes of compelling the teaching of falsehood, and of preventing the teaching of the Lord's plan of freedom. Although the underlying philosophy of secret combinations includes these objectives, it goes even further. Their aim is to totally destroy freedom by abolishing the right of private property. When the state controls the very means by which life is sustained and freedom is exercised, it is able to dictate and control virtually every human activity including that of education.

This underlying philosophy and purpose is revealed by the following excerpt from a letter written by Giddianhi, the leader of the secret band to Lachoneus, the leader of the Nephites. In this letter he threatens to exterminate the Nephites unless they surrender their property voluntarily:

> Therefore I write unto you, desiring that ye would yield up unto this my people, your cities, your lands, and your possessions, rather than that they should visit you with the sword and that destruction should come upon you.
>
> Or in other words, yield yourselves up unto us, and unite with us and become acquainted with our secret works, and become our brethren that ye may be like unto us—not our slaves, but our brethren and partners of all our substance. (3 Ne. 3:6, 7)

This excerpt reveals two important facts: (1) The Gadianton Band was practicing communism and, (2) They were trying to compel the Nephites to "be like unto us," and engage in it also. What else could Giddianhi have meant by the term, "partners of all our substance?" What other meaning can be placed on his threat to destroy the Nephites unless they "yield up unto this my people, your cities, your lands, and your possessions?"

Communism Appeals To The Baser Instincts Of Men

Communism has a greater appeal to the evil in men than any other political philosophy. While enforced priestcraft provides government jobs only for teachers, priests, educators and those who administer the system, under Communism where the state owns all the property and all means for the production and distribution of goods and services, state jobs are created for every activity whatsoever. Also the opportunity to exercise unrighteous dominion is increased to its maximum. And finally those who control government also control all of the things of this world, which lie within their jurisdiction. It is for these reasons that Communism has such an irresistible appeal to the proud, the power-hungry and those who seek to live on the labor of others. It is the perfect system for wickedness of all kinds.

Members of secret combinations use it to commit murder and plunder in their own interest. But to obtain and maintain their power, they appeal to the evil in men. To the poor and the indolent they offer a living without work. To the power hungry they offer countless opportunities to rule over others. To those who desire to destroy the work of God, they provide a police force which will kill the saints and the prophets. To those who desire to commit sin without punishment, they offer a set of laws which either do not punish iniquity, or which enable the wicked to escape punishment by the payment of money. A completely corrupted government is truly the MOTHER OF ABOMINATIONS.

THE NEPHITE VOTERS WERE SEDUCED INTO ADOPTING COMMUNISM

With the foregoing observations in mind, let us note what the record says regarding the reasons for the Communist takeover of the Nephite government the first time. The following quotes tell us that the laws had been corrupted by the voice of the people:

> . . . they had altered and trampled under their feet the law of Mosiah, or that which the Lord commanded him to give unto the people; . . . (Hela. 4:22)
>
> For as their laws and their governments were established by the voice of the people, and those who chose evil were more numerous than they who chose good, therefore they were ripening for destruction, for the laws had become corrupted. (Hela. 5:2)

Then in the following verses we are told the role of the Gadianton Band in the corruption of these laws:

> And it came to pass that the Lamanites did hunt the band of robbers of Gadianton; and they did preach the word of God among the more wicked part of them, insomuch that this band of robbers was utterly destroyed from among the Lamanites.
>
> And it came to pass on the other hand, that the Nephites did build them up and support them, beginning at the more wicked part of them, until they had overspread all the land of the Nephites, and had seduced the more part of the righteous until they had come down to believe in their works and partake of their spoils, and to join with them in their secret murders and combinations. (Hela. 6:37, 38)

This quote states that even the more part of the righteous Nephites were seduced to partake of the spoils of government. These spoils of course, are the fruits of Communism. It is obvious that the Band had induced the voters to adopt welfare state programs into the laws of the land. It will be recalled that the Nephite voters had the power to impose taxes and thus enrich themselves from the public trough. This should explain one of the main reasons the laws had been corrupted. The Book of Mormon gives a concise description of the consequences of this corruption. Let us note what it says. Nephi, who had resigned his position as chief judge, and had been in the land northward preaching, returned to Zarahemla to find this situation:

> And seeing the people in a state of such awful wickedness, and those Gadianton robbers filling the judgment seats—having usurped the power and authority of the land; laying aside the commandments of God, and not in the least aright before him; doing no justice unto the children of men;
>
> Condemning the righteous because of their righteousness; letting the guilty and the wicked go unpunished because of their money; and moreover to be held in office at the head of government, to rule and do according to their wills, that they might get gain and glory of the world, and, moreover, that they might the more easily commit adultery, and steal, and kill, and do according to their own wills. (Hela. 7:4, 5)

Has anyone written a more accurate and concise description of Communism than this? It is Satan's ultimate plan of wickedness and it's effective operation requires the abolition of private property. Obviously the Lord's Church cannot function under such a system. Not only would such a government jail or murder those who attempted to operate the Church, but without the ownership and control of private property, there could be no building of chapels and temples; no printing of books and literature; no support of missionaries and similar activities carried on by religious denominations. If the Church were permitted to exist at all in a

Communist country, it would continually face restraints which would prevent it from functioning properly.

Character Weakness Caused Nephite Voters To Adopt Communism?

Nephi, the son of Helaman II, who was the prophet at this time, delivered a speech to the Nephite people regarding the corruption of their laws. He accused them of uniting themselves to the Gadianton band and listed in some detail the reasons for their having done so. A portion of that speech is found in the seventh and eighth chapters of Helaman. We quote the following therefrom:

> But behold, it is to get gain, to be praised of men, yea, and that ye might get gold and silver. And ye have set your hearts upon the riches and the vain things of this world, for the which ye do murder, and plunder, and steal, and bear false witness against your neighbor, and do all manner of iniquity.
>
> Yea, wo be unto you because of that great abomination which has come among you; and ye have united yourselves unto it, yea, to that secret band which was established by Gadianton!
>
> Yea, wo shall come unto you because of that pride which ye have suffered to enter your hearts . . . (Hela. 7:21, 25, 26)

Once again, as was the case with those who favored enforced priestcraft, it was the sin of pride which induced the people to corrupt their government.

The Lord Permitted The Nephites To Escape From The Gadianton Band

It appears that because the Nephites had been seduced and deceived into accepting Satan's plan this first time, the Lord was merciful to them and permitted them to repent and restore His government of freedom. This repentance however did not come without extensive suffering. With Satan's forces in control, civil war broke out and became so widespread that the entire nation faced extinction. At that point the Lord sent a famine which stopped the fighting but threatened mass starvation. Only when faced with annihilation from this source did the Nephites listen to the words of their prophet, repent, and cleanse their government of secret combinations. (Hela. 11)

Tens Of Thousands Continued To Join The Secret Combinations

The Nephite experience with Gadianton robbers, civil war, and famine, ended in the 76th year of the reign of the judges. However it was only four years thereafter that the Band formed again and enticed tens of thousands of Nephites and Lamanites to join it. In the eighty second year of the reign of the judges, which was only the seventh year after the first destruction of the Band, the record states that it had increased to such an enormous size that it threatened the combined armies of the Nephites and the Lamanites:

> And the robbers did still increase and wax strong, insomuch that they did defy the whole armies of the Nephites, and also of the Lamanites; and they did cause great fear to come unto the people upon all the face of the land.
>
> Yea, for they did visit many parts of the land, and did do great destruction unto them; yea, did kill many, and did carry away others captive into the wilderness, yea and more especially their women and their children. (Hela. 11:32, 33)

It was at this point in his labors as a historian that Mormon paused to comment upon the rapidity with which his people forgot the consequences of their awful iniquity and returned to it time and again. As usual he attributes their troubles to pride:

> O how foolish, and how vain, and how evil, and devilish, . . . and to set their hearts upon the vain things of this world! Yea, how quick to be lifted up in pride; yea, how quick to boast, and do all manner of that which is iniquity . . . (Hela. 12:4, 5)

The Secret Combinations Finally Destroyed The Nephite Government

During the forty years immediately preceding the coming of the

Lord, the Band continued to form time after time and many thousands of both Nephites and Lamanites continued to join it and fight and die for it as they repeatedly attempted to conquer the Nephite government. At one point the robbers became so numerous, and the threat of destruction so serious, that the righteous who opposed them found it necessary to gather up all of their possessions including a seven-year food supply, and retire to a relatively small area where they could better defend themselves.

The robbers, not having anything to steal, and having exhausted almost all the wild game in the mountains, found themselves in such a weakened condition that they decided to temporarily abandon their efforts to conquer and retire to the land northward. They were headed in their flight and annihilated. All of them were either killed or compelled to enter into a covenant of peace. The record relates that this was the most sanguinary war ever fought among the descendants of Lehi up to that time. It ended about eight years prior to the coming of the Lord.

The enormous relief the people felt when the threat of their extinction was removed, deeply humbled them. The record says:

> Therefore they did forsake all their sins, and their abominations, and their whoredoms, and did serve God with all diligence day and night. (3 Ne. 5:3)

As impossible as it may seem, it was only five years until the Nephites once again reverted to extreme wickedness. Things became so bad that,

> In the thirtieth year the church was broken up in all the land save it were among a few of the Lamanites who were converted unto the true faith, and they would not depart from it. . . (3 Ne. 6:14)

Once again the source of their problem was pride:

> Now the cause of this iniquity of the people was this—Satan had great power, unto the stirring up of the people to do all manner of iniquity, and to the puffing them up with pride, tempting them to seek for power, and authority, and riches, and the vain things of the world. (3 Ne. 6:15)

Apparently pride had once again caused the corruption of government because we are told that when the prophets tried to call them to repentance,

> There were many of the people who were exceedingly angry because of those who testified of these things; and those who were angry were chiefly the chief judges, and they who had been high priests and lawyers; yea, all those who were lawyers were angry with those who testified of these things. (3 Ne. 6:21)

So angry were the lawyers and the judges that they took the prophets and put them to death secretly so that the knowledge of their death did not come to the attention of the governor of the land who alone had the power to authorize the death penalty. There was then an attempt made to bring these murderers to justice. However they and their relatives and friends formed a secret combination and murdered the chief judge. This together with the other wickedness of the people, brought down the government. The people then broke up into tribes.

It is interesting to observe that when the people corrupted their laws this time, they sinned knowingly for the record says:

> Now they did not sin ignorantly, for they knew the will of God concerning them, for it had been taught unto them, therefore they did willfully rebel against their God. (3 Ne. 6:18)

This willful violation of God's laws brought terrible and swift retribution.

GOD WILL NOT ALLOW PROPHET-MURDER TO GO UNPUNISHED

It was at this point that the Lord virtually exterminated the Nephite nation. After the tempests, earthquakes, fires, whirlwinds and upheavals had ceased, the Lord's voice was heard proclaiming the extent of the disaster. He mentioned sixteen prominent cities which had been obliterated. He described the fate of the city of Jacobugath which was the principal city of the Gadianton robbers, in these words:

> And behold, that great city Jacobugath, which was inhabited by the people of king Jacob, have I caused to be burned with fire because of their sins and their wickedness, which was above all the wickedness of the whole earth because of their secret murders and combinations; for it was they that did destroy the peace of my people and the government of the land; therefore I did cause them to be burned, to destroy them from before

> my face, that the blood of the prophets and the saints should not come up unto me any more against them. (3 Ne. 9:9)

In describing the fate of the sixteen cities he had destroyed, the Lord mentioned six different times that he was avenging the blood of the prophets and saints who had been slain. It also seems significant that in the above quote the Lord describes the wickedness of the Gadianton robbers as being above all the wickedness of the whole earth. Moroni confirms that they are the ultimate in wickedness in the following verse:

> And it came to pass that they (the Jaredites) formed a secret combination, even as they of old; which combination is most abominable and wicked above all, in the sight of God: (Ether 8:18)

In his statement regarding the position of the Church on Communism, President McKay declared that it is the greatest satanical threat . . . on the face of the earth, and that it is diametrically opposed to everything for which the Church stands. Thus we have been warned against Satan's organizations by prophets both ancient and modern.

What Lessons Should The Gentiles Learn From The Nephite Experience With Self-Government?

We have now completed our review of the Nephite experience with self-government. What lessons should we learn from all of these stories of war and bloodshed? Do they have an important message for us today? Are political beliefs important in the sight of God? Can we condemn ourselves eternally merely by opposing or failing to support the Lord's plan of freedom? We have seen how hundreds of thousands of Nephites and Lamanites perished fighting over opposing political philosophies. The Lord established a government among them subject to the voice of the people. Then He allowed Satan to offer the voters enforced priestcraft and Communism. Has He done the same thing for us today? Is it our failure to heed this message of the Book of Mormon which has placed the whole Church under condemnation as stated in D&C 84:54-59? Is our pride leading us to accept the plan of Satan as it did the former inhabitants of this holy land? In subsequent chapters we shall consider this possibility.

XIII

Secret Combinations

Division Between The Just And The Unjust

The Lord has decreed that in the next life, those who are just will be separated from those who are not. There will be a resurrection of the just, and another of the unjust. The concept of justice is summed up by the Lord in these words from the Sermon on the Mount:

> Therefore all things whatsoever ye would that men should do to you, do ye even so to them: for this is the law and the prophets. (Matt. 7:12; 3 Ne. 14:12)

The importance of obeying this law which has come to be known among men as THE GOLDEN RULE, cannot be overemphasized, for the Lord has declared it to be the law and the prophets. Its coverage then is very broad. It forms the basis or the foundation for all human action. If one does not treat his fellow man as he would be treated, he has violated this universally known rule and subjected himself to the penalty of being placed with all others who do not obey it. These will be the unjust.

The Lord measures to every man according to the measure which he has measured to his fellow man. (D&C 1:10; Alma 41:3-7) The Lord can use this law to judge all mankind because everyone knows it, even from childhood. It is universally known, thoroughly understood, even by the young and the simple, and easily applied. Each normal person knows what harms him and this knowledge lets him know what harms others. It is quite simple for men to apply this rule of justice in their personal relationships. Those who fail to give it observance are excluded from polite society. They are labelled as rude, impolite. Our desire to be accepted by others induces most of us to obey it on a personal basis.

But that which is understood so clearly on a personal basis, is ofttimes not seen when men act in groups and especially when they act in the name of government. Regardless of that fact, the rule should still apply and when it is not applied, the government becomes corrupt and wicked to the same extent. Those who approve, support and favor unjust laws, although they may not be criticized here, will surely be condemned by the Lord and branded as unjust. On the other hand when a government adopts unjust laws, those who oppose them are ofttimes criticized and condemned by those who favor them.

When such unjust laws become common, they will completely corrupt the morals of the society and it is almost impossible for parents to keep their children from going along with the crowd.

1. The secret combination has destroyed every civilization which has lived on this promised land. That includes the antediluvians, the Jaredites, and the Nephites. The inhabitants of the land today have been specifically warned against them and threatened with destruction unless we repent.

2. That the secret combinations destroyed the people in the days of Noah is indicated not only by the books of Moses and Abraham, but also by the Book of Mormon. The secret combinations got started among the Jaredites when the daughter of Jared, seeing the sorrow of her father at the loss of his kingdom, suggested to him the following plan:

> . . .Whereby hath my father so much sorrow? Hath he not read the record which our fathers brought across the great deep? Behold, is there not an account concerning them of old that they by their secret plans did obtain kingdoms and great glory?
>
> And it was the daughter of Jared who put it into his heart to search up these things of old; . . .
>
> And it came to pass that they formed a secret combination, even as they of old; which combination is most abominable and wicked above all, in the sight of God.
>
> And they have caused the destruction of this people of whom I am now speaking, and also the destruction of the people of Nephi. (Ether 8:9, 17, 18, 21)

> Wherefore, O ye Gentiles, it is wisdom in God that these things should be shown unto you, that thereby ye may repent of your sins, and suffer not that these murderous combinations shall get above you, which are built up to get power and gain—and the work, yea, even the work of destruction come upon you, yea, even the sword of the justice of the Eternal God shall fall upon you, to your overthrow and destruction if ye shall suffer these things to be.
>
> Wherefore, the Lord commandeth you, when ye shall see these things come among you that ye shall awake to a sense of your awful situation, because of this secret combination which shall be among you; or wo be unto it, because of the blood of them who have been slain; for they cry from the dust for vengeance upon it, and also upon those who built it up. (Ether 8:9, 17, 18, 21, 23, 24)

The secret combination has largely achieved its deadly work in these latter days in that the Great and Abominable Church of the Devil has spread over all the earth and has dominion over every nation kindred, tongue and people.

We will be wiped out just as the other three civilizations were unless we recognize this monstrous evil and take steps to prevent it from bringing us down to destruction spiritually and physically. (1 Ne. 14) Fathers must turn their hearts to their children and teach them to love the Lord before they can be corrupted by this terrible evil. Only those who do this or who are beyond reach of the Great and Abominable can expect to survive the great destruction.

Why is the Secret Combination so objectionable to the Lord? For one thing it kills the prophets and does so through the use of government. Such murders go unpunished and

> . . . the Lord will not suffer that the blood of his saints, which shall be shed by them, shall always cry unto him from the ground for vengeance upon them and yet he avenge them not. (Ether 8:22)

But another reason is that the secret combination corrupts the hearts of all the people so there are no righteous left. Little children growing up in a society which has been corrupted by the secret combinations have no opportunity to learn the truth and so the Lord puts an end to such a people. Only eight adults survived the flood; two survived the Jaredite destruction and only one righteous man survived the war which destroyed the Nephites.

The secret combinations among the Jaredites corrupted the hearts of all the people until there were only thirty individuals which survived the destruction which came to that group.

Violence fills the earth because governments refuse to carry out the death penalty for murder as the Lord has commanded and because corrupt governments have taught the people to be corrupt. They have destroyed faith in God, in moral law and have taught that there need be no need to respect the right of private property. Corrupt governments teach their people to steal.

Several instances of the awful consequences of a corrupt government are given in the Book of Mormon. In one case the Jaredite nation almost became extinct because of the spread of these murderous combinations. Let the record tell the story:

> For so great had been the spreading of this wicked and secret society that it had corrupted the hearts of all the people; therefore Jared was murdered upon his throne and Akish reigned in his stead.
>
> And there began to be a war between the sons of Akish and Akish, which lasted for the space of many years, yea, unto the destruction of nearly all the people of the kingdom, yea, even all, save it were thirty souls, and they who fled with the house of Omer. (Ether 9:6, 12, See also Ether 11:7, 22)

The secret combinations corrupted the hearts of nearly all the Nephites at one time to the extent that only the prophet Nephi and his brother, Lehi were left to warn the people. Even the more part of the righteous had come down to believe in the works of the secret combinations and partake of their spoils. (Hela. 6:38)

Secret Combinations During The Patriarchal Reign

When the whole earth was filled with violence the Lord destroyed the people. Obviously there was not then a righteous government punishing violence.

During Book of Mormon times, large bodies of people were condemned to eternal misery for supporting Satan's political programs. Very often they divided over the issue of enforced priestcraft. (Alma 3:26, 27; 28:10-14; 34:34, 35; 50:21, 22) Other times it was over the issue of total Communism. (3 Ne. 3:7; 1:27-30; 2:11-19; Mor. 9:14)

Unless The Fathers Turn Their Hearts To Their Children And Teach Them To Reject Satan's Plan, All Flesh Will Be Wasted At The Lord's Coming

1. The Gentiles have been warned repeatedly that we will be destroyed as a nation unless we repent. (1 Ne. 14; 2 Ne. 6:12; 3 Ne. 16:10-15; 20:15-16; 21:14; 30:1, 2; Mor. 5:22-24; 8:34-41; Ether 2:9-12 4:6-19; 8:23-26; D&C 84:54-59)

2. These scriptures admonish us to repent of our pride, priestcrafts, secret combinations, and adultery among other sins. While many may assume that they are not guilty of these sins, if we approve of, or fail to disapprove of laws through which these sins are being committed by our governments we are guilty.

Unless We Apply The Golden Rule To Government Action, We Almost Certainly Will Be Deceived

This rule is the law and the prophets. It is God's law, and unless we use it to help us to avoid exercising unrighteous dominion through government, we will find ourselves classified among the many who are guilty of this sin. (D&C 121:34-40)

The Scriptures Indicate That When Civilizations Come To This Chosen Land And Ripen In Iniquity, The Lord Wipes Them From The Face Of The Earth

Indeed this is the decree of the Lord repeated four different times in as many verses in Ether 2. The examples given by the scriptures indicate that at least three civilizations have suffered this fate. The Lord has threatened this civilization with extinction unless we turn our hearts to our children and our fathers. We are told how this might be done and are also warned that unless we do so, we will be moved out of our place.

When a society becomes wicked it is almost impossible for children growing up therein to avoid accepting the false beliefs of their fathers and becoming proud unless special measures are taken by parents in the home to prevent this. Fortunately we have been given the remedy and unless this is applied, another civilization will disappear because of wickedness.

THE CONSTITUTION REQUIRES OUR LOYALTY AND SUPPORT

I reverence the Constitution of the United States as a sacred document. To me its words are akin to the revelations of God, for God has put His stamp of approval on the Constitution of this land. I testify that the God of heaven sent some of His choicest spirits to lay the foundation of this government, and He has sent other choice spirits—even you who read my words—to preserve it. (Ezra Taft Benson, *The Constitution, A Heavenly Banner*)

XIV

The Constitution Of The United States Of America

We Have A Debt To The Lord For The Book Of Mormon And The Constitution

Having considered the Nephite experience with self-government, we shall now consider our own. Our purpose will be to apply the lessons taught in their record to our own problems. The Book of Mormon and the Constitution are two of the greatest documents on freedom ever written. Each was prepared under the direction and inspiration of the Almighty. As American citizens we owe an unpayable debt of gratitude to Him who has placed them in our hands.

From them we can come to a full realization that He is indeed the author of liberty, and that He has provided the citizens of this nation with a greater degree of freedom than the world has heretofore known. In addition thereto, He has given us in the Book of Mormon, that knowledge which is essential to the preservation of our freedom.

There Are Two Basic Requirements For Local Self-Government

Like the Book of Mormon, the Constitution is so profound and its virtues so numerous, that it would take many volumes to discuss even its most important provisions. In this chapter we shall consider the two principal provisions which give the citizens the right to govern themselves.

There are two main aspects of self-government: (1) the right of the people on a local level to make, amend and repeal laws, and (2) the right of the people on a local level to judge those accused of breaking them. Local government is the very heart and soul of liberty, and freedom is greatest under that government which permits these two functions to be performed at the lowest level practicable. Thomas Jefferson has expressed his feelings on this matter as follows:

> . . . the way to have good and safe government is not to trust it all to one; but to divide it among the many, distributing to everyone exactly the functions he is competent to. Let the national government be entrusted with the defense of the nation, and its foreign and federal relations; the state governments with civil rights, laws, police and administration of what concerns the state generally; the counties with the local concerns of the counties and each ward direct the interests within itself. It is by dividing and subdividing these republics, from the great national one down through all its subordinations, until it ends in the administration of every man's farm and affairs by himself; by placing under every one what his own eye may superintend, that all will be done for the best. What has destroyed the liberty and the rights of man in every government which has ever existed under the sun? The generalizing and concentrating all cares and powers into one body, no matter whether of the autocrats of Russia or France, or the aristocrats of a Venetian senate. (Thomas Jefferson, *Works* 6:543)

Is There A Comparison Of Self-Rule By The Nephites And U.S. Citizens?

It appears that the power of the Nephite voters to make, alter and repeal their laws at the local level was at least equal to that possessed under the Constitution. While our laws are mainly made by legislatures, nothing is said in the Book of Mormon regarding representative government in the making of laws. At the outset the laws then in force, were approved by the voice of the people, and thereafter any changes appeared to require a mere majority vote. Thus, the Nephite voter's voice in making laws was apparently more direct than our own.

However, the Nephite citizen did not have as direct a control over the judging process as is provided for under the Constitution. Whereas, elected judges appeared to have the exclusive power to judge those accused of violating Nephite laws, under the Constitution, the people are given the primary right to handle this infinitely important power of self government. It provides that "the trial of all crimes, except in the cases of impeachment, shall be by jury . . ." (Art. 3, Sec., 2; see also the 6th Am.) In civil cases where the amount in controversy exceeds twenty dollars, either of the litigating parties may demand a jury trial. (7th Am.)

Regardless of these differences, under both systems the power to determine what the laws should be and how they should be enforced was placed in the hands of the people. They could control the making and also the judging of their laws either directly or indirectly. They could, by majority vote, decide whether or not the laws of God are enforced. These fundamental rights which were provided by the Lord, placed the responsibility for government directly on the people in both nations.

THERE ARE PENALTIES FOR ABUSING THE POWER OF SELF-RULE

The Nephites were told that if the time should come when the voice of the people, meaning the majority of them,

> . . . doth choose iniquity, then is the time that the judgments of God will come upon you; yea, then is the time he will visit you with great destruction even as he has hitherto visited this land. (Mosiah 29:27)

It is assumed herein that this divine decree applies equally to the Gentiles, for our own scriptures declare that the Lord,

> . . . holds men accountable for their acts in relation to them, (governments) both in making laws and administering them for the good and safety of society. (D&C 134:1)

THE RIGHTS OF SELF-GOVERNMENT MAY BE FORFEITED

While both the Nephites and the Gentiles living under the Constitution were accorded the power of self-rule, this power may be easily forfeited. The Lord has declared with respect to the duties of those living under the Constitution:

> Wherefore, honest men and wise men should be sought for diligently, and good men and wise men ye should observe to uphold; otherwise whatsoever is less than these cometh of evil. (D&C 98:10)

If either by default or intention we allow politicians to take office, who either do not know the laws of God, or do not believe in them, the consequences will be as the Lord has stated:

> Nevertheless, when the wicked rule, the people mourn. (D&C 98:9)

It is also apparent that if the enlightened members of society who are able to dispense justice, decline to serve on juries thus leaving the high and sacred function of judging to the idle, the uninformed and those whose main interest is to earn a jury fee, the inestimable privilege of jury trial may fall into disrepute and be abandoned. The citizens would thus forfeit the most important part of their right of self-government under the Constitution.

If it could be assumed that those elected to public office would adopt only laws which are constitutional, and if we could rest assured that those who serve on juries would dispense justice, then it would make no difference whether we exercised our right to vote or do jury duty. The retention of freedom demands effort, and without such it will be lost.

The Lord Has Commanded Us To Preserve Freedom

Not only is it a privilege to preserve freedom, but a commandment of the Lord. Our obligation to obey God's laws concerning the laws of the land is found in the following quote:

> And now, verily I say unto you concerning the laws of the land, it is my will that my people should observe to do all things whatsoever I command them. (D&C 98:4)

Let us next cite the scripture which states what His commandments consist of:

> And that law of the land which is constitutional, supporting that principle of freedom in maintaining rights and privileges, belongs to all mankind, and is justifiable before me.
>
> Therefore, I, the Lord, justify you, and your brethren of my church, in befriending that law which is the constitutional law of the land;
>
> And as pertaining to law of man, whatsoever is more or less than this, cometh of evil. (D&C 98:5-7)

This scripture permits no latitude to alter the Lord's laws. It declares that whatsoever is more or less than those laws which have His approval, cometh of evil. This strictness is in accord with the requirement of obedience to divine laws generally:

> There is a law, irrevocably decreed in heaven before the foundations of this world, upon which all blessings are predicated—
>
> And when we obtain any blessing from God, it is by obedience to that law upon which it is predicated. (D&C 130:20, 21)

Is The Constitution Subject To Change?

Those interested in obeying the Lord's commandments regarding the laws of the land will be intensely interested in being able to precisely distinguish between those laws which are, and those which are not constitutional. Some may claim that this is a question which cannot be answered with certainty. Others may state that what constitutes constitutionality, changes with the differing interpretations placed upon that document by a majority of the judges on the Supreme Court of the United States.

Still others say that since there is a provision in the Constitution permitting amendments, if that provision is followed correctly and the amendment properly adopted, and if it has the effect of making laws constitutional which prior thereto were not, the Lord thereby permits us to befriend a different set of laws. Are the Lord's laws thus changeable according to the whims of men?

Men Are Forbidden To Change Those Laws Protecting Freedom

If we believe the statement quoted above from D&C 130 which states that "there is a law irrevocably decreed," we know the Lord's laws do not change. The word "irrevocable" means unchangeable and neither judges nor democratic majorities have the authority to change divinely decreed laws. Does this mean then that the Lord has forbidden all constitutional amendments and differing interpretations? Let us carefully read what He said regarding the law we are to befriend:

> And that law of the land which is constitutional, supporting that principle of freedom in maintaining rights and privileges, belongs to all mankind, . . . (D&C 98:4)

Here the Lord identifies clearly the laws of which He speaks. They are those which support freedom and maintain rights and privileges that we are forbidden to tamper with. Such laws are eternal and should not be altered because they belong to all mankind, whether they lived before, during, or after the Constitution was framed. The following scripture confirms this view:

> According to the laws and constitution of the people, which I have suffered to be established, and should be maintained for the rights and protection of all flesh, according to just and holy principles; (D&C 101:77)

Since the laws and constitution should be maintained for the rights and protection of all flesh, regardless of the age or country in which they live, any alterations adversely affecting such rights and protection are forbidden. Thus, it would appear that while some types of changes in the Constitution would not offend, others would. For example, there have been amendments extending the voting privilege and changing the date when congress convenes, which appear to have little if any affect upon freedom. Some may feel that the right to vote is a freedom. Surely it may be so regarded but it is extremely rare when one person's vote affects freedom one way or another. How he votes will surely affect the extent of his freedom in the hereafter, but seldom if ever will it alter the laws affecting his, or any other person's freedom here on earth.

The Penalties For Violating God's Laws Are Not The Same For All

While discussing the inviolability of God's laws, it seems important to observe that while His laws are changeless, the penalties imposed for their violation may differ from person to person in order to achieve justice. The scriptures teach:

> For of him unto whom much is given much is required; and he who sins against the greater light shall receive the greater condemnation. (D&C 82:3)

Here is stated an eternal principle of justice which is as applicable to the judgments rendered by man against man, as to those imposed by the Lord in the hereafter. Men should be punished only to the extent they have violated conscience. (D&C 134:4; Alma 30:7-11) We do not punish infants and mental incompetents because they are incapable of forming the criminal intent. In accordance with this rule of justice, we should not punish a person for the harm he does, but for that which he intends.

While we can generally assume that a person intends the natural and probable consequences of his acts, this is only a presumption and other considerations may prove it false. When punishment is imposed, its severity should depend upon the accused's knowledge of God's laws. We are always justified in assuming that a rational defendant is familiar with the Lord's fundamental law called the Golden Rule and that he justifies doing to the accused as he sought to do to others. (Matt. 7:1, 2)

Some may be tempted to conclude that to escape punishment, it would be wise to remain ignorant concerning those laws which are constitutional. When we remember that it is impossible for a man to be saved in ignorance, we see that this is not the answer. A man can obey only those laws of which he is aware, and thus if he wants freedom, which is the blessing predicated upon obedience to the Lord's laws concerning government, we must be informed sufficiently to merit freedom or slavery. In any event, as shall be pointed out more fully later, men already are familiar with the Golden Rule which is the basic law we must obey in government.

Is There Difficulty In Agreeing Upon Constitutional Laws Affecting Freedom?

Since there is so much contention and dispute regarding which laws are constitutional, some may despair of being able to know the Lord's will concerning them. Others may believe it impossible to come to a unity on something so controversial. In response to such attitudes, let us first note that the Lord never has, and never will, give a commandment to members of His Church which is beyond the capacity of the ordinary person to obey. Furthermore, compliance will not require an unreasonable expenditure of time and means. If the Lord has commanded us to come to an agreement regarding which laws we should befriend, we may rest assured that such is possible. We have already taken one step toward this goal in noting that He requires agreement only on those laws affecting freedom. We have also determined the Lord's laws concerning freedom are the same in every dispensation.

Words of President Benson

The formula for successful relationships with others boils down to that divine code known as the Golden Rule. "Therefore, all things whatsoever ye would that men should do to you, do ye even so to them." [Matthew 7:12] (Ezra Taft Benson, *Teachings*, p. 44)

XV

THE GOLDEN RULE AND THAT LAW WHICH IS CONSTITUTIONAL

BOTH THE "LAWS" AND THE "CONSTITUTION" WERE ESTABLISHED BY THE LORD

Having considered the Nephite experience under a divinely established government of self-rule, let us now consider a similar experience by Gentiles living under the United States Constitution. Our purpose will be to describe our constitutional system and then apply to our problems, the lessons taught by the Nephite record. We first observe that the Lord stated that He suffered both the laws and the Constitution to be established. (D&C 101:77) What might be the difference between the two? In trying to answer this question let us observe that there are two main types of laws: (1) those called "substantive" which declare the God-given rights and privileges of the people, and (2) those called "procedural" which specify how government must proceed in adopting and executing substantive laws.

Even though the Constitution is often described as the supreme law of the land, it might be more properly called the power to make and execute laws. It establishes the machinery of government, divides its powers into legislative, executive and judicial departments, and then specifies the manner in which those powers must be exercised. Thus it deals more with procedural than with substantive laws.

In reality governments have no power to make substantive laws. Their power is limited to declaring those God-given rights and privileges which already exist. The Constitution does declare what those rights and privileges are and it forbids the government to abridge them. But the inalienable rights of man are one thing, and the method of protecting and enforcing them another. Perhaps it was this distinction the Lord meant to make in using the words, the laws and Constitution. To the officers in government the Constitution certainly is the supreme law of the land because it places limits on their powers and directs the manner in which they are to proceed. There is another limitation on their powers which is inherent in our constitutional system and to which we call attention. It is the limit which derives from the fact that all powers possessed by them come from the people.

The preamble to the Constitution says in part:

> We, the people of the United States . . . do ordain and establish this Constitution for the United States of America.

According to this statement it was and is the people themselves who adopt the Constitution and not a government nor its officers. Through this document, the people confer certain powers on their servants in government. This being so, the people are the source of all powers possessed by those servants. Since it is a fundamental maxim that a power can rise no higher than its source, those officers do not and cannot possess any power which the people do not have. This restriction is of transcendent importance in a government of the people, by the people, and for the people. It is the touchstone by which the propriety of all governmental actions may be tested.

In this chapter we will consider the nature and limit of the powers which the people possess, and which are delegable by them to government. We will observe that the right of a person to use force on another is limited by the principles of private morality declared by the Golden Rule. This being true, this same restriction limits the powers of their agents in government.

In the chapter following this, we will consider those constitutional procedures which must be followed by government officers in the exercise of their powers.

The Lord's Substantive Laws Protecting Freedom Are Eternal

The Lord in giving commandments regarding the laws of the land in this last dispensation, specifically pointed out that His laws pertaining to freedom are always the same. In the revelations given to the prophet Joseph concerning the duty of Church members to obey His will concerning constitutional laws, He made these statements:

> And that law of the land which is constitutional, supporting that prin-

> ciple of freedom in maintaining rights and privileges, belongs to all mankind, and is justifiable before me. (D&C 98:5)
>
> According to the laws and constitution of the people, which I have suffered to be established, and should be maintained for the rights and protection of all flesh, according to just and holy principles. (D&C 101:77)
>
> Have mercy, O Lord, upon all the nations of the earth; have mercy upon the rulers of our land; may those principles, which were so honorably and nobly defended, namely, the Constitution of our land, by our fathers, be established forever. (D&C 109:54)

If the constitutional laws and principles which the Lord has established in this dispensation, belong(s) to all mankind, are for the rights and protection of all flesh, and should be established forever, it is obvious that they are eternal and unchangeable. They are the same in this dispensation as in others. This being true, we may distinguish between those laws that are constitutional and those which are not, by referring to the commandments the Lord has given regarding laws and governments in other ages. In particular we can use the Ten Commandments and the Golden Rule with perfect confidence that they are in complete harmony with that law which is constitutional. We can test the constitutionality of any substantive law by noting whether it violates either of these two codes.

The Fundamental Law Of Human Relations Is The Golden Rule

When the Lord came to earth in the meridian of time, He gave to His followers in Palestine and in the Americas, a law or rule of behavior which is so fundamental and so complete that it comprehends and includes all other laws pertaining to human relations. Among men it is known as the Golden Rule and was stated by the Lord as follows:

> Therefore all things whatsoever ye would that men should do to you, do ye even so to them; for this is the law and the prophets. (Matt. 7:12; 3 Ne. 14:12)

This same law was given to the children of Israel as part of the Mosaic code, but was stated somewhat differently: . . . Thou shalt love thy neighbor as thy self. (Lev. 19:18)

One who loves his neighbors as himself will, of course, obey the Golden Rule by treating them as he would be treated.

The Golden Rule Is A Complete Law With Rewards And Penalties

In what way is the Golden Rule a law? That is, if it is a law as the Lord stated, what are the rewards for obedience and the penalties for disobedience? Simply this: as we do unto others, so shall it be done unto us. This was made plain by Christ in another statement in the sermon on the mount wherein He said:

> Judge not unrighteously, that ye be not judged; but judge righteous judgment.
>
> For with what judgment ye judge, ye shall be judged; and with what measure ye mete, it shall be measured to you again. (Matt. 7:2, 3; JST)

It is noted that the word judgment is used in the Bible to mean a penalty or a punishment imposed by government or by the Lord. For example, after having Moses give the Ten Commandments to the Children of Israel, He told him:

> Now these are the judgments which thou shalt set before them. (Exodus 21:1)

The Lord then proceeded to reveal to Moses the punishments which the judges should inflict upon those who violated His commandments and statutes.

Harmony Between The Golden Rule And The Law Of Moses

The penalties prescribed by the law of Moses were essentially those mandated by the Golden Rule. Those guilty of offenses were to be treated or dealt with as they had dealt with their victims. The measure which they had meted out, was to be measured to them again as is indicated by the following familiar decree:

> And thine eye shall not pity; but life shall go for life, eye for eye, tooth for tooth, hand for hand, foot for foot. (Deut. 12:21)

In this passage, the application of the Lord's fundamental rule of justice is set forth in simplicity and plainness. However the following explanations seem necessary to avoid unwarranted conclusions regarding its meaning: (1) The accused was judged by his intent to do evil rather than by the amount of harm he had caused. Actions serve merely as evidence of intent. However, experience teaches that we are usually justified in assuming that a person intends the natural and probable consequences of his actions. In other words, when a person causes harm, we are usually safe in assuming he intended to do so. Nevertheless if it is discovered that the injury was inflicted accidentally or in justifiable self-defense for example, no punishment should be imposed even though it may be proper to compel him to make restitution. (2) In accordance with the fundamental tenet of the Golden Rule, the judge should mentally place himself in the position of the accused before imposing sentence. By so doing he can better determine the real intent of the accused and thus establish a fair standard for judging him. The Lord has warned however that: "Thine eye shall not pity" that evil might be done away from among you. (3) Except in cases like murder where restitution is impossible, the wrongdoer in a criminal case was not required to suffer in the same manner as did his victim if he was able to atone for his crime otherwise such as by making restitution with goods or services. (Ex.21:18, 19; 21:30) (4) In cases of theft or malicious destruction of property, the wrongdoer was required to pay his victim several times the value of the property taken. This was apparently necessary for two reasons: (A) To effectively deter crimes of this nature and, (B) To more adequately compensate the victim not only for his lost property, but also for lost time, trouble and inconvenience. (Ex. 22:1) (5) In non-criminal cases, that is in those situations where one person had caused harm negligently and without intending to do so, he was required to make restitution equal to the damage inflicted and thus suffer only to the extent he had caused another to suffer. It is submitted that observance of the Golden Rule would require adherence to the foregoing.

THE GOLDEN RULE PLACES LIMITATIONS ON GOVERNMENT POWER

Not only does the Golden Rule provide government with a precise standard regarding what it should do, but it sets up an equally precise standard regarding what it should not do. The rule applies to all of the actions of men whether they are committed alone or while acting in concert with others and thus places the same restraints on governments as on individuals.

This conclusion may seem novel to some since the rule is generally thought of as having application only to individual behavior. But there are compelling reasons why men should obey it when they act under the authority of the state. Before enumerating them we desire to point out that when men act through government they use force and the threat thereof. This fact seems to be so little understood and so commonly overlooked that it requires special and repeated attention.

There are two methods of influencing human behavior: one is by compulsion, the other by persuasion. A distinct line separates these methods. Let us examine it. When compulsion is used the one being compelled is not allowed his choice in the matter. He is commanded or forbidden to act in a specified manner and if he fails to do so he is physically punished until he complies. If he resists he is overpowered or punished until his resistance ceases. Punishment consists of depriving him of one of those possessions which every person desires to retain—life, liberty or property. When persuasion is used the one doing the persuading may use argument, pleading, logic or even the offer of a bribe. However, the one being influenced is left free to make his own decision. He knows that if he decides not to obey, he may incur the displeasure of his persuader but nothing more. Neither his life, liberty nor property are in jeopardy. No physical punishment is inflicted or threatened; otherwise the case is one of compulsion.

When governments act they use the compulsion method. Every law, regulation or rule which they adopt contains a penalty clause which directs the officers to take either the life, the liberty or the property of those who disobey. Unless a law provides for the loss of one of these possessions it cannot be properly termed a law. It is nothing more than a request or a recommendation which the people are as free to disregard after its enactment as before.

The Effect Of Using Force Is The Same Whether Used By The State Or Individuals

It cannot be denied that the nature and consequence of an act of force is not altered merely by changing the number engaged in its use.

The effect is the same whether done by one person or a million. The one against whom it is used is just as dead and just as surely bereft of his liberty or property in the one case as the other. Insofar as he is concerned it makes not the slightest difference from whence the force proceeds.

Furthermore the mere passing of a law which legalizes an act of violence has no effect either. Clothing force in the robes of legality may obscure or hide the naked fact from view, but it does nothing to change its nature. Legislatures, monarchs and democratic majorities are as powerless to alter the effect of an act of compulsion on a human as to alter the effect of the law of gravity on him.

Therefore if it would be wrong, and a violation of a person's rights for him to suffer at the hands of an individual, it would be equally wrong for him to suffer at the hands of the multitude. If the act is reprehensible, it remains so regardless of who does it.

On the other hand, if the use of force is proper; that is, if the one against whom it is employed deserves to be punished or compelled to pay a debt—the effect upon him is again the same regardless of its source. This being so, logic requires that we use the same standard to determine the propriety of its use in both cases. If the Golden Rule is a proper rule for the individual, it is proper for the group. If it is a proper standard for the citizen, it is a proper standard for the state.

THE GOLDEN RULE IS A UNIVERSAL CODE OF JUSTICE

The need and desire for justice seems to be inherent in every person who believes in moral values and who accepts the fact that there is a distinction between good and evil. Those who believe in good and evil also believe that the good should be rewarded and the evil punished. Or to state the matter otherwise, when people believe in right and wrong, they also believe that when wrong is committed it remains so until proper punishment is imposed, a correct restitution is made, or both. Their sense of justice is satisfied only when this occurs.

Furthermore the punishment must fit the crime and the restitution be equal to the injury. If the penalty is either too severe or too lenient, or the restitution too great or small, to this same extent, justice has not been done.

It is submitted that by enforcing the Golden Rule, man's desire for justice is satisfied. it is also submitted that there is no other standard of justice upon which men can agree. Thus the Lord's Golden Rule is not only the fundamental code of justice for Christians, but for the entire human race. It is the only code that has universal acceptance. One who is punished or compelled to make restitution according to this standard has no grounds for complaint. By his actions toward others he has set a standard of behavior. He has indicated how he wants to treat others. Can he complain when others treat him according to that same standard? Is this not what he would consider just if he were the injured party or the one administering justice? No case is being made here for revenge nor for disobeying the commandment to forgive. We are merely stating here an eternal law of the harvest which the Lord has repeated in every dispensation. (Ex. 20; Matt. 7; D&C 1:10)

This is one of those irrevocable laws decreed in heaven before the foundations of the earth, and the blessing of freedom is available only to those who learn and obey it. To comply with the law, it is as necessary to punish evil as to reward virtue. The Lord obeys the law Himself, and if we are just, we will do likewise.

The Golden Rule Is Universally Known And Easily Applied By All

It seems incredible that the entire law as well as the prophets could be comprehended in one short sentence. However mature reflection will show this to be so. The Lord in His infinite wisdom has provided humanity with a complete standard of behavior in language both clear and concise. In those few words He has stated not only the law, but also the reward for obedience and the penalty for violation.

The Golden Rule is easily understood and remembered even by the young, the simple and the uneducated. It rests solidly upon a universally known standard of morality which arises out of the common knowledge that what is good and bad for ourselves is equally so for others. It has the indispensable virtue of being unchangeable and therefore predictable. It incorporates into the administration of justice those elements of certainty and stability so essential to public tranquility. Let that person who would reject it as a standard, undertake to formulate another to take its place.

XVI

The Reign Of Divine Law

Prefatory Statement

In this chapter we commence our task of demonstrating that the Golden Rule should apply to the actions of government. Recognizing that there may be those who doubt that it should constitute "the law and the prophets" as the Bible states it to be, or who, because they do not accept the Christian religion, consider themselves not bound by it, we shall undertake to demonstrate in this and the following chapters, that it constitutes a logically sound rule which appeals to reason regardless of one's faith or lack thereof. Herein we present the arguments showing that the first step in the solution of our problem is to discover those divine laws of nature which prevail in this field, and which must be obeyed to achieve the goals we seek.

Can All Men Be Expected To Agree That Precise Divine Laws Reign In The Field Of Political Science?

The scriptures indicate that the laws governing in the field of political science are very exact and precise. There is no latitude for error. Strict obedience is demanded. Any deviation from "that law of the land which is constitutional . . . cometh of evil." There is a law irrevocably decreed upon which all blessings are predicated. (D&C 130:20, 21)

While those who believe these scriptures to be the revealed word of God will accept the truths stated therein on faith, can we expect those of different religious beliefs to accept them? Can it be shown logically that eternal and immutable divine law governs in the field of government as it does in the physical world? In what follows we shall attempt to do so.

Definition Of Divine Law

The term "divine law" is used herein to mean a statement of an unvarying relationship between cause and effect. It is a description of change which, according to all that is known, will invariably follow a given cause. Thus, divine laws constitute that entire body of laws which exist independently of the dictates of men. Their operation is unrelated to the will of democratic majorities, the enactments of legislatures or the decrees of monarchs. They are above and beyond man. He is powerless to alter or affect them in any way. His ignorance of them, his refusal to accept them, or his mistaken beliefs regarding how they function, have not the slightest effect upon their operation. The only way he can obtain the results which are predicated upon obedience is to learn and obey them.

The Reign Of Law In The Physical World Is Universally Recognized

Civilized man realizes that he lives in a physical universe governed by inexorable, immutable law. He has learned that to accomplish any given result he must discover and precisely obey the laws upon which that result depends. If he complies partially or imperfectly, he may expect only a partial or an imperfect result.

The reign of law in the physical world is not questioned by intelligent people. Scientists as well as others have proved over and over again the unvarying nature of the rules which govern changes relating to energy and matter such as the laws of gravity, electricity and thermodynamics. All reliable evidence proves the existence of immutable laws in the physical world and nothing man has observed has disproved their existence. Therefore, they are taken for granted. The large sums of money spent on research is evidence of man's faith in the reign of law. By conducting such research he tries to discover new laws which he assumes to exist and which he knows he must obey to achieve his purposes. Never yet has he been disappointed in his assumption that law governs in the physical world.

The Use Of Intelligence Is Dependent Upon Divine Law

We now propose to demonstrate that the existence of divine law is so essential that it is impossible to use intelligence in its absence. Intelligence has been defined as:

> The ability to apprehend the interrelationships of presented facts in such a way as to guide action toward a desired goal.

Using this definition we might define intelligent conduct as compliance with law to obtain a desired goal. One cannot work toward a goal unless he can foresee the consequences of his actions. One cannot foresee the consequences of his actions unless laws exist which decree that the same results will follow the same causes.

From this we must conclude that intelligent conduct is possible only in the presence of law. Only where one can predict the consequences of what he does can he guide action toward a desired goal. Where law prevails and is understood, one is able to predetermine the results which will flow from any given course of conduct and thus choose that course which will accomplish his purposes.

It is difficult, if not impossible to visualize an environment in which law does not exist. If such were possible, chaos would reign. Nothing could be depended upon to happen the same way twice. Past events and conditions would bear no relation to future occurrences. Man could not survive in such an environment. Being unable to foresee the results of his actions, he could not feed and clothe himself. Memory, judgment, knowledge, foresight, reason or any other qualities of the mind would be of no avail. In the absence of law, intelligent conduct would be impossible and intelligence unusable.

The Exercise Of Freedom Impossible Without Divine Law

In deciding that the use of intelligence would be impossible in the absence of law, it would necessarily follow that making choices would also be impossible in its absence. However, the proposition that the exercise of free agency depends upon the existence of law is so important to the entire theme of this work, we make a special point of it here.

When one exercises freedom he chooses between alternatives. This means he elects to accept the consequences which flow from pursuing one course of action while rejecting those which would result from another. But unless laws exist which predetermine the consequences he is choosing between, he could not anticipate them; therefore a choice would be impossible.

As we shall point out more fully later, individual freedom is the transcendent need and desire of all people. Furthermore, it is indispensable to joy and happiness. These, the ultimate goals of existence would be completely beyond the reach of man were it not for the prevalence of divine laws which make choices possible.

The Reign Of Law In The Field Of Political Science Has Long Been Recognized

The proposition that law controls in the field of government has been recognized and stated by the sages, prophets and great thinkers of the past. The people of the Old Testament regarded God as the source of their civil laws. The Ten Commandments together with the related statutes and judgments which came to them through the prophet Moses, constituted the essence of their legal code and was enforced among them just as civil laws are enforced today. Even the penalties imposed for violation were accepted by them as having been divinely revealed. (Deut. 5:1-33) To the Israelites, the laws of God and the laws of nature were one and the same—immutable, inexorable and eternal.

The notion that there is a law of nature which emanates from God and governs political activities had its advocates among the Romans. Cicero, a statesman and orator of some stature, proclaimed his acceptance of this belief in the following passage:

> Of all these things respecting which learned men dispute there is none more important than clearly to understand that we are born for justice, and that right is founded not in opinion but in nature. There is indeed a true law (lex), right reason, agreeing with nature and diffused among all, unchanging, everlasting, which calls to duty by commanding, deters from wrong by forbidding. . . It is not allowable to alter this law nor to deviate from it. Nor can it be abrogated. Nor can we be released from this law either by the senate or by the people. Nor is any person required to explain or interpret

> it. Nor is it one law at Rome and another at Athens, one law today and another thereafter; but the same law, everlasting and unchangeable, will bind all nations and all times; and there will be one common Lord and ruler of all, even God, the framer and proposer of this law. (De Legibus II, 4, 10)

Accompanying and following the reformation, the doctrine of a supreme and controlling law of nature found acceptance and reiteration by recognized authorities in the fields of social and political science. The english philosopher, John Locke, sometimes called the intellectual ruler of the eighteenth century, had this to say in his second essay concerning civil government which made its appearance around 1689:

> Thus the law of nature stands as an eternal rule to all men, legislators as well as others. The rules that they make for other men's actions, must...be conformable to the law of nature—i.e., to the will of God, of which that is a declaration, and the fundamental law of nature being the preservation of mankind, no human sanction can be good or valid against it. (*Second Essay Concerning Civil Government*, Par. 135)

Sir William Blackstone, a famous english jurist, and one of the best legal minds in any country, wrote this in his commentaries on the laws of England published in 1765:

> Man, considered as a creature, must necessarily be subject to the laws of his creator. . . This will of his maker is called the law of nature. . . This law of nature, being co-eval with mankind, and dictated by God himself, is of course superior in obligation to any other. It is binding over all the globe, in all countries, and at all times; no human laws are of any validity, if contrary to this; and such of them as are valid derive all their force and all their authority, mediately and immediately, from this original. . . Upon these two foundations, the law of nature and the law of revelation, depend all human laws; that is to say no human law should be suffered to contradict these. . . Nay, if any human law should allow or enjoin us to commit it, we are bound to transgress that human law, or else we offend both the natural and the divine. (V. I, pp. 41-43)

The U.S. Constitution Based Upon The Divine Law Concept

It is generally conceded that both Locke and Blackstone wielded an immense influence on the thinking of the men who established the

Constitution and laws of the United States. Certainly those founding fathers believed in the supremacy of natural law. The Declaration of Independence is itself an affirmation of the view that natural law is superior to the authority of civil rulers. In this document the doctrine of the law of nature is transmuted into the doctrine of the "unalienable rights of man," the essence of which is contained in the following excerpt:

> We hold these truths to be self-evident, that all men are created equal; they are endowed by their creator with certain unalienable rights; that among these are life, liberty, and the pursuit of happiness. That to secure these rights, governments are instituted among men, deriving their just powers from the consent of the governed; that, whenever any form of government becomes destructive of these ends, it is the right of the people to alter or to abolish it. . . (Declaration of Independence)

The thought here expressed, that men possess from their creator certain rights which are unalienable and which no government can rightfully take from them, is a statement of the divine law concept in slightly different form. Here, as in the other quotes, it is asserted that there are natural limitations on the power of civil rulers. Deviation from these natural laws (or the protection of natural rights) is not allowable. But if such does occur it is the right of the people to abolish such a government and replace it with one which exercises only those powers naturally possessed.

The Constitution itself contains more clauses placing restraints on the power of government than clauses granting it powers. Thus this document which constitutes the supreme law of the land, rests upon the natural law concept that the rights of man come from God and are beyond the reach of government. There have been many cases brought before the courts wherein state and federal statutes have been declared unconstitutional. In these cases the courts have recognized that the restraints placed on government are real and that the rights of the individual are indeed, unalienable and untouchable.

There Is Agreement Of Logic, Tradition And The Constitution With The Scriptures

In this chapter we have attempted to demonstrate the truth of the scriptural statements that there are eternal immutable divine laws prevailing in the field of government. In support of this point we have shown that intelligence cannot be used to solve the problems of government unless such is the case. We have quoted noted authorities of the past who have been in agreement. Finally, we have shown that our constitutional system of government rests upon this principle.

Assuming the reign of divine laws, we are now prepared to see if we can come to agreement on the purpose or purposes government should have. If we can do this, then we will be able to identify those laws which must be obeyed to reach that common goal.

Words of Ezra Taft Benson

It is generally agreed that the most important single function of government is to secure the rights and freedoms of individual citizens. But, what are those rights? And what is their source? Until these questions are answered there is little likelihood that we can correctly determine *how* government can best secure them. Thomas Paine, back in the days of the American Revolution, explained that:

> Rights are not gifts from one man to another, nor from one class of men to another . . . It is important to discover any origin of rights otherwise than in the origin of man; it consequently follows that rights appertain to man in right of his existence, and must therefore be equal to every man. (*P.P.N.S.*, p. 134)
>
> The great Thomas Jefferson asked:
>
> Can the liberties of a nation be thought secure when we have removed their only firm basis, a conviction in the minds of the people that these liberties are of the gift of God? That they are not to be violated but with his wrath? (*Works,* 8:404; *P.P.N.S.*, p. 141)

(Ezra Taft Benson, *The Proper Role of Government*, p. 3)

XVII

Individual Freedom—The Transcendent Purpose Of Government

Prefatory Statement

We have seen that the first and most fundamental lesson man can learn is that of obedience to divine law. Until he does this it is impossible for him to knowingly accomplish any purpose whatsoever. That basic truth is the starting point for the acquisition of knowledge in every discipline and applies with as much force to the study of government as to other fields. In view of this fact, we are pursuing our attempt to reach agreement that the Golden Rule should apply to the actions of government, by seeking to identify those laws which must be obeyed to achieve the purposes we seek through the agency of the state. However before proceeding to this task, it will be necessary to agree upon the purpose or purposes to be accomplished. Unless we are all willing to give priority to a single objective, or unless the various goals set for government are harmonious, it will be impossible to find a set of laws, obedience to which will accommodate everyone. An antagonism in purposes would require a sacrifice of one goal to accomplish another—a violation of the laws leading to one result in order to obey those which lead to results inconsistent therewith. Let us commence our search by noting the Lord's purpose in establishing governments.

The Lord's Purpose In Establishing Governments

The scriptures indicate that the primary purpose of the Lord in establishing a government in the United States was to protect the freedom of the people. This purpose is set forth in the following quotations:

> According to the laws and constitution of the people, which I have suffered to be established . . . that every man may act . . . according to the moral agency which I have given unto him . . . (D&C 101:77, 78)

> Therefore it is not right that any man should be in bondage one to another. And for this purpose have I established the Constitution of this land, by the hands of wise men whom I raised up unto this very purpose, and redeemed the land by the shedding of blood. (D&C 101:79-80)

> And that law of the land which is constitutional, supporting that principle of freedom in maintaining rights and privileges, belongs to all mankind, and is justifiable before me. (D&C 98:5)

The Lord's purpose then in establishing our laws and Constitution was to provide free agency. When it is remembered that the war in heaven was fought over this same issue, the importance of government in the Lord's plan for man here on earth becomes more apparent.

The Purposes Of The Founding Fathers

Since the wise men who drafted and implemented the provisions of the United States Constitution did so under the inspiration of the Almighty, it can only be expected that their purposes agreed with His. These were stated in the preamble which reads as follows:

> We, the people of the United States, in order to form a more perfect union, establish justice, insure domestic tranquility, provide for the common defense, promote the general welfare, and secure the blessings of liberty to ourselves and our posterity, do ordain and establish this Constitution for the Unites States of America.

There are six different purposes enumerated in this preamble. However liberty is one of them and all of the others must be in harmony therewith. We shall now undertake to show that individual freedom is the first and foremost need and desire of all men in all countries and ages, and therefore we can make it not only the first, but the exclusive purpose of government.

Can All Reach Agreement On A Single Purpose For Government?

People are so diverse in their interests and aims that it may appear impossible to pass a single set of man-made laws which serve the needs and desires of all people equally. While some are religious, others deny the existence of God; while some are devoted to much learning, others are content to remain uneducated; while some love art, music and the theatre, others prefer science, engineering or sports; while some desire palatial homes, rich food and expensive clothing, others are content with the simpler things of life.

Furthermore any one person is subject to constant change so that his objectives and values at one point in life may be replaced by a different set later on. Do these infinitely diverse and ever-changing purposes and interests make it impossible for the members of society to reach agreement upon a single and controlling purpose for government?

It Is Logical To Require That Freedom Be The Goal Of Government

Fortunately there is a common need and desire which all share and which takes precedence over all other considerations: this is the need and desire to be free. Every person regardless of the age or country in which he lives, desires his own liberty of action. While we may differ widely in the goals we use freedom to obtain, every person wants the freedom to carry out his own purposes whatever they may be. Thus every person with a goal will have an accompanying desire to be free to achieve it.

Not only does every person desire freedom, but this desire takes precedence over every other consideration. To become and remain free is paramount because when a person is in bondage, he must first free himself before he can pursue any other purpose. This truism applies to partial as well as to total restraint. If servitude in any degree makes impossible the attainment of an objective, the removal of the restraint must occur before the goal can be reached.

Freedom May Be Made The Exclusive Purpose Of Government

Assuming that a state of freedom is transcendent above all other needs, it should constitute the supreme and controlling objective of government. No other purpose can be allowed to take precedence over it, and if any other goal is found to be in conflict therewith, or to diminish in any degree the freedom of the individual, it must be abandoned as being opposed to the paramount need and desire of all men.

So considered we may establish freedom not only as the supreme, but the exclusive purpose of government. If freedom exists, every other achievement within the power of man is made possible, while without it every other goal is beyond reach. Thus regardless of differences in religious beliefs, culture, background and experience, the transcendent purpose which all people have for government is in complete harmony with the Lord's.

The Elements Of Freedom

Since every person desires freedom, every person desires those possessions without which the exercise of freedom is impossible. They are:

1. Life and some degree of physical and mental health and strength.
2. Liberty of action or the absence of restraint and coercion.
3. Knowledge of those laws which must be obeyed to achieve one's goals.
4. The right and control of property.

Let us observe that each of these four possessions is indispensable to the exercise of freedom and that each person wants his own protected against injury and loss.

Life

To strive toward any goal demands some degree of physical health and strength. Therefore the desire for life is at least as strong as the desire to accomplish goals. Every person wants bodily health and strength not only because it means freedom from pain and suffering, but also because the greater the vigor of mind and body, the more able he is to exercise freedom and accomplish his purposes.

Of course there are those abnormal individuals who intentionally abuse and injure their bodies and some even take measures to bring their existence to an end. But even such people want to determine for themselves when and by what means they shall suffer or terminate their lives. They would strenuously object if others undertook to make these decisions for them.

Also, since every person desires to be born with a disease-free body and wants the care, support and protection during infancy and childhood which only the family can properly provide, every rational person knows that illicit sex relations are evil and harmful. They are primarily responsible for destroying the family unit and transmitting disease and misery.

And so throughout history, moral man has recognized that such crimes as murder, mayhem, assault, battery and adultery are evil and should be prohibited and punished. They are so regarded because they injure and destroy life—that element of freedom which everyone desires and wants protected. In view of this, each person wants government to enforce laws which protect his life against injury and destruction.

Freedom From Restraint And Coercion

Another desire which all share is freedom from control and regimentation. When a person is restrained or coerced, he is compelled to fulfill the purposes of those using the compulsion rather than his own; consequently he cannot exercise freedom.

Admittedly, there are those who prefer to have others direct their lives in some areas, thus saving them the trouble of thinking and making decisions. It is very common for people to subject their time and talents to the direction and control of others in exchange for money or property. And this should be their privilege. They should have the right to bargain with anyone they choose and determine which of their activities and what portion of their time is subject to supervision by others.

But even though some desire relief from self-supervision with its accompanying responsibilities, the desire to be free from coercion and restraint is universal. Everyone objects to being enslaved and wants protection against those who would place him in bondage, thus preventing him from accomplishing his purposes.

From this we may conclude that every person favors the enforcement of laws which prevent his enslavement.

KNOWLEDGE

The third element of freedom mentioned is knowledge—sufficient knowledge of facts and laws to enable one to achieve his purposes. It will be remembered that law reigns in every area in which intelligence can be used and that no goal can be reached without complying with that law upon which the desired result depends. But one cannot obey a law of which he is ignorant; therefor, a knowledge of law is indispensable to the exercise of freedom. Also the desire for it will be somewhat proportional to the desire for freedom.

That this desire varies from person to person is admitted. But everyone objects to being deceived or having the knowledge he does possess corrupted by falsehood. If one bases his actions on false principles and erroneous information, his efforts are futile, his failure certain and the exercise of freedom frustrated. Therefore every person wants to be protected against deception. He wants laws enforced which will forbid and punish lying and deception.

THE RIGHT AND CONTROL OF PROPERTY

The fourth element of freedom, the right and control of property, requires a more extensive discussion than do the other three because the need for it may not be as easily recognized. However, an accurate understanding of the nature of this right and its relationship to the other three, will demonstrate that without it there is no freedom.

Property consists of the earth's raw materials and energy which have been organized into usable products such as food, clothing and shelter. Unless one is free to acquire and utilize these forms of wealth, his existence ceases, and it is of the greatest importance to recognize that if he must depend upon others for sustenance, he is not free. He is subject to the direction and control of those who support him and will do nearly anything they command merely to stay alive.

And it matters not whether it be an individual or an organization such as government which feeds him. His subservience is as certain as his desire for life. When this fact is recognized, it is plainly seen that the right to acquire, own, and control property is as essential to the exercise of freedom as life itself.

Not only must one own and control his own sustenance to be free, but he must have the right and control of property to accomplish his every purpose. Property is the means to all ends because no goal of any consequence can be achieved unless one is free to use property to aid him in reaching it.

It is with property that we build our homes and support families; acquire a farm, an office, a factory, machinery and tools and enter the occupation of our choice. We utilize property to construct churches and exercise freedom of religion; obtain a printing press, a lecture hall, a radio or television station and exercise freedom of press and speech. We gain an education by using property to pay for instruction and to support ourselves while we learn. Not any of these freedoms can be exercised without the right and control of property.

Let us also recognize that it is with property that we purchase the skill, experience and labor of others by which we accomplish objectives beyond our own ability, time and talents.

While men differ widely in the amount of property they desire to own and control, everyone wants enough to sustain life and enable him to achieve his purposes. Therefore everyone wants his property protected against theft and destruction. He wants government to adopt and enforce any laws necessary for these purposes.

The Mutual Dependence Of The Elements Of Freedom One Upon Another

In the foregoing discussion it has been observed that the freedom elements are closely interrelated and mutually dependent one upon another. This fact seems sufficiently important to merit special attention. If it be true that not one of these four possessions is usable unless the other three are present, the necessity of government protecting them all becomes most apparent. Viewed in this light each possession is equally important. No three of them is of value unless the fourth is present.

There is no difficulty in recognizing that the other elements are valueless without life. It is also clear that without liberty or knowledge the other elements would be unusable. But the right and control of property is equally necessary for without it, life cannot be sustained, liberty exercised, nor knowledge utilized.

Let it also be recognized that a partial denial of the right and control of property diminishes the value of the others accordingly. Since a loss of property reduces one's ability to carry out his purposes, the utility of life, liberty and knowledge is reduced in like manner.

Scriptural Support For The Protection Of The Freedom Elements

The scriptures support the foregoing conclusions. The Ten Commandments together with their related statutes not only provide for punishing the destruction of the elements of freedom, but also for compelling those responsible for such injuries to make restitution.

These principles are also reiterated in modern day scriptures:

> We believe that no government can exist in peace, except such laws are framed and held inviolate as will secure to each individual the free exercise of conscience, the right and control of property, and the protection of life. (D&C 134:2)

> We believe that the commission of crime should be punished according to the nature of the offense; that murder, treason, robbery, theft, and breach of the general peace, in all respects, should be punished according to their criminality and their tendency to evil among men . . . (D&C 134:8)

The Constitution Adopted To Protect The Rights Of Man

The central purpose for the adoption of our constitutional system of government was the protection of the rights of man. Those who established it did so under the assumption that each individual possesses certain unalienable rights and that governments are formed to secure them. The essence of this rights of man philosophy is expressed in the Declaration of Independence in these words:

> We hold these truths to be self-evident, that all men are created equal; that they are endowed by their Creator with certain unalienable rights; that among these are life, liberty, and the pursuit of happiness. That to secure these rights, governments are instituted among men . . .

While this statement specifically identifies some of man's rights, by its very wording it does not presume to list them all. However, the fact that life and liberty are named, necessarily implies that the other two elements of freedom—property and knowledge—are among them. This is so because the four elements are indivisible and inseparable. Not one of them is usable unless the other three are also present.

But even though the Declaration of Independence does not specifically list property as one of the unalienable rights of man, the Constitution does so as is indicated in the 5th amendment:

> No person shall . . . be deprived of life, liberty, or property, without due process of law; nor shall private property be taken for public use, without just compensation.

From the foregoing quote it is apparent that those who founded the American system of government regarded the protection of property equally as important as the protection of life and liberty. It is observed that although the element of knowledge is not mentioned in the fifth amendment, the right to the free exchange of knowledge is protected by the first amendment which says:

> Congress shall make no law respecting an establishment of religion, or prohibiting the free exercise thereof; or abridging the freedom of speech, or of the press; or the right of the people peaceably to assemble, and to petition the government for a redress of grievances.

The Necessity Of Recognizing That Every Right Is Represented By A Corresponding Duty

It is assumed that all people will agree that the protection of the four elements of freedom should be the transcendent purpose of government. However the natural laws which must be obeyed to achieve this goal will be much more readily discernible if we first recognize that every human right is represented by a human duty, and that governments can protect rights only by enforcing those duties. Therefore in the following chapter we will identify those duties which must be enforced to protect rights.

XVIII

The Duties Of Man

Prefatory Statement

In pursuing our goal of demonstrating that the Golden Rule should apply to the actions of government, we have shown that: (1) Only by complying with divine natural law can we hope to achieve any goal; (2) That all people, regardless of other differences, want freedom above any other possession; (3) That only by protecting man's rights to life, liberty, property and knowledge, can government protect freedom.

In this chapter we consider the fact that a right in one person is always represented by a duty in another, and that the only way a right can be protected is by compelling those who owe the corresponding duty, to observe and discharge it.

We shall classify rights and duties as being either natural or acquired and shall show that regardless of their type, they involve the elements of freedom. We shall also show that only governments may properly enforce duties and therefore all men have a duty to support it in doing so.

Rights Exist Only If Represented By Duties

If it is assumed that all men are endowed by their Creator with a set of unalienable rights to the four elements of freedom, it must also be assumed that all men are burdened with a corresponding set of duties respecting those rights. Basic to an understanding of a right is a realization that it cannot exist without a matching duty; for what can a right consist of other than the enforcement of a duty concerning it? By very definition a right cannot exist in one person unless there is a corresponding duty in another. Unless there is someone who can be compelled to do, or refrain from doing something to give the right meaning, it has no substance.

Rights and duties are as inseparable as are the concepts of light and darkness, positive and negative, good and evil. One term standing alone is meaningless because it can neither be comprehended nor explained without considering its opposite with which it must be contrasted.

Once this fact is recognized it becomes apparent that if all men have been endowed with a right to the four elements of freedom, all men have had imposed upon them a set of duties concerning these rights. And what is the nature of these reciprocal rights and duties? Each member of society is entitled to have all others refrain from injuring or taking his life, liberty, property or knowledge, and each is obligated in turn to refrain from invading or violating these endowments of his fellow men.

Natural Rights And Duties

Let us denominate the rights and duties just described as "natural" because we are born with them. They have been conferred upon us and imposed upon us without any conscious action on our part. Our Creator in granting each of us our rights, of necessity imposed upon us the duty of respecting the rights of others.

These "natural" duties may be regarded as negative in nature because they obligate us to refrain from acting. We are required to abstain from that conduct which will cause harm to others. Only when we have violated this negative duty by committing a wrong, are we obligated to take affirmative action and make amends for the injury inflicted.

Acquired Rights And Duties

But in addition to our natural negative duties which require us to refrain from acting, there are also what might be termed acquired or assumed duties which require us to take some positive action. These are brought into existence only when we voluntarily agree to assume them. They are acquired and assumed as a result of a deliberate and premeditated intent that we do so.

The most common and familiar type of such rights and duties arises out of the business contract. In the typical case the parties enter into a binding agreement under the terms of which one party assumes an obligation to deliver goods or perform services in exchange for the right to receive money. The other party assumes the duty to pay the money, and acquires the right to compel delivery of the goods or performance of the services.

Another type of acquired rights and duties arises out of the family relationship. Under the marriage contract each party acquires legally enforceable rights against the other and assumes obligations in exchange therefor. The rights and duties between parents and children are different in some respects from those created by agreement, but are nonetheless real. Even though no formal agreement is entered into, when parents bring a child into the world they voluntarily assume the duty to support and care for that helpless infant until he is able to fend for himself. In exchange for such benefits, the child owes the parents obedience and also the duty to provide for their needs if their positions become reversed with the parents becoming helpless and the child able to sustain them.

It is observed that the rights and duties which we acquire concern the elements of freedom just as do those which we have called natural. The rights acquired under a business contract or because of a family relationship, entitle the holder thereof to have his life or liberty maintained, or his property or knowledge increased. On the other hand the duty assumed requires an expenditure or utilization of these possessions. Whether the right is natural or acquired, the owner thereof is entitled to have others observe a duty respecting the elements of freedom—either to refrain from injuring them or to take some affirmative action concerning them.

Rights and Duties Without Substance Unless Enforced

Just as a right does not exist without a duty, neither rights nor duties exist unless enforced. Unless the person who violates a right is compelled to atone for the wrong and make restitution for the injury, it is a misuse of the term to call it a right.

The substance of a right consists of the power to compel the invader of the right to do something, and the substance of a duty consists of being compelled to perform. Unless the performance of the duty is compelled, the right is without a remedy and the failure to perform without a penalty. It is enforcement which brings both into existence and gives them substance.

The doctrine of the rights of man then necessarily includes the use of force on humans for without such physical violence and the threat thereof, they would not exist.

Government Necessary For The Enforcement Of Rights And Duties

If it be true that rights and duties do not exist unless enforced, it is also true that they exist incompletely or not at all in the absence of government; this being the only agency which is at once powerful enough and impartial enough to exercise the force required.

Government is the supreme physical force in society. To perform its functions it must be supplied with sufficient manpower and means to enforce its will against all persons and groups. Only with such power can it adequately enforce human rights.

When government functions properly it enforces rights and duties in a just manner. It is not subject to bias or partisan pressure. It correctly appraises the character of the wrong committed, the restitution required and the punishment deserved. This combination of superior force and impartial judgment is indispensable if human rights are properly protected. It is most apparent that if each person had to rely on his own resources to enforce his rights, many would remain unenforced and would therefore not exist. The strong and cunning would prevail over the weak regardless of whose rights had been invaded. Thus, in the great majority of cases, rights and duties would disappear for want of enforcement.

And in those cases where the strong happened to be in the wrong, there would be little chance for justice since the natural bias of men makes them unfit to be judges in their own cases. In view of these facts, we can conclude that the rights of man are in essence the right to use the force of government to punish wrong and compel the performance of duties. This is in harmony with the philosophy of the Declaration of Independence which says:

> To secure these rights, governments are instituted among men . . .

It is also in harmony with the scriptures. The right to use the force of government to punish crime and compel the performance of duties is taught by the Bible, the Book of Mormon and the Doctrine and Covenants. The following scripture from the Book of Mormon for example, states the right of a creditor to compel payment of a debt:

> Now if a man owed another, and he would not pay that which he did owe, he was complained of to the judge; and the judge executed authority, and sent forth officers that the man should be brought before him; and he judged the man according to the law and the evidences which were brought against him, and thus the man was compelled to pay that which he owed, or be stripped, or be cast out from among the people as a thief and a robber. (Alma 11:2)

The Duty To Support Government

The list of man's rights and duties would be incomplete without noting his right to call upon government for protection and his duty to support it in doing so. It has been seen that only the agency of government can properly protect rights. Once it is established and assumes this responsibility, each citizen is entitled to call upon it for protection of his own rights. But no one can lay claim to this right without assuming a corresponding duty; and the duty in this instance is to provide the means and manpower required for this purpose. Government cannot operate unless supported, and such support must be provided by those it protects.

From this it must be concluded that the duty to support government is an integral and indispensable part of the doctrine of the rights of man. Human rights do not exist unless this duty is performed. And let it be recalled that a duty is without substance unless enforced; therefore government must have the power to compel those it protects to pay taxes and perform other necessary duties such as serve in the armed forces and on juries.

As long as government restricts itself to the function of protecting the elements of freedom, and as long as it apportions the taxes and other essential duties equitably, no one can justly complain about his own political obligations.

Since everyone desires and needs to have his rights protected, and since government is the only practical means by which this can be done, everyone should realize that for his own benefit it must be supported.

Each should be able to see that it would be unjust and destructive of his own rights if others were permitted to withhold their support. Therefore, if he fails to bear his fair share, he knows he is shirking a duty which is rightfully his. Logic tells him that force may be properly used to compel him to perform. As is stated by the scriptures:

> We believe that all men are bound to sustain and uphold the respective governments in which they reside, while protected in their inherent and inalienable rights by the laws of such governments; . . . (D&C 134:5)

Having defined the task of protecting human freedom as being that of enforcing the duties of man, we are now prepared to discuss in chapters which follow, those divine natural laws governments must obey in performing this function.

XIX

The Four Laws Government Must Obey To Protect Human Rights

The Four Subdivisions Of The Golden Rule

The purpose of government is to protect our rights to those four possessions without which the exercise of freedom is impossible. Those four possessions or elements of freedom are: (1) Life, (2) Liberty, (3) Property, and (4) Knowledge. However it can do this only by (1) punishing those who intentionally violate their duty not to injure these rights, and by (2) compelling those who owe a duty to discharge it. In performing these two functions, governments carry out the provisions of the Golden Rule.

But ofttimes governments punish those who have intended no evil, and compel the performance of duties which are not owed. Such abuses of power are obviously contrary to the Golden Rule. The four sub-rules then which governments must comply with in carrying out their functions in accordance with the Golden Rule are: In punishing evil government must:

1. punish the intentional violation of duties;
2. punish nothing except the intentional violation of duties;

In enforcing rights government must:

3. enforce existing duties;
4. never create nor abolish duties.

We shall now undertake to demonstrate that governments must obey each of these four subdivisions to the Golden Rule in order to protect the four elements of freedom.

Law One: Government Must Punish The Intentional Violation Of Duties

Probably every one agrees that governments must punish crime to some extent. While there may be differences of opinion regarding what constitutes a crime and how severe penalties should be, everyone desires that government protect his life, liberty, property and knowledge. Since the only way such protection can be afforded is by punishing the evil which causes the loss, everyone favors punishing some crimes. Let us attempt then to come to a unity of belief regarding what crimes should be punished and how severe the punishment should be.

We first observe that whenever government fails to punish some intentional violation of a duty, it fails to protect the right which is destroyed by that violation. Hence, for every right which society desires to protect, it must penalize that breach of duty which injures or destroys the right.

In view of these facts, if we can all agree on what rights should be protected, then we should all be able to agree on what constitutes a punishable crime. But we reach agreement on this when we recognize that all want life, liberty, property and knowledge protected against those who would intentionally destroy these possessions. In other words if all of us desire freedom, and regard as evil any unjustified attempt to destroy those possessions which are essential to its exercise, we have thereby come to an agreement on what constitutes a punishable crime.

But this is exactly the same test for determining punishable evil as is decreed by the Golden Rule. Therefore unless we have made an error in assuming that all want the four elements of freedom protected, we have proved that the Golden Rule provides a universally acceptable standard regarding what evil should be punished. All have thus reached agreement on this crucial matter regardless of their religious beliefs or lack thereof.

How Severe Should The Punishment Of A Crime Be?

Punishments must be severe enough to deter the crime we are seeking to restrain, otherwise the right involved is not protected. On the other hand if the penalty exceeds this, to this same extent it is unnecessarily severe and will cause an injustice to the criminal.

The only standard for punishment ever devised which meets both of these requirements is the one decreed by the Golden Rule. If the offender is made to suffer to the same extent that he intended for his victim, and if he is compelled to make full restitution for the injury, the punishment has proved sufficiently severe to deter the evil. At the same time the offender has no grounds for complaint. By treating his victim in a specified manner, he has established a standard of behavior. Surely he cannot justifiably complain when he is dealt with according to that same standard.

The foregoing analysis demonstrates that everyone, regardless of differences in religious beliefs, should accept the Golden Rule as a standard for the actions of government in the punishment of crime, not only because it comes from the supreme Lawgiver of mankind, but because of self-interest as well. Only by punishing crime according to this standard are the elements of freedom properly protected, and this is a goal desired by every rational being.

Law Two: Government Must Punish Nothing Except The Intentional Violation Of Duties.

All human conduct may be divided into two categories: (1) Those acts committed or omitted with an intent to do evil—that is to violate the Golden Rule, and (2) Those committed or omitted without such an intent. All criminal laws may be divided into two categories: (1) Those which provide for punishing conduct of the first type; and (2) Those which provide for punishing that of the second.

When a government adopts laws which provide for punishing conduct of the first type, it has reached the natural limits of its power to punish. All criminal laws other than these have the effect of punishing innocent behavior, and this itself is a crime. Even the threat to punish innocent behavior is a crime because those who obey the law out of fear are denied a rightful freedom. While men should not feel free to do evil without fear of punishment, their freedom to do good should be unrestricted. When this is taken from them by the passage of unjust laws, the effect is the destruction of freedom rather than its preservation.

The same considerations which require that the elements of freedom be protected from unjustified destruction by those outside of government, require that they be protected from those within its framework. Men in government should comply with the same moral code which they compel others to obey. History is replete with instances where those in control of the police power and the armed forces have murdered, plundered and enslaved the citizens of their own nation.

Therefore it is of the utmost importance that a precise limit be placed upon the power of government to punish. According to this second subdivision of the Golden Rule, this limit has been reached when intentional violations of duty have been punished. Unless a citizen has undertaken without justification to destroy or injure an element of freedom, he should not be punished.

It Is Illogical To Punish One Whose Conscience Is Clear

Both humanity and justice require that we refrain from punishing a person who has intended no evil. Logic also requires observance of this rule. The purpose of punishment is to restrain and prevent the evil which almost invariably arises from an attempt to commit evil; not to prevent the good which almost always results from an attempt to do good.

When a person undertakes to do good, or in other words increase the elements of freedom, he ordinarily accomplishes this purpose. At least he seldom does the opposite. Therefore, punishing such conduct deprives society of the good which results when people are left free to engage in beneficial activities. Punishing the innocent also destroys one of the elements of his freedom—either life, liberty or property.

Even though a person who undertakes to do good inadvertently causes harm, it is still illogical to punish him. A well-meaning person need not be punished to induce him to try to avoid injuring others. This he does voluntarily. And if he has unintentionally caused harm and has failed to make restitution, the injured party may recover in a civil suit. A criminal action is not brought for this purpose.

Does this second law agree with the Golden Rule? It would be difficult to imagine a more flagrant violation of that rule than that of punishing an innocent person. The rule demands that we treat a person as he has intended to treat others. Therefore to inflict injury on one who has acted innocently, is in direct opposition to the rule. Also since the one inflicting punishment would object to being punished for an act committed with a clear conscience, he must refrain from doing such to others.

The following scriptures assure us that the Lord approves of punishment only when the accused has violated his conscience:

> Judge not unrighteously, that ye be not judged, but judge righteous judgment. For with what judgment ye judge, ye shall be judged; and with what measure ye mete, it shall be measured to you again. (Matt. 7:2, 3, JST)

> . . . the civil magistrate should restrain crime, but never control conscience; should punish guilt, but never suppress the freedom of the soul. (D&C 134:4; See also Alma 30:7-11)

LAW THREE: GOVERNMENTS MUST ENFORCE EXISTING DUTIES

Having considered those two subdivisions of the Golden Rule pertaining to punishments, let us now examine those which determine when government should enforce duties. Once it is recognized that an individual has a right to the elements of freedom, it is also assumed he has a right to recover damages from anyone who unjustifiably injures them. The one causing the injury has violated his duty to refrain from doing so and may properly be compelled to make restitution.

But unless the duty can be enforced, the right which it represents does not exist. Therefore, government must be available to compel the performance of every enforceable duty whether natural or assumed, and determine whether the breach is intentional or due to negligence.

In the situation where the breach of the duty is intentional, compelling the wrongdoer to make restitution is in addition to punishing him. If government does no more than punish such breaches, the victim suffers a loss which remains unredressed. Therefore, he must be able to recover damages in the case where the injury is intentional as well as where it is due to negligence. Under the Law of Moses, both punishment and restitution were handled in the same proceeding. Under other systems of jurisprudence such as our own, two proceedings are used: One to punish the crime and another to assess and compel payment of damages.

Today in our society, the types or classes of laws under which government compels the performance of duties have been divided up into the following categories:

1. Tort laws
2. Contract laws
3. Family relations laws
4. Tax laws, military conscription laws and similar enactments which specify the citizens' duty toward government.

Tort laws provide for restitution usually in cases where the rights violated are "natural" rather than "acquired." (The term "natural right" is used herein to describe a right with which we are born. The term "acquired right" is used to describe a right acquired under contract or agreement) However tort laws sometimes permit recovery for injuries to acquired rights as well. Injuries inflicted in these instances are generally due to the intentional or negligent conduct of the wrongdoer and the tort laws provide for redress in either case.

If the rights injured and the duties breached are "acquired" rather than "natural," relief is usually available under either the law of contracts or that of family relations. In these cases the breach of the duty usually consists of a failure to act. If one fails to discharge duties he has assumed under a business contract or a family relationship, the injured party may obtain the aid of government to compel performance or recover damages caused by nonperformance.

Duties owed to government are enforced under tax laws, laws providing for military conscription, jury duty and similar enactments.

In the foregoing discussion we have treated "punishment" and "compelling performance" as though they are two distinctly different methods of protecting freedom. While it is true that punishment should be imposed only in those cases where there has been an intentional injury, whereas compelling performance is usually limited to those instances where there has been a failure to perform a duty, there are instances where punishment is appropriate in the latter situation. If a person who is obligated to perform, deliberately refuses to do so even though able, punishment may be necessary. But let it be recognized that in such an event, the violation of the duty would be intentional and therefore properly punishable.

Since every rational person wants others to discharge their debts to him, he cannot, under the principles of the Golden Rule, object to laws which compel him to discharge his debts to others. Thus the rule that government must stand ready to compel the performance of existing duties is in conformity with that universal standard of justice. The Book of Mormon confirms these conclusion:

> Now if a man owed another, and he would not pay that which he did owe, he was complained of to the judge; and the judge executed authority, and sent forth officers that the man should be brought before him; and he judged the man according to the law and the evidences which were brought against him, and thus the man was compelled to pay that which he owed, or be stripped, or be cast out from the people as a thief and a robber. (Alma 11:2)

LAW FOUR: GOVERNMENTS MUST NEVER CREATE NOR ABOLISH DUTIES

People will generally agree that governments should not possess the power to put a person to death, put him in jail or take from him his property unless he has committed some crime or failed to discharge his debts. This is the restraint placed upon the federal government by the following provision of the Constitution:

> No person shall be ... deprived of life, liberty or property, without due process of law; nor shall private property be taken for public use, without just compensation. (5th Amend.)

The only exception to this rule allowed by the Constitution pertains to the case of bankruptcy where government is given the power to take charge of the assets of an insolvent debtor, distribute them equitably among his creditors, and release him from all debts remaining unpaid. This, of course has the effect of abolishing the property rights of those creditors who are not paid in full, but it is considered necessary in order to distribute the debtor's assets equitably and to give him a chance to make a fresh start. But most people would probably agree that it would be unjust for government to directly abolish property rights for reasons other than this.

The fundamental moral law which forbids governments to create rights and duties, should be plainly obvious to everyone. However, because people tend to fix their attention on the creation of rights, and fail to recognize that rights cannot exist without duties, the necessity of obeying this moral law is not clearly seen.

It is impossible for rights to exist in one person unless there are corresponding duties in others. Therefore, when governments "create rights," they must at the same time, "create duties." But when they create duties, they destroy rights. Those upon whom the "created duties" are imposed, lose their rights just as surely as if government had passed a law taking them directly. Thus it is impossible for government to create a right in one person without destroying the right of another.

An explanation of what happens when rights are created under a welfare state law will make this clear. When such a law is passed, it provides welfare benefits for some group. But at the same time other laws must be enacted which compels taxpayers to pay those benefits. Government cannot possibly give to one, that which it does not take from another. But this is a forcible taking of property to pay debts not owed, and the obligor is unjustly deprived of an element of freedom.

When government takes property from a person only to the extent necessary to enforce existing duties, the one from whom it is taken loses nothing to which he is entitled because no one has a right to refuse to perform a duty. But if force is used to compel the performance of duties not owed, at that point government crosses that precise line which divides the protection of rights from their destruction, and acts directly contrary to the purpose for which it is formed.

Those in government have no more authority to arbitrarily impose new duties than do the citizens they represent. If an individual undertook to impose and enforce a duty to which he had no right, his act would be regarded as a crime. It is no less so when performed by men acting in the name of government. Since citizens have no power to create rights, and since the only powers governments possess are those given them by the people, the creation of rights by government is a usurpation of power.

Men surrender none of their rights when they establish government. They merely delegate to that agency the power of enforcing existing rights. Neither do they assume any new duties. In the absence of government, each man would be under the necessity of enforcing and protecting his own rights—and doubtless at great cost. Therefore, when we support government we do not perform a new duty. We only discharge in a more effective and economical manner an obligation which already existed—that of protecting our own rights. These fundamental truths underlie the American constitutional system of government and are expressed in the Declaration of Independence in these words:

> That to secure these rights, governments are instituted among men, deriving their just powers from the consent of the governed; that, whenever any form of government becomes destructive of these ends, it is the right of the people to alter or to abolish it, and to institute a new government . . .

Jefferson, who is generally regarded as the author of the above words, provided a more complete exposition of his views in a letter written to Francis Gilmer in 1816 which reads in part as follows:

> Our legislators are not sufficiently apprized of the rightful limits of their power; that their true office is to declare and enforce only our natural rights and duties, and to take none of them from us.
>
> No man has a natural right to commit aggression on the equal rights of another; and this is all from which the laws ought to restrain him; every man is under the natural duty of contributing to the necessities of the society; and this is all the laws should enforce on him; and, no man having a natural right to be the judge between himself and another, it is his natural duty to submit to the umpirage of an impartial third.
>
> When the laws have declared and enforced all this, they have fulfilled their functions, and the idea is quite unfounded, that on entering into society we give up any natural right. The trial of every law by one of these tests, would lessen much the labors of the legislators, and lighten equally our municipal codes. — (*Works of Thomas Jefferson, Federal Edition*, G.P. Putnam & Sons, [1905], V. XI, PP. 533-534)

Since no person whether within government or without, can honestly claim that he would consider it just to have others impose duties upon him which he had never agreed to and did not owe, he cannot in good conscience favor laws which do that very thing unto others. Such would be an obvious violation of the principle of the Golden Rule which requires that we treat others as we would be treated.

That Precise Line Between Laws Which Are Constitutional And Those Which Are Not

We have heretofore noted the necessity of precisely distinguishing between those laws which are, and those which are not, constitutional. It is submitted that the four laws discussed in this chapter enable us to do this.

According to the first two laws, punishments should be inflicted for the intentional violation of a duty but in no other instance. This of course requires that in passing judgment on a law which imposes a penalty for violation, we must answer this simple question: Does it require proof of an evil intent in order to convict? If it does, and if the punishment provided is just, then the law is in accordance with the Golden Rule and the Constitution. If it does not, then it is one of those laws which, although as law-abiding citizens we should obey, we should never befriend. We should seek its repeal.

It should be observed that an evil intent does not exist merely because one intentionally violates a law. There are numerous laws today at every level of government which provide for punishing those who have neither intended evil nor caused harm. Such laws can easily be violated by a person who has no evil intent. The true test of the constitutionality of a criminal law is whether or not it provides for punishment only if the defendant violated his conscience by breaking the Golden Rule.

Let us now consider the last two laws which require that government enforce existing rights, but never create nor abolish them. To decide the constitutionality of a law involving these two rules, again it is necessary to answer one key question: Does the law provide for enforcing existing duties only? If it either creates rights or abolishes them, it destroys freedom and is unconstitutional. While as law-abiding citizens we should obey it, never should we befriend it.

Citizens Fully Competent To Pass Upon Constitutionality Of Laws

The ordinary person is fully capable of comprehending these four rules, and establishing the two crucial facts involved in their application. No specialized legal training is required for this. Therefore in requiring that the people befriend only those laws which are constitutional, the Lord did not ask something beyond the ability and time of the citizenry. In fact in mandating the jury trial in all criminal cases, He placed responsibility for doing so directly on the ordinary person in all such instances.

XX

Governments Shall Punish The Intentional Violation Of Duties

How The Nephites Laid Aside The Political Commandments Of God

In our discussion of the Nephite experience with self-government, we saw that around the sixty and second year of the reign of the judges, the Nephites had completely corrupted their laws. Among the perversions of which the record says they were guilty are the following:

> 1. Laying aside the commandments of God;
>
> 2. Doing no justice;
>
> 3. Condemning the righteous;
>
> 4. Letting the guilty and the wicked go unpunished
>
> 5. Being held in office at the head of government . . . that they might get gain and glory of the world, and, moreover, that they might the more easily commit adultery, and steal, and kill . . . (Hela. 7:4, 5)

In this and following chapters, we shall consider the extent to which the Gentiles on this land of promise may have laid aside the commandments of God, and become guilty of these same offenses. In this chapter we shall consider the sin of letting the guilty and the wicked go unpunished.

The Lord's Laws Should Be Obeyed In The Punishment Of Crime

It may be true that there is no field of inquiry in which the need for a knowledge of the Lord's laws is more essential than in political science. Especially does this seem so with respect to criminal laws. Since here we use violence on humans and forcibly deprive them of life, liberty and property, it is of the utmost importance that we know the rules we should follow before acting. If we go blundering ignorantly along using guesswork, opinion, and prejudice as we inflict death, imprisonment and fine, this is obviously one of the most inexcusable sins we can commit.

On the other hand, if the life, liberty and property of innocent people can be protected only by inflicting the proper penalties for crime, then our failure to impose just punishments is again, a sin of serious magnitude. Let it be noted that if there is a fixed divine law which should be followed here, very few are obeying it correctly because there is almost total disagreement today regarding what that law is. It may truthfully be said that much of the wickedness of men consists of our failure to properly punish evil on the one hand and our use of government to unjustly punish the innocent on the other.

Only by inflicting the punishments decreed by the Lord in the Golden Rule, the Ten Commandments, and the principles of the Constitution, is justice done both to society and the offender. By causing the offender to suffer as he has caused others to suffer, and by compelling him to make any restitution possible, the crime is restrained and society is protected. Justice is done to the criminal when he is dealt with as he has dealt with others.

The failure however of governments to inflict punishments according to this rule, is proving to be a sad tragedy in the world today because society is not receiving protection against criminals. Also the people are being taught to condone and accept wickedness. Punishing that conduct which is motivated by a desire to destroy freedom, and refraining from punishing any other, is one of the most effective means of teaching the people to distinguish accurately between good and evil. Any deviation from this rule will tend to have the opposite effect. Especially is this true in the case of murder, adultery and abortion.

Consequences Of The Failure To Punish Murder

Murder is the one crime for which the Lord has always specified the death penalty. According to the Mosaic Code:

> The land cannot be cleansed of the blood that is shed therein, but by the blood of him that shed it. (Num. 35:33)

Furthermore as Alma told Nehor who was contending that he should not be executed for the murder of Gideon:

> And thou hast shed the blood of a righteous man, yea, a man who has done much good among this people; and were we to spare thee his blood would come upon us for vengeance. (Alma 1:13)

The Lord will surely demand an accounting for man's failure to carry out His decreed penalty in this matter. In this connection we should consider the awful penalty which will be inflicted upon that society which permits millions of abortions to not only not be condemned, but financed by government funds!

There are circumstances under which abortions are considered justified. These include cases of forcible rape, incest, and to save the life of the mother. However in other instances how can a woman who undergoes an abortion logically contend that she is treating her offspring as she would have been treated by her own mother. Her feelings of awful guilt may haunt her throughout this life and beyond. And how can any doctor hope to escape the penalty which will surely be imposed for having destroyed human life for hire. To put an unborn child to death for no other purpose than to make money, hide adultery or avoid the inconvenience of parenthood, seems to be among the most despicable and horrible of all sins.

Consequences Of The Failure To Punish Sex Sins

The second most serious sin listed among the Ten Commandments is that of adultery. Although severely punishable under the Mosaic law, today there is not even a pretense of doing so in many areas. There seem to be few adults left who can cast the first stone with a clear conscience. The consequence is that this and similar sex crimes have become common and acceptable. The disastrous influence this is having upon the beliefs and practices of our youth, is plain for all to see.

Some try to justify their sex sins by arguing that the matter is purely personal, and should not be punishable. They contend that society is not being harmed by adultery, fornication, prostitution and homosexuality, and therefore these things should not be a concern for the law. How can anyone blind himself to the disease, the broken homes and hearts, the illegitimacy, the abortions, the teen-age pregnancies and the enormous welfare costs being caused by their wickedness?

Or applying the Golden Rule to the situation, is there a person who lives who dares claim that it makes no difference to him that he is born blind or with a disease-ridden body; that his mother is a prostitute; that he is illegitimate and his father unknown; that he lives on welfare at the expense of others; that during infancy and childhood he lacked the love and affection which only parents can properly give?

Even those who refuse to believe in the eternal punishments decreed by the Lord for those who prostitute the powers of procreation are compelled by logic to admit that such sins should be punished. Their own self-interest makes this conclusion inescapable.

The home is the fundamental unit of society and when it goes, society goes. Sex sins are primarily responsible for the destruction of the home, and any nation which fails to prevent its destruction by punishing the crimes which cause it, is doomed. Society has as much right to punish sex sins as it does to punish murder, mayhem, robbery and theft; its own self-preservation demands that it do so.

The two greatest powers God has given are to create and destroy life. When these powers are abused and prostituted from their proper purposes, and when governments fail to punish such crimes, then the Lord will do so by destroying those who are guilty. Those who imagine they can violate these laws of God with impunity should recall the fiery fate of Sodom and Gomorrah. They might also reflect upon the possibility that the A.I.D.S. epidemic now sweeping the earth is the desolating or overflowing scourge the Lord has decreed for this generation. (D&C 5:19; 45:31; Isa. 28:15) It appears that Isaiah was speaking of this horrible disease in the following passage:

> The shew of their countenance doth witness against them; and they declare their sin as Sodom, they hide it not. Woe unto their soul! for they have rewarded evil unto themselves. (Isa. 3:9; 2 Ne. 13:9)

Consequences Of The Failure To Punish Crimes Generally

The Lord God of Heaven has issued an everlasting decree concerning nations who inhabit this promised land. One of His statements is spoken directly to the Gentiles and reads as follows:

> For behold, this is a land which is choice above all other lands; wherefore he that doth possess it shall serve God or shall be swept off; for it is the everlasting decree of God. And it is not until the fulness of iniquity among the children of the land, that they are swept off.
>
> And this cometh unto you, O ye Gentiles, that ye may know the decrees of God—that ye may repent, and not continue in your iniquities until the fulness come, that ye may not bring down the fulness of the wrath of God upon you as the inhabitants of the land have hitherto done. (Ether 2:10, 11)

What must be done to avoid the destruction spoken of? It would seem that one of the things most urgent is to enforce God's laws by condemning and punishing those sins forbidden by His Ten Commandments.

In our society today there are an enormous number of crimes which go undetected. But there are many others which are known but not properly punished. A variety of reasons are assigned for this failure. One of the most regrettable of these is that when the people become wicked, they neglect to punish the sins of which they themselves are guilty. Another cause is the overburdening of the judicial machinery with cases arising out of unjust regulatory, licensing and welfare state laws.

When the Nephites got themselves into this same situation, (Hela. 7:4, 5) anarchy and civil war broke out. (Hela. 11:1, 2) To save the people from total destruction from this fratricidal conflict, the Lord sent a famine which finally brought the survivors to their senses. Only after thousands had perished from hunger did they repent and cleanse their government of its iniquity.

I also spoke at length for the repeal of the ordinance of the city licensing merchants, hawkers, taverns, and ordinaries, desiring that this people might be a free people, and enjoy equal rights and privileges, and the ordinances were repealed. (Joseph Smith, History of the Church, Vol. V, p. 8)

There is a glaring paradox in our society. On the one hand, legislation has been enacted allegedly to prevent one business or combination of business (a monopoly) from disrupting or eliminating competitors in the market. On the other hand, we have yet to awaken fully to the worst form of monopolistic practice currently impeding the free market. I refer to government monopoly, when government either by ownership or regulation prevents the full freedom of action by sellers. This, of course, regulates and controls prices. (Ezra Taft Benson, *This Nation Shall Endure*, p. 109)

XXI

Government Shall Punish Nothing Except The Intentional Violation Of Duties—Licensing Laws

Prefatory Statement

By enforcing licensing laws, governments not only punish those who lack an evil intent, but they enforce rights which do not exist. Such laws have the effect of destroying freedom by destroying the right of private property. They deny the people their inalienable right to make a living and, at the same time, prevent the buying public from purchasing goods and services from whom they choose.

We shall first define licensing laws and then show that they are not adopted either to punish crime or to protect property rights. Their enforcement constitutes a violation of the Golden Rule. Finally we shall discuss why some people favor them.

Licensing Laws Have The Effect Of Condemning The Righteous

In prior chapters we observed that when the Nephites corrupted their laws, one of the sins of which they were guilty was that of "condemning the righteous because of their righteousness." (Hela. 7:5) The Book of Mormon does not state what particular type of righteousness was being condemned. But does it matter? The condemnation and punishment of a righteous act is wicked regardless of the type.

The Lord has issued the commandment, "six days shalt thou labor." He has also condemned idleness. Therefore any law which condemns a man for working at a legitimate occupation is evil. In this chapter we shall demonstrate that by enforcing licensing laws, we are using government to commit the same sin of which the Nephites were guilty: that of punishing the righteous.

WHAT IS A LICENSING LAW?

A licensing law is one which makes it a crime for a person to enter into some particular profession, trade, business or occupation without first obtaining permission from the state. Permission is granted only to those who fulfill certain requirements which vary from one type of occupation to another.

For the professions and trades such as medicine, law, engineering, dentistry, plumbing, electrical contracting, general contracting, barbering, burying the dead and nursing, etc., the applicant is usually required to graduate from some professional or trade school, obtain a minimum amount of experience, and pass an examination. The level of difficulty of the exam is varied from time to time so that only a limited number will be able to successfully pass it and obtain a license. Or as an alternative, the number permitted to apprentice or to enter college to take the required course work, may be limited for the same reason.

Usually licenses to enter businesses such as banking, insurance, savings and loan associations, etc., may be obtained only by those who have a specified minimum amount of investment capital and a business location situated in an area zoned for that purpose. Experience in the business may also be required.

Licenses to carry on a transportation or communication business are usually difficult to obtain because the number issued is ofttimes limited to a favored few. Certificates of convenience and necessity are usually required. With respect to licenses to operate a utilities business such as a water, electricity or gas company, there is usually one license granted for each type of service in a given area and that licence is usually given to a local government. This, of course, constitutes socialism.

Certain types of labor laws also have the effect of granting monopolies to a favored group. Laws which make it difficult or impossible for those who lack membership in a union to obtain employment are of this type. The employer is forbidden by law to make his own contract with the employee, and the law may also prevent the employee from obtaining employment in the unionized industry otherwise.

Licenses called quotas or bases, are sometimes required before one can produce and sell certain types of dairy and agriculture products. Following is an example of a licensing law:

> It is unlawful to engage in the practice of medicine in this state without first obtaining a license. Any person who engages in the practice of medicine without a license shall be guilty of a felony—UTAH CODE ANN. SEC. 58-12-30

Licensing Laws Neither Punish Evil Nor Enforce Rights; They Do Restrain Competition

Although licensing laws always provide for punishing those who violate them, it is not necessary to prove that the defendant either intended evil or caused harm in order to convict him. Such laws can have no effect on the punishment of crime. The reason is that existing criminal laws already cover every type of criminal offence which one might commit in carrying on a business or trade.

Neither are they necessary to permit an injured party to recover damages. Tort and contract laws exist which provide relief for such injuries.

Licensing laws restrain competition. They grant exclusive monopolies to those who hold them and make it a crime for others to compete. They also prevent the buying public from purchasing goods and services from anyone except the licensees. Although the law seldom mentions buyers, the restriction on their freedom is the same as if they did for if the seller cannot sell, the buyer cannot buy.

Licensing Laws Violate The Golden Rule By Creating Duties

Not only do licensing laws violate the Golden Rule by punishing the innocent, but they have the effect of creating duties which should not exist.

By enforcing licensing laws, governments create new rights in the licensees and in doing so they create new duties in all others. All unlicensed people lose certain rights because they are forbidden to enter the licensed occupation except at a cost in time and money they do not feel they can afford. Also they are forbidden to patronize anyone except the licensees.

No one has a duty to refrain from entering a legitimate occupation and selling his products and services to anyone he chooses. Nor does the buying public have a duty to refrain from patronizing anyone they choose. Nevertheless by adopting licensing laws, governments undertake to create and enforce all of these duties. But it lacks the power to do so. All power it has comes from the people and since the people have no right to create such duties, neither does government.

Do Licensing Laws Protect The Public Against Incompetence?

One argument used to justify licensing laws is that they serve to protect the public against incompetence, inexperience and lack of adequate training. The feeling seems to be that only those who are the best qualified have a right to serve the public.

Let us examine this argument.

We will commence with the trite observation that no one is perfect. No matter how old or young, how educated or ignorant, how experienced or untried, everyone is subject to making mistakes. Each person who lives a full and ordinary life, commences in a state of utter incompetence at birth, increases in ability until he reaches his prime (which is always short of perfection), and then returns again to utter incompetence at death. While some may largely retain their mental faculties until the end, physical deterioration is as certain as death itself.

Since all men are imperfect and prone to make mistakes, virtually every act of any consequence we perform might possibly injure someone. No matter how careful, how well-trained or well-intentioned we may be, the possibility of human error is always present to threaten the well-being of others.

No physician or nurse ever becomes so skillful and wise that he is free from the danger of taking the life he/she is trying to save. No mechanic, builder, machine operator or craftsman ever becomes so proficient that he can claim that his efforts will always be constructive but never destructive; or that the product of his work will be free from dangerous defects. No teacher ever becomes so knowledgeable and wise that he can be certain that he will always teach truth and never error.

Being human beings that we are, we are forever subject to failure of mind and body; to malfunction of brain and muscle; to heart attack, lapse of memory and mistake of judgment. Especially is this true in view of man's inability to fully understand and control the elements of nature. Who can erect a structure which will withstand every earthquake or storm? Who can construct a piece of machinery so perfectly that it might not fail because of metal fatigue or some other unpredictable defect? Who understands the diversity of minds and bodies well enough that he can foresee the effect of a given medicine or piece of information on any particular person?

Furthermore everyone is constantly changing. We are continually learning and forgetting; acquiring a skill only to lose it again; gaining vigor and health during one period and then losing them in another.

Now is it possible for any licensing agency (who are erring humans themselves) to classify this infinite and ever-changing diversity of human imperfection into two groups—the qualified, and the unqualified—and be just to everyone? Any line which is drawn must be purely arbitrary with nothing more to support it than the prejudice or selfish interest of the one who drew it because all he has to choose between is varying degrees of constantly changing ignorance, incompetence and inexperience.

And even though it were possible to distinguish between the fit and the unfit, due to the constant changes taking place in people, this classification would not be valid for more than a brief period. There would be those close to the line who would be constantly crossing over it going both directions.

One of the worst aspects of licensing laws is that those who already hold the licenses wield the political power by which they prevent those on the outside from getting in. They make the rules and erect the hurdles which prevent others from competing. In many instances they erect those hurdles just high enough to maximize their own incomes.

Do Not Licensing Laws Provide The Public With Only Those Who Are Best Qualified?

Even admitting the practical impossibility of distinguishing between the qualified and the unqualified, some may contend that licensing laws protect the public by allowing only the best qualified to serve them.

But who are the best qualified? If there is a sound reason why only the most superior should be permitted to make a living at law, medicine, engineering, banking and plumbing, then why don't we permit only the top ten percent of those now engaging in these activities to have licenses? If the public is entitled to have only the best, why allow this other ninety percent to sell their inferior goods and services?

The obvious answer to this proposal is that it would have the effect of eliminating approximately ninety percent of the goods and services now being produced. That which the less qualified group is providing is needed even though it is somewhat inferior. It would be harmful to the public to prevent them from working merely because they are less skillful and more apt to make mistakes than the superior ten percent.

But where does this argument lead to? If we follow it through the next step, we must conclude that existing licensing laws are even now denying the public an untold amount of goods and services which would otherwise be available. If they were abolished so that twice as many people could enter into a given trade or occupation, we might find approximately twice as much being produced. If that were true, the buying public would be benefitted enormously because the price would necessarily have to be lowered to sell that much.

The demand for goods and services is literally unlimited. There are millions of people who now need dental, medical, legal, engineering and other professional assistance who cannot afford to pay the fees charged by those who have been compelled to spend a large portion of their lives and tens of thousands of dollars obtaining a license. The same can be said of trades, occupations and businesses of all kinds. If the bars were removed, the unemployed and other venturesome souls would flood into these areas, become proficient and begin exchanging goods and services with each other to the benefit of everyone—except possibly present license holders and the bureaucrats who serve them.

Do Not Licensing Boards Provide The Public With Valuable Information?

It is generally true that those who serve the public the best, gain a deserved reputation for doing so. Nevertheless there are those who feel that licensing laws serve a valuable purpose in compelling those who hold licenses to attain some minimum level of education, experience and competence. Thus in the absence of a reputation, the public can use this fact to help them choose someone who is qualified. Are not licensing laws valuable for this purpose?

It is assumed that in the absence of licensing laws, those who consider themselves professionals in a given field, would band together in a professional association, establish minimum standards for membership, and proceed to advertise their superiority. Thus the public would still be provided with information regarding who the professionals consider professional. And certainly it is the right of doctors, lawyers, engineers, accountants and others to do this very thing. Furthermore anyone who falsely claimed membership in such a group, should be prosecuted for false advertising. No harm would result from such associations and doubtless much good would be accomplished by them.

If those who consider themselves better qualified want to prove their excellence, they could then do so in the open market. But why should they be allowed to establish government enforced monopolies which compel customers to patronize them or go without? If they feel that buyers might not be able to distinguish between them and those less skilled, they can still set up their own rules for membership in their organization and deny admittance to any they feel to be unqualified.

But at the same time why should the public be denied their freedom to reject their claims of superiority? Or why should not the public be permitted to purchase products and services of an inferior quality and doubtless at a cheaper price if they desire? In other words, why should we continue to allow licensing laws to deny people their freedom of contract?

Why Are Licensing Laws Adopted?

In an unregulated economy, the only ones in business are those who have customers who come to them voluntarily and in preference to anyone else. They are producing goods and services which the public want and are willing to pay for. What other test is there for being qualified? This is the only one which is relevant and fair, and many there are who have failed it. The consuming public is discriminating and demanding. They are also merciless. They can be counted on to keep the unqualified from serving them. No licensing board or government agency is needed for this purpose.

When we deny men their freedom to be productive because we fear they might possibly cause harm, we act foolishly and unjustly. If a person intends to do good, he will do infinitely more good than harm. One who enters a business or profession, is well aware that he must serve the public satisfactorily or go bankrupt.

No honest and sensible person will undertake a job which he knows he cannot do even if he could find a customer who would permit him to try. He knows that he must produce what is contracted for or subject himself to lawsuits for breach of contract, false advertising and even criminal negligence. If he is not honest and sensible, if he misleads the public by false advertising, or injures them by selling injurious goods and services, then of course he should be punished and compelled to make restitution. But before we convict him, let us give him a fair trial before an impartial tribunal. Let us not send him before a board of licensees or their hirelings who have already judged him guilty even though he has intended no evil and caused no harm. Let us not prevent him from making a living at our licensed profession solely on the arrogant supposition that we are better qualified than he to serve the public.

Licensing Laws Are Adopted Because Of Pride

In D&C Sec. 121, the Lord has said that many are called but few are chosen because the many set their hearts "so much upon the things of this world and aspire to the honors of men" that they fail to learn a crucial lesson regarding the principles of righteousness. He also says in this same section that:

> When we undertake to cover our sins, or to gratify our pride, our vain ambition, or to exercise control or dominion or compulsion upon the souls of the children of men in any degree of unrighteousness, . . . Amen to the

priesthood or the authority of that man. (V. 37)

Is there a person who cherishes and utilizes a government issued license who is not guilty of each of the sins mentioned in this scripture? If we tried to use force to prevent competition outside of government we would be guilty of racketeering and extortion. Do we not cover these sins with licensing laws? Are we not gratifying our pride, our vain ambition, and exercising unrighteous compulsion when we forcibly prevent others from competing?

There is scarcely an adult in our society today who does not hold one or more government granted licenses, certificates, honors, titles, degrees, letters or privileges, affirming him to be something special and/or granting him some economic advantage. The Nephites were destroyed for their pride. Is not the time ripe for us to repent of this sin and repeal those laws which are enabling government to gratify it in this manner?

Of course it must be recognized that since licenses are required for virtually all occupations, if we are to earn a living in these areas and at the same time obey the law, we must obtain the required license. However if we befriend, uphold and support laws which are so clearly contrary to the principles of the Constitution, how can we hope to escape the condemnation of a just God? And if we fail to abolish them voluntarily, will not the Lord force a cleansing as he did when the Nephites corrupted their laws?

WORDS OF PRESIDENT BENSON

My attitude toward government is succinctly expressed be the following provision taken from the Alabama Constitution:

> That the sole object and only legitimate end of government is to protect the citizen in the enjoyment of life, liberty, and property, and when the government assumes other functions it is usurpation and oppression. (Art. 1, Sec. 35)

An important test I use in passing judgment upon an act of government is this: If it were up to me as an individual to punish my neighbor for violating a given law, would it offend my conscience to do so? Since my conscience will never permit me to physically punish my fellowman unless he has done something evil, or unless he has failed to do something which I have a moral right to require of him to do, I will never knowingly authorize my agent, the government, to do this on my behalf.

I realize that when I give my consent to the adoption of a law, I specifically instruct the police—the government—to take either the life, liberty, or property of anyone who disobeys that law. Furthermore, I tell them if anyone resists the enforcement of the law, they are to use any means necessary—yeas, even putting the law-breaker to death or putting him in jail—to overcome such resistance. These are extreme measures but unless laws are enforced, anarchy results.

As John Locke explained many years ago:

> The end of law is not to abolish or restrain, but to preserve and enlarge freedom. For in all the states of created beings, capable of laws, *where there is no law there is no freedom.* For liberty is to be free from restraint and violence from others, which cannot be where there is no law; and is not, as we are told, "a liberty for every man to do what he lists." For who could be free, when every other man's humour might domineer over him? But a liberty to dispose and order freely as he lists his person, actions, possessions, and his whole property within the allowance of those laws under which he is, and therein not to be subject to the arbitrary will of another, but freely follow his own. [*Two Treatises of Civil Government, II, 57; P.P.N.S.*, p. 101]

(Ezra Taft Benson, *An Enemy Hath Done This*, p. 132-33)

XXII

Government Must Punish Nothing Except The Intentional Violation Of Duties—Regulatory Laws

Definition Of A Regulatory Law

We shall use the term regulatory law to mean any rule, regulation or government decree, the purpose of which is to regulate the business and private affairs of the people. While this definition is broad enough to cover licensing laws and some types of welfare state laws, those are special types of regulatory laws which we treat separately. Therefore our discussion in this chapter will cover types of regulatory laws other than those.

Regulatory Laws Violate The Golden Rule

We have seen in the previous chapter that licensing laws have the effect of violating the Golden Rule. Herein we will see that regulatory laws have this same effect. In both instances when the laws are enforced the innocent are punished, the right of private property is abridged and the power of government over the people is increased.

Regulatory laws are often confused with criminal laws because they contain a penalty clause making it a criminal offense to violate them. Nevertheless, they are not adopted for the purpose of punishing crime. They are useless for this purpose because criminal laws already cover all types of crimes which one can commit in the operation of his business and private affairs.

The fundamental and all-important difference between a regulatory law and a criminal law is this: proof of an evil intent is essential to convict one of violating a criminal law, but is not necessary for conviction under a regulatory law. Since regulatory laws provide for inflicting penalties on those who are innocent of an evil intent, they are in direct conflict with our second law which decrees that government shall punish nothing other than the intentional violation of duties.

Some may imagine that regulatory laws are necessary to permit one who has been injured by a business to recover damages therefor. But this is not true since tort and contract laws already make provision for all such cases.

What Motivates The Adoption Of Regulatory Laws?

We see clearly why licensing laws are adopted: Their purpose is to give special interest groups government enforced monopolies. But the reasons which motivate the passage of regulatory laws are not that easily identified. This is especially true since they so obviously violate the Golden Rule and the principles of private morality.

As individuals, we have no desire to regulate the private and business affairs of one another. Usually our own difficulties and problems consume all of our time and energy. Neither do we have any right to do so. Any person who would undertake to force others to operate their businesses or conduct their private affairs as he dictated, would be excluded from polite society and probably end up in jail.

Also, since as individual citizens we have no authority to interfere in each others private and business affairs, we cannot convey such a power to government; and if this cannot be done, regulatory laws constitute a usurpation of power. Why then do we tolerate regulatory laws? Could it be because almost all men have the disposition to exercise unrighteous dominion as soon as they get a little authority? Is it because we have been deceived into believing regulation is necessary?

The Iron Law Of Stewardship Makes Regulation Unnecessary

Those who favor government interference with the operation of private businesses seem unaware of the iron law of stewardship which decrees that an owner of private property must use that property for the benefit of others, lose it to those who will, or suffer the losses which the ownership of idle property always brings. In an unregulated economy, business owners must conduct their businesses in such a manner that they serve the buying public on their own terms or go bankrupt. They must also share what they produce with employees.

Owners of businesses are caught between the conflicting demands of customers who are always asking for better quality at lower prices, and those of employees who are always seeking higher wages which requires an increase in prices. He needs no government regulatory agency to compel him to try to satisfy both of these two groups because unless he does he will lose them. He can be depended upon to operate his business as efficiently as possible and to do whatever is necessary to retain both his customers and his employees.

When government steps in and forces him to comply with a new set of demands, this always reduces the efficiency of his operation and raises his costs, including taxes. Of course these burdens must be passed on to the consumers in the form of increased selling prices.

Since, as noted above, regulatory laws are useless either for the punishment of crime or for the recovery of damages, and since they do nothing but increase selling prices and taxes, everyone should oppose them on practical grounds if nothing else. But there is another consequence of regulatory laws which is far more serious than this which we shall now discuss.

Regulatory Laws Help Achieve The Communist Goal Thereby Preventing The Operation Of The Law Of Stewardship

It is apparent that when regulatory laws are numerous enough, the communist goal of abolition of private property is largely achieved without government becoming the owner. If regulatory laws enable it to dictate the purposes for, and the manner in which private property may be used, it possesses many of the powers which ownership would give.

We own property so that we may use it to achieve our own purposes. But if government has the power to dictate what those purposes are and how they shall be achieved, private ownership is largely denied. To the extent government regulations exist, the constitutional guarantee that, "no person shall . . . be deprived of life, liberty or property without due process of law," is denied. Also to this same extent the Communist goal of "abolition of private property" is achieved.

The Lord, in describing His reasons for establishing the laws and Constitution of the United States said:

> Therefore, it is not right that any man should be in bondage one to another.
>
> And for this purpose have I established the Constitution of this land, by the hands of wise men whom I raised up unto this very purpose, and redeemed the land by the shedding of blood. (D&C 101:79-80)

Government constitutes the greatest threat to human freedom on earth and one of the easiest ways of bringing citizens into bondage is by regulating and controlling their property. Any person who believes that the Lord has commanded men to befriend only those laws which are constitutional, and at the same time realizes that the support of Communist objectives is one of the worst sins he can commit, will hesitate before supporting regulatory laws.

It is also apparent that to the extent that regulatory laws exist, they prevent the operation of the iron law of stewardship. The owner is compelled to do as the bureaucrat dictates rather than as the customers demand. If it be true that everyone is benefitted by the operation of the law of stewardship, then it is to the interest of consumers, employees and taxpayers alike to see that regulatory laws are abolished so that its operation is not interfered with.

If businessmen commit crimes, let them be punished under the criminal laws. If they cause injury, let those who suffer, recover damages in a civil suit. But in all other situations, businessmen should be free from the control of government so that they may serve the public on its own terms.

SHOULD GOVERNMENT OWNERSHIP BE PREFERRED OVER PRIVATE OWNERSHIP?

Only governments are able to escape the inexorable demands of the iron law of stewardship. They are not faced with the necessity of solving the problems faced by the private owner. They do not need to put their property to productive use in order to continue to own it. And even if they operate it, they need not do so efficiently. They can always compel the public to pay their losses through increased taxes.

The monopolies which men should fear are those of governments and gangsters. Government is the one organization which can legally use its ownership and control of property to make slaves and paupers of the people. That is the one owner which can sit on the wealth of a nation and permit it to lie idle. In a socialist nation where the state owns the land and regulates and controls the use to which it may be put, the people are literally in bondage to their own government. One of the Ten Points of the Communist Manifesto reads as follows:

> Abolition of property in land and application of all rents of land to public purposes.

Unregulated Businesses Provide Maximum Benefits For All

When the free enterprise system is allowed to operate without interference, the rich do not get richer while the poor get poorer, but the poor benefit far more than do the so-called rich. The rich can neither gain nor retain large amounts of wealth except by serving both the public and their employees.

To operate a large enterprise, the owner must not only serve many consumers and do so on their terms, but he must hire large numbers of employees on their terms. In doing this he must allow these groups to reap nearly all of the benefits from the operation of the business. In every large business, the consumers and employees consume a hundred fold more of what is produced than do the owners, and this is the true test as to who benefits from the operation of that business.

Because of envy, greed, and the spreading of false doctrines, large businesses ofttimes become the object of hate campaigns. The truth is that the public is always better off with such businesses in operation than without, because it is the public which consumes nearly all the businesses produce. The real concern of the public should be that their governments never adopt laws which give such businesses special privileges and monopolies, thus preventing others from entering the field and serving them also. Licensing laws always harm society by preventing the unrestricted operation of the law of stewardship.

But socializing a business by transferring its ownership to government is the worst alternative of all. In doing so, the stewardship law is abolished, thus causing the greatest injury possible to employees and consumers alike.

When one compares the poverty and want in socialist countries with the prosperity and well being of the people who live under a government which protects the right of private property, the benefits of the operation of the Lord's system of stewardship is plain to see. Today it is impossible to compare a completely unregulated economy with one which is regulated, because the former does not exist. However any fair observer will find that other things being equal, the less the regulation, the greater the prosperity of everyone.

It is strange indeed that the private capitalist which the people should trust, they tend to fear; while the government owner and regulator which they should fear, they tend to place their faith in.

What About Public Nuisances?

Suppose that business owners produce obnoxious or harmful sights, sounds, smells or chemicals on their property. Are not regulatory laws necessary to prevent such? Anyone who wants to obey the Golden Rule and give businessmen the same just treatment he would desire, will insist that one charged with committing a public nuisance be granted his day in court. If a defendant is charged with having caused an injury either intentionally or negligently, let those making the charge prove their case in a court of law if they are able, and let the defendant present his defense.

Regulatory agencies are unnecessary for the prosecution and trial of public nuisances. On the other hand, to have a case tried before those whose very jobs depend upon prosecuting and judging nuisance cases, may result in biased decisions, bribery, or both. Only by assigning cases of public nuisances to regular courts of law can a defendant expect to receive a fair trial.

REGULATION IS COSTLY

It would be difficult to make a close guess as to the total cost of regulatory laws. It is so enormous, and results from so many different aspects of regulation, that the estimator cannot be certain he has taken everything into account. He can count bureaucratic noses and add up the cost of office space, secretaries, telephone bills, travel and other operating costs. But who can estimate the number of man hours which businesses are forced to devote to preparing the never-ending and ever-increasing reports, answering the questionnaires and correspondence, conferring with, placating, and obeying the orders of government employees who are charged with regulating them?

Who can estimate the value of the goods and services the public has been denied by the interference of regulatory agencies? Who can guess how many businesses have failed for no other reason than that they could not bear the expense of preparing the paperwork and complying with other regulations of the bureaucracy? The cost may run into hundreds of billions of dollars annually.

HOW CAN WE STOP THE ENFORCEMENT OF REGULATORY LAWS?

The Constitution of the United States provides for trial by jury in all criminal cases. If this practice were followed in all jurisdictions, the people acting as jurors would have the power to prevent enforcement of any regulatory law inimical to their interests. They would have an absolute veto on every law under which government attempts to impose a criminal penalty. They would have the power to compel obedience to the second subdivision of the Golden Rule which decrees:

> Government shall punish nothing except the intentional violation of duties.

Another method of abolishing the bureaucracy is to elect men to office who will repeal the laws which created it.

Words of Ezra Taft Benson

In reply to the argument that a little bit of socialism is good so long as it doesn't go too far, it is tempting to say that, in like fashion, just a little bit of theft or a little bit of cancer is all right, too! History proves that the growth of the welfare state is difficult to check before it comes to its full flower of dictatorship. But let us hope that this time around, the trend can be reversed. If not, then we will see the inevitability of complete socialism, probably within our lifetime.

This brings up the next question: How is it possible to cut out the various welfare-state features of our government which have already fastened themselves like cancer cells onto the body politic? Isn't drastic surgery already necessary, and can it be performed without endangering the patient? In answer, it is obvious that drastic measures *are* called for. No half-way or compromise actions will suffice. Like all surgery, it will not be without discomfort and perhaps even some scar tissue for a long time to come. But it must be done if the patient is to be saved, and it can be done without undue risk. (Ezra Taft Benson, *The Proper Role of Government,* p. 19)

XXIII

Governments Shall Never Create Nor Abolish Duties—Welfare State Laws

Prefatory Statement

In this chapter we discuss the fourth and last of the four sub-rules of the Golden Rule. It forbids government to either create or abolish rights or duties. The moral principle which underlies this law is this: When government creates a right in one person or group, of necessity it must destroy rights by creating duties in some other person or group. The creation of a duty destroys the obligor's rights by compelling him to give up some element of his freedom when he discharges it.

That They Might The More Easily...Steal.

We have heretofore observed that when the Gadianton band captured control of the Nephite government around the year 30 B.C., they did so by a combination of murder, intrigue, and seducing the Nephite voters to join with them in partaking of the spoils of government. (Hela. 6:38) We also observed that in describing the conditions which existed when the robbers came into power, Mormon stated that they were, "Held in office at the head of government, ... that they might get gain ... and, moreover, that they might the more easily ... steal ..." (Hela. 7:5)

It is probably true that the principal reason these secret combinations were called Gadianton Robbers, was because their main goal was to seize control of government so that they could use it to commit plunder. In this chapter we shall consider the extent to which we have fallen victims to the same satanic plot.

Definition Of A Welfare State Law

By the term "welfare state law," we mean one under which government transfers public funds, property or services without receiving a fair consideration in return. Included within this definition are all of those public welfare programs which provide aid to the young, the old, the sick, the disadvantaged, the unemployed, the uneducated, the widows, the orphans, the victims of natural disasters, victims of man-made disasters, etc.

Under this definition, we include those laws which provide for food stamps, social security, medicare, old age benefits, industrial insurance and unemployment insurance. While under some of these programs the government compels the recipient to contribute some of his own money which, in theory, is to be returned to him, he usually receives at least twice as much as he puts in because at least one half of his benefits come from employers or other taxpayers. Also taxpayers pay the cost of administering these programs.

Welfare State Laws Create New Duties And Destroy The Right Of Private Property

By adopting laws which permit or direct that public funds be paid to welfare recipients, government thereby creates a duty on the part of taxpayers to support the welfare recipients. To this same extent it violates the right of private property. Every taxpayer has a duty to pay his fair share of the cost of defending freedom. But he has no morally enforceable obligation to pay taxes for the support of those to whom he owes no natural or assumed duty. Neither does the recipient have the right to demand that he do so.

It is generally assumed that robbery, plunder, and theft, when committed outside of government violate the rules of morality. We all object to being victims of such crimes and know that they are contrary to the divine commandment: "Thou shalt not steal."

Does the fact that government does the taking and the giving alter anything? Does that which is evil suddenly become good by the adoption of a man-made law which legalizes the taking? It is difficult to find any meaningful difference between the two situations. Everything which government gives to one, it must take from another, and the taking is always done under laws which compel the victim to pay.

Welfare State Programs Threaten The Existence Of Our Constitutional System Of Government

Welfare state practices can be extended until they equalize all incomes and thus create a completely socialized nation. But they can also be extended until they bankrupt the national treasury and create such a financial crisis that our constitutional system of government is overthrown. They are in large measure, the cause of budget deficits and the enormous, interest bearing debt which increases by many billions of dollars each year. The answer to these problems is not merely to decrease welfare state programs, but abolish them entirely. Once such practices are commenced, there is no logical stopping place. Experience shows that politicians who find they can raid the public treasury in exchange for votes, have difficulty restraining themselves.

Welfare State Programs Are Diametrically Opposed To The Principles Of The Constitution

Governments which have been established by the Lord are obligated to protect private property against the avarice of those in government as well as those outside. The following provision from the United States Constitution prohibits theft by government:

> No person shall be ... deprived of life, liberty, or property, without due process of law; nor shall private property be taken for public use, without just compensation. (5th Amendment)

The commandment, Thou shalt not steal which is one of the ten most important laws ever given, has never been repealed. This commandment applies as much to groups as to individuals and no man-made law can possibly revoke or alter it. Nor can any person who participates in robbery by government avoid being condemned by the Lord unless he repents.

THE LORD'S COMMANDMENTS REGARDING WORK

When Adam was driven from the Garden of Eden, the Lord told him:

> In the sweat of thy face shalt thou eat bread, till thou return unto the ground; . . . (Gen. 3:19)

One of the Ten Commandments reads:

> Six days shalt thou labor and do all thy work. (Ex. 20:9)

The Lord has also decreed:

> Thou shalt not be idle; for he that is idle shall not eat the bread nor wear the garments of the laborer. (D&C 42:42)

So grievous is the sin of idleness that the Lord has decreed that unless there is repentance, one shall lose his place in the Church:

> . . . And the idler shall not have place in the Church, except he repent and mend his ways. (D&C 75:29; See also D&C 56:17; 60:13)

Even though very few, if any, have been excommunicated for idleness in this life, can we doubt but that the Lord will divide the industrious from the indolent in the next?

The laws of man which limit or prohibit the young or the old from working, and which provide welfare state benefits which relieve us of the necessity of earning our own living, are directly contrary to the above laws and instructions. An enormous amount of idleness and laziness is being caused by our welfare-state system.

WHY IS IT SO IMPORTANT THAT WE OBEY THE COMMANDMENT TO WORK?

No person ever has or ever will accomplish any task, or develop any talent, without work. He will remain largely useless until he overcomes the natural tendency to be idle. Thus the importance of work lies in the fact that without it we are nothing, while through it we can reach every desired height. One who fails to learn to work in this life has failed to grasp one of its most important opportunities. Every blessing is predicated upon obedience to law. But obedience requires work—earnest, persistent effort. Leonardo Da Vinci has said, "O God, you sell us everything for the price of an effort."

One who fails to learn to work has a sad future and may lose many of the benefits he earned in the past. Notice the severity of the Lord's condemnation of the man who buried his talent:

> Thou wicked and slothful servant . . . Take therefore the talent from him, and give it unto him which had ten talents. . . . And cast ye the unprofitable servant into outer darkness: there shall be weeping and gnashing of teeth. (Matt. 25:26, 28, 30)

The Book of Mormon describes the terrible fate of Church members who waste their time thus:

> But wo unto him that has the law given, yea, that has all the commandments of God, like unto us, and that transgresseth them, and that wasteth the days of his probation, for awful is his state! (2 Ne. 9:27)

The Lord's Plan To Teach Us To Work

By giving us mortal bodies with their unceasing need for food, clothing and shelter, the Lord placed us in a situation where someone must work or we all die. We have had the sentence of labor for life passed upon us. Through the organization of the family, the Lord provided for our periods of helplessness with the parents taking care of the children during the time of their inability, and with the children caring for the parents when their situations are reversed.

While cooperation between family members can and should take care of the incapacity of infancy, old age and periods of sickness in most cases, there are always the poor among us who are not provided for. The Lord's commandments to provide for them are most clear and contain severe penalties for violation:

> And it is my purpose to provide for my saints, for all things are mine.
>
> But it must needs be done in mine own way; and behold this is the way that I, the Lord, have decreed to provide for my saints, that the poor shall be exalted, in that the rich are made low.

> Therefore, if any man shall take of the abundance which I have made, and impart not his portion, according to the law of my gospel, unto the poor and the needy, he shall with the wicked, lift up his eyes in hell, being in torment. (D&C 104:15, 16, 18)

Welfare state laws are contrary to every aspect of the Lord's plan. They legalize plunder and teach people to believe it is their right to live at the expense of others. They tend to remove the necessity of obeying the commandment to labor. They encourage idleness and tend to abolish the need for charitable giving. They destroy the sanctity of family relationships by removing the interdependence which should exist therein.

Modern Prophets Condemn The Welfare State

The late President David O. McKay in a letter written to the faculty and administration at the Brigham Young University in 1967, said this:

> This trend to a welfare state in which people look to and worship government more than their God, is certain to sap the individual ambitions and moral fiber of our youth unless they are warned and rewarned of the consequences. History, of course, is replete with the downfall of nations who, instead of assuming their own responsibility for their religious and economic welfare, mistakenly attempted to shift their individual responsibility to government.
>
> I am aware that a university has the responsibility of acquainting its students with the theories and doctrines which are prevalent in the various disciplines, but I hope that no one on the faculty of Brigham Young University will advocate positions which cannot be harmonized with the views of every prophet of the Church, from the prophet Joseph Smith on down, concerning our belief that we should be strong and self-reliant individuals, not dependent upon the largess or benefactions of government. None of the doctrines of our Church give any sanction to the concept of a socialistic state.

The Relationship Between The Welfare State And Secret Combinations

In our discussion of Nephite history, we showed that the secret combinations of that era were communistic. (3 Ne. 3:7) At one point this evil group worked itself into control of Nephite government by seducing even the more part of the righteous to "believe in their works and partake of their spoils." (Hela. 6:38) It appears that they used the welfare state approach.

The Nephite prophets have warned us that if we allow the secret combination to get "above us," it will destroy us as it did the Nephites and the Jaredites. (Ether 8) Just how many hundreds of billions of dollars must be spent per year on welfare state programs before it can be said that the communist movement is "above us," is not known. But if we have already gone so far that we cannot stop the practice, we have reached the point of no return.

This may in part be what President Benson was referring to when he said:

> Our nation will continue to degenerate unless we read and heed the words of the God of this land, Jesus Christ, and quit building up and upholding secret combinations, . . . (*Ensign*, July 1988, p. 80)
>
> I testify that wickedness is rapidly expanding in every segment of our society. (See D&C 1:14-16; 84:49-53) It is more highly organized, more cleverly disguised, and more powerfully promoted than ever before. Secret combinations lusting for power, gain, and glory are flourishing. A secret combination that seeks to overthrow the freedom of all lands, nations, and countries is increasing its evil influence and control over America and the entire world. [See Ether 8:18-25] (*Ensign*, November 1988, p. 87)

THE PREDICAMENT OF THOSE WHO DESIRE TO THROW OFF THE WELFARE STATE

Welfare state handouts have become so enormous and pervasive in the United States, that one almost despairs of trying to formulate a plan through which they could be eliminated. Governments at every level engage in such practices. Many different kinds of programs have been adopted, some of which compel those who receive benefits to contribute to the funds from which they are paid. In such instances the contributor justifiably feels that he has a vested interest in the program and should be entitled to receive back the amount of his contribution plus a fair return. However the effects of inflation makes it almost impossible to determine how much that should be.

Another serious problem which must be faced by those who would abolish government handouts, is that the recipients who have become accustomed to them would experience great difficulty if they were terminated suddenly. Perhaps a phase-out program should be considered.

Regardless of how difficult the problem is, it seems certain that unless we solve it voluntarily, the Lord will do so for us and His method may be far more painful than any we would devise.

XXIV

The Destruction Of Rights By Use Of Irredeemable Paper Money

Prefatory Comment

Our discussion of the preservation of rights under the United States Constitution would be incomplete if we did not mention the provision it contains prohibiting the government from destroying property rights through the use of irredeemable paper money. Today throughout the world, many governments finance themselves largely by the printing of irredeemable currency.

The Lord inspired the Founding Fathers to place in the Constitution a provision prohibiting this practice. In spite of this, laws have been adopted and upheld in the United States, permitting the federal government to print and circulate irredeemable paper money and make it a tender in payment of debts.

Does The Lord Recommend A Monetary System?

The Book of Mormon contains relatively few details regarding the functioning of the Nephite economy. But one thing it does provide is a careful description of their monetary system. This is found in Alma 11:3-19. In these few verses we learn that prior to the time of the reign of the judges, the people altered their monetary system from generation to generation, "according to the minds and the circumstances of the people."

However when king Mosiah established a government subject to majority vote, laws were adopted which fixed a monetary system consisting of gold and silver coins of various denominations and specifically related values. Those laws also fixed an exchange rate between the coins, a measure of grain, and a days work for a judge.

Unless this information is valuable, why would Mormon have taken the trouble to engrave it upon the plates? Can it be that the Lord wants us to know that a monetary system consisting of gold and silver coins is the one He approves of, and that such a system is vital to our well-being? It is difficult to discern any other reason.

Certain it is that when the Founding Fathers, acting under the inspiration of the Almighty, established our constitutional system, they provided for a monetary system consisting of gold and silver coins. In doing so they forbade the use of anything else as a tender in payment of debts. The provision making this the constitutional law of the land follows:

> No state shall . . . make anything but gold and silver coin a tender in payment of debts. (Art. 1, Sec. 10)

The states were not permitted to coin their own money because to have allowed this would have opened up the way for as many different denominations of gold and silver coins as there are states. A uniform monetary system which would circulate throughout all the states was desirable and so the power to coin the money was given to the federal government in this clause:

> The congress shall have power . . . to coin money, regulate the value thereof, and of foreign coin, and fix the standard of weights and measures. (Art. 1, Sec. 8)

The power here given to coin money, is nothing more than the power to weigh, alloy, shape and stamp coins in such a manner that one can see at a glance how many grains of the indicated metal the coin contains. (A grain is a small measure of weight equal to the weight of a grain of wheat.)

The power given to "regulate the value thereof," was necessary because there was more than one metal chosen as legal tender. Since only a fixed number of grains of one of the metals could be used as a standard for the nation's money, the number of grains of the other metal having a value equivalent thereto, would have to be regulated or changed from time to time as the relative values of the two metals varied in the open market. Had the relative values of the two metals been fixed, as appears to have been the case with the Nephite system, this power to regulate would not have been necessary. In modern times however, this power was essential because of the constant fluctuation between the two metals in the world market.

Or to explain the matter according to what actually occurred, by the first coinage act of 1792, Congress chose silver rather than gold as the standard metal, and made 371.25 grains of pure silver the basic unit of our entire monetary system. They called this unit the dollar, and regulated the value of gold at fifteen times that of silver. In other words they stated that one grain of gold was equivalent in value to 15 grains of silver.

The 1792 act also authorized the minting of gold and silver coins and declared both to be "a lawful tender in all payments whatsoever." (1 Stat. at Large, P. 250) In 1834, due to an increase in the value of gold relative to silver, Congress changed the ratio between the two metals from 15 to 1, to almost 16 to 1.

THE GOLD AND SILVER MONETARY SYSTEM HAS BEEN ABANDONED

The Founding Fathers and those who understood the transcendent importance of a sound monetary system, maintained it until the time of the Civil War. However during that grave national crisis, the northern states commenced the alteration of the system. Congress adopted laws authorizing the printing of paper money and making it a tender in payment of debts. It also commenced regulating and controlling private banks. The supreme court in a series of split decisions, finally held these measures to be constitutional.

A number of years after the end of the Civil War, the nation reverted to a hard money standard, but used gold, rather than silver as the standard of value. This lasted until the great depression of the 1930's. During this second national crisis another series of laws were adopted resulting in the complete abandonment of a sound monetary system. In another series of split decisions, the supreme court held such laws to be constitutional. All of this occurred in spite of the fact that the original constitutional provision regarding gold and silver coin had never been changed.

DOES THE CONSTITUTION PERMIT GOVERNMENT TO PRINT PAPER MONEY?

Some may believe that the wording of the Constitution can be reasonably interpreted to allow for the use of irredeemable paper as money. Since in our opinion, the provision regarding money is of enormous importance and needs to be understood by all, we will briefly discuss this issue.

The only power the Constitution gave to the federal government regarding money was to coin it and borrow it. The power to print it is nowhere mentioned.

Furthermore we are faced with the fact that the Constitution forbids the states to make anything but gold and silver coin a tender in payment of debts. If we respect this mandate, how can we possibly believe that the federal government has the power to compel them to use anything else? To believe that the federal government has the right to compel the states to violate the Constitution is against all reason.

But if any further proof is needed that the Federal has no constitutional power to "emit bills of credit," or print and circulate paper as money, it may be found in the debates of the Constitutional Convention. A proposal was made therein to give the Congress this very power and it was rejected by a vote of nine to two.

In a footnote explaining his vote in favor of denying the power, James Madison says:

> This vote in the affirmative by Virginia was occasioned by the acquiescence of Mr. Madison, who became satisfied that striking out the words would not disable the government from the use of public notes, as far as they could be safe and proper; and would only cut off the pretext for a "paper currency," and particularly for making the bills a "tender" either for public or private debts." (*Madison's notes on the Federal Convention*, Aug. 16, 1787)

WHY IS A MONETARY SYSTEM OF GOLD AND SILVER COINS IMPORTANT?

Those who believe the Constitution to be the handiwork of the Lord, need no other reason than this to favor the gold and silver monetary system for which it provides. It cannot be doubted that this is one of those provisions which is necessary to protect the rights which belong to all mankind, and therefore we are under commandment to leave it unchanged. Let us observe what rights are adversely affected by an irredeemable paper system.

The Federal Government Now Has Unlimited Power To Manufacture Money And To Spend It

The unlimited power of a government to print and circulate irredeemable paper as money is one of the most formidable and dangerous powers a government can possibly have. Who can imagine a device better calculated to give it control over the economy and the people? When a government can purchase goods and services and force the sellers to accept worthless paper as payment therefor, where is the restraint on its power to purchase?

When politicians, without risking their popularity by raising taxes, can conveniently and unobtrusively obtain the means by which to raid the public treasury to satisfy the demands of constituents whose favor they seek to purchase, where is the restraint on the power to corrupt?

A Corrupted Monetary System Grants An Unlimited Power To Tax

Those wise men who drafted the Constitution, carefully limited the power of the federal government to impose taxes. They denied it the power to impose direct taxes except when apportioned among the states on the basis of population. Since this is an extremely unpopular method of taxation, the restraint was most effective until the income tax amendment was adopted which made incomes subject to direct federal taxation without apportionment.

But the power to inflate the currency, which has been called the cruelest tax of all, has now been usurped by the federal government, and all of the carefully laid plans of those Founding Fathers to limit its taxing and spending powers have been brought to naught. The result has been most dramatic.

Back in the early 1930's when the nation was on the gold standard, the national annual budget was between four and five billion dollars. Today it is far more than a hundred times that amount and is growing by many billions more each year.

CORRUPTED MONETARY SYSTEM GRANTS AN UNLIMITED POWER TO INCUR DEBT

When a government can pay its debts only with gold and silver coin or with goods and services of an equivalent value, and when it cannot obtain these except through taxation and borrowing, its credit is subject to close scrutiny and creditors will lend no more than they believe it can repay.

Thus a redeemable currency puts a definite limit on the power of a government to borrow. When it attempts to borrow in excess of its credit as the North did during the Civil War, the value of its obligations declines in the market place. If the decline continues, creditors cease to loan except at a discount which is so high, that the attempt to borrow is rendered futile.

But when a government has the power to print unlimited quantities of paper money with which to pay its debts, creditors have little fear of lending or collecting. This removes virtually all restraints on the power of government to borrow. Let us note what has happened to the United States national debt since the nation abandoned the gold standard during the great depression.

At the beginning of that period, the national debt was between twenty five and thirty billion dollars. Today it is over three trillion and it continues its upward spiral as the orgy of printing, spending, and borrowing continues. This trend threatens the very existence of our Republican form of government.

A CORRUPTED MONETARY SYSTEM IMPAIRS THE OBLIGATION OF CONTRACT

Contained within the United States Constitution is this restraint on the powers of the states:

> No state shall ... pass any ...law impairing the obligation of contracts. (Art 1, Sec.10)

No device was ever invented which more cunningly and deceptively impairs the obligation of contract than a corrupted monetary system. The depreciation of the purchasing power of the money received by the creditor often goes unnoticed because he receives the same number of monetary units bargained for. However in the United States alone, creditors lose many billions of dollars in property rights each year because of the inflation caused by our irredeemable monetary system.

The government, being the largest debtor, benefits more than any others from this silent method of destroying property rights. It is a most disgraceful spectacle to see our government which was organized to establish justice, resort to injustice on such a gigantic scale.

A Corrupted Monetary System Discourages Investments

Another destructive consequence of an irredeemable paper monetary system is that it discourages and prevents the formation of investment capital. Mass production of goods and services is completely dependent upon the formation of investment capital with which the production facilities are acquired. But inflation destroys the incentive to save and, when rapid enough, makes saving virtually impossible for the great majority of the people.

Since the rate of inflation can never be accurately predicted, it is impossible for debtors and creditors to make contracts upon which they can depend. This destroys confidence between man and man, prevents the exercise of sound business judgment, discourages the very idea of investment, and subjects one's economic future to the machinations of politicians.

A Corrupted Monetary System Centralizes Political Control

To the extent that local and state governments receive their funds from a centralized government, to this same extent the right of citizens to control the affairs of their counties and cities is denied. Local government officials become subject to direction from those who crank the printing presses and supply their funds, rather than from those who elect them to office. Furthermore the voters have lost control of the purse strings. Their control over those who furnish the funds is almost non-existent.

Therefore when the federal government has the unlimited power to print paper money, and when it uses that power to finance state and local programs, the power of the citizens over their local affairs is largely destroyed. Irredeemable paper money is one of the most dangerous threats to freedom which exists.

A Corrupted Monetary System Is Proposed By The Communists

It should be of grave concern to those who accept the words of the prophets regarding the dangers of secret combinations, to note that in abandoning the Lord's monetary system, we have adopted the essential features of the system proposed by the adversary. Point number five of the Communist Manifesto provides for:

> Centralization of credit in the hands of the state by means of a national bank with state capital and an exclusive monopoly.

Today the federal government has an exclusive monopoly on the printing and issuance of money. Existing laws make it prohibitive for private banks to issue notes redeemable in gold and silver coin as they were able to do prior to the Civil War. While in theory banks are privately owned, through licensing requirements and regulations, the controls exercised over them by governments are so extensive, that many of the incidents of private ownership are denied, and the aims of the Communists achieved.

In concluding this Chapter, from Ezra Taft Benson we read:

> I believe in honest money, the gold and silver coinage of the Constitution, and a circulating medium convertible into such money without loss. I regard it as a flagrant violation of the explicit provisions of the Constitution for the federal government to make it a criminal offense to use gold or silver as legal tender or to issue irredeemable paper money. (Ezra Taft Benson, *An Enemy Hath Done This,* p. 145)

XXV

Public Schools

Scope Of Chapter

The last violation of constitutional principles which we will discuss is that of government schools. The institution of public education is so universally accepted today that many readers are apt to scoff at the idea that the control of education by government and the use of public funds for its support is contrary to moral law. Before rejecting the idea as absurd, one might ponder these facts which will be discussed more fully herein:

1. Point number ten of the Communist Manifesto contains the following proposal:

   Free education for all children in public schools. (App. III)

2. When public education was first proposed in the state of Utah, the leadership of the Church was unalterably opposed to it.

Education Is A Huge Enterprise

By any standard, education is one of the largest ventures not only in the United States but in the world. Furthermore the great bulk of it is public education. There are an enormous number of people whose income is derived from the taxes imposed to support this activity. Not only are there millions of teachers, administrators, janitors, food handlers and other types of direct employees, but there are many others who receive their income from building and maintaining school buildings and related facilities. There are those who spend endless hours writing text books and manuals for use by the students. There are others who manufacture and sell a wide variety of equipment for transportation of students, laboratories, sports, music, art, drama, etc.

The clientele for this enormous enterprise is, of course everyone. It is rare indeed to find in western countries at least, a person who has not received formal training in either private or public schools.

History records that in prior dispensations there were church sponsored programs for adults engaged in learning about religion, and sometimes these programs were financed by public funds. But government programs for taking children out of their homes and giving them years of training in secular subjects at public expense seems to be novel to this generation.

Does The Concept Of Public Education Agree With The Golden Rule?

Typically, public education laws adopted in the United States provide that parents, under threat of punishment for not doing so, must send children between the ages of six and sixteen, to some school there to be taught courses prescribed by the state. In the overwhelming majority of cases the school is a government school whose teachers and administrators are state employees and the course work is almost exclusively secular in nature. For all practical purposes, the teaching of religion in public institutions is forbidden. Taxpayers, whether they patronize the system or not, are compelled to finance the operation.

Any moral person would be horrified at the proposal that he do personally that which the proponent of public education does through government. The very idea of going to a neighbor and threatening him with punishment unless he sends his children to school at a certain age is repulsive to most people. Then to specify the type of instruction the child must be given, and finally tell him he must finance the scheme with his own funds—this would usually be considered one of the most obvious violations of human rights and of the rules of common decency of which one is capable.

It would be a forcible violation of two of the human rights which people hold dear above all others—the right of personal liberty and the right of property. Children are not to be allowed to use their time as they or their parents want it spent. But they must use it getting an education, and it must be the particular type of education which professional educators dictate. They might contend that this enslavement of the child is for his benefit, but they cannot logically deny that if it were done outside of government, it would constitute the crime of enslavement.

Parents are not to be allowed to spend their money as they choose, but they must spend it as educators consider best. They might contend that this is for the child's best good and that the particular type of education they have selected is indispensable for their welfare. But they cannot deny that if they were to do this directly, it would constitute a despicable crime against the right of private property.

Or let us suppose that you are a public school teacher or administrator. Can you imagine yourself gathering your neighbors together and threatening them with violence unless they patronize your school and pay your salary? Suppose that a chain of food stores claiming to have a necessary brand of children's food were to induce the government to issue a decree that all parents must feed their children that particular brand of food or else. Furthermore suppose that the law specified that even though the parents bought this particular food from some other source, they must nevertheless support the X chain of food stores with their tax money. Would you agree with such a law?

Most people would probably agree that the foregoing examples would be completely unjustifiable intrusions into the most sacred of family relationships. They would obviously constitute serious violations of the Golden Rule. Will anyone seriously admit that he would be willing to have his neighbor do these things to him outside of government? But does it alter anything when done by a group in the name of the state?

Can Men Alter Moral Law By The Passage Of Man-Made Laws?

Even if there is no moral justification for individuals using force on one another to compel children to be educated in a certain manner, can we justify government doing these things? It may be contended that the Golden Rule does not apply to actions committed through government and that some different standard must be used when men act in concert. Others may believe that even though the same moral laws applies to groups as to individuals, the individual is not held morally accountable for what government does. Let us examine these arguments.

Everyone will agree that the consequence of using force is not altered by changing the number of people who are engaged in using it. A person is just as surely bereft of his life, liberty or property when they are taken from him by a group as when they are taken by an individual. Neither does the passage of a law legalizing the use of force alter the consequences of its use. Clothing force in the robes of legality may disguise its nature but it does nothing whatsoever to change the effect of the force on the one against whom it is used.

It should also be apparent to anyone that if it is wrong or evil to put a person to death, enslave him, or deprive him of his property, the immoral nature of the act cannot be changed by man-made law. Men are as powerless to alter the laws of morality as they are to alter the laws of physics or chemistry. If the use of force on a person is evil, it remains so regardless of the fact that some legislature, dictator, or democratic majority has formally declared it to be otherwise.

On the other hand if a person deserves to be put to death, jailed or fined, such punishments would be just even though the law declared otherwise. The principles of justice are eternal, unchanging and everlasting and are completely beyond the power of man to change.

The final question we must answer then is whether the individual members of society are answerable for evil done in the name of government. It is first observed that the organization called government cannot be held morally accountable. The actions of governments are the actions of men, performed by men at the command of men, and only they can be either rewarded or punished for what governments do. Among the beliefs of members of the Church of Jesus Christ of Latter-day Saints is this:

> We believe that governments were instituted of God for the benefit of man; and that he holds men accountable for their acts in relation to them, both in making laws and administering them for the good and safety of society. (D&C 134:1)

While the foregoing scripture states that the Lord holds men accountable for the actions of government, it does not specify which men. Since God is just, those who commit or cause the actions, or who fail to do their political duty, must be held accountable. There are scriptures such as the twenty-ninth chapter of the Book of Mosiah which explain upon whom political responsibility rests. Under a monarchy, major credit or blame for what government does may rest upon the king and his appointees. However under a government subject to the voice of the people, responsibility for what government does or fails to do, rests directly on the voting citizens.

If the foregoing analysis is correct, a person should test the rightness or wrongness of any act of government by asking if it would be moral for the individual to commit the act himself. If it would be immoral for the individual to control the education of children, it is no less wrong for him to do so in cooperation with others and by using the power of government.

What Do The Scriptures Say About Public Education?

Let us first note that the Lord holds parents personally accountable for the teaching of their children and if they fail to discharge this duty properly, the sins of the children rest upon the parents. (D&C 68:25; 2 Ne. 4:5, 6) If parents are to be held accountable, then they must be given the right to control what is taught to their children and who teaches them. Both of these rights are denied under the typical laws providing for public schools.

If parents permit others to help train their children, they certainly should have the right to determine who they are and should follow the scriptures in making the choice. The following scriptures state who might safely be trusted to teach children:

> And also trust no one to be your teacher nor your minister, except he be a man of God, walking in his ways and keeping his commandments. (Mosiah 23:14)

> . . . and if ye receive not the Spirit ye shall not teach. (D&C 42:14)

> He (the Lord) commandeth that there shall be no priestcrafts; for, behold, priestcrafts are that men preach and set themselves up for a light unto the world, that they may get gain and praise of the world; but they seek not the welfare of Zion.
>
> Behold, the Lord hath forbidden this thing . . . (2 Ne. 26:29, 30)

Inasmuch as socialized education allows parents virtually no control over who teaches their children, they cannot insure that those who do so have the Lord's approval.

THE SCRIPTURES AND TEACHING CHILDREN

The following scripture states the distinction between what should, and what should not be taught:

> For behold, thus saith the Lord God: I will give unto the children of men line upon line, precept upon precept, here a little and there a little; and blessed are those who hearken unto my precepts, and lend an ear unto my counsel, for they shall learn wisdom; . . .
>
> Cursed is he that . . . shall hearken unto the precepts of men, save their precepts shall be given by the power of the Holy Ghost. (2 Ne. 28:30, 31)

Another scripture which underlines the danger of the precepts of men, even to the humble followers of Christ, is this prophecy concerning latter day conditions:

> They wear stiff necks and high heads; yea, and because of pride, and wickedness, and abominations, and whoredoms, they have all gone astray save it be a few, who are the humble followers of Christ; nevertheless, they are led, that in many instances they do err because they are taught by the precepts of men. (2 Ne. 28:14)

Apparently these humble followers of Christ who do err in so many instances are being taught by teachers who do not have the power of the Holy Ghost. Another scripture which speaks of the effect of the evil influence of the precepts of men in these latter days is this:

> And when the times of the Gentiles is come in, a light shall break forth among them that sit in darkness, and it shall be the fulness of my gospel;
>
> But they receive it not; for they perceive not the light, and they turn their hearts from me because of the precepts of men. (D&C 45:28, 29)

The precepts of men, as being taught in these latter days, are having an evil effect upon everyone including the humble followers of Christ. Everyone is falling victim to Satan's cunning plan which is to give men learning, make them proud and unwilling to hearken unto the counsel of God. The awful consequence of this plan is that it's victims perish.

Not only did Nephi prophesy universal pride and deception in these latter days, but Moroni who also had a vision of latter-day conditions saw the same situation:

> Behold, I speak unto you as if ye were present, and yet ye are not. But behold, Jesus Christ hath shown you unto me, and I know your doing.
>
> And I know that ye do walk in the pride of your hearts; and there are none save a few only who do not lift themselves up in the pride of their hearts, unto the wearing of very fine apparel, unto envying, and strifes, and malice, and persecutions, and all manner of iniquities; and your churches, yea, even every one, have become polluted because of the pride of your hearts.
>
> O ye pollutions, ye hypocrites, ye teachers who sell yourselves for that which will canker, why have ye polluted the holy church of God? (Morm. 8:35, 36, 38)

That both Nephi and Moroni were speaking of members of the Lord's Church in these prophecies there can be no question. Neither can one doubt but that Moroni saw priestcraft and false teaching in the Holy Church of God. The following prophesy of the Lord confirms the existence of pride, priestcraft and a multitude of other sins among the Gentile members of His Church in these latter days:

> And thus commandeth the Father that I should say unto you: At that day when the Gentiles shall sin against my gospel, and shall reject the fulness of my gospel, and shall be lifted up in the pride of their hearts above all nations, and above all the people of the whole earth, and shall be filled with all manner of lyings, and of deceits, and of mischiefs, and all manner of hypocrisy, and murders, and priestcrafts, and whoredoms, and of secret abominations; and if they shall do all these things, and shall reject the fulness of my gospel, behold, saith the Father, I will bring the fulness of my gospel from among them. (3 Ne. 16:10)

From the above scriptures it is difficult to avoid the conclusion that public education laws which compel the teaching of the precepts of men while prohibiting the teaching of the counsels of God in connection therewith, is implementing Satan's cunning plan. According to the foregoing scriptures the victims of this plan will be cursed and will perish unless they receive spiritual enlightenment from some other source and humble themselves sufficiently to accept it.

To forcibly subject little children to this risk by placing them under the tutelage of those who do not teach by the "power of the Holy Ghost," and who are not walking in the ways of the Lord nor "keeping his commandments" is a sin of great magnitude. The Book of Mormon relates an example of the teaching of the precepts of men without the precepts of the Lord, and the result was fatal to the eternal welfare of the learners. (Mosiah 24:1-7)

THE DANGER OF BEING A TEACHER

In former dispensations there were relatively few teachers who taught for money. Especially was this true of the teaching of children which was done largely by parents in the home. The organized teaching of children only is not discussed in the scriptures.

The establishment of an organization for the specific purpose of teaching was probably never considered. Not only because the taking of children from parents was considered a deprivation of one of the greatest blessings of parenthood but because the hiring of teachers to train children was far too costly for anyone except royalty. Parents training children to work because of the contribution they could make to the family while learning a trade or skill probably was the norm.

Today all that is changed. Ofttimes both father and mother work outside the home at jobs which do not permit the training or even the presence of children. The majority are being reared by day care centers, T.V. and public schools where religious teaching is forbidden by the supreme court. The following scriptures indicate that there is no profession of greater danger to the welfare of the human soul than that of teaching little children. Matt. 18:1-9 indicates that to teach falsehoods to adults is one thing, but to teach falsehoods to little children—can there be a greater sin than to receive pay for destroying the faith of a little child who believes in Christ? Better for such a person that he be drowned in the depths of the sea with a millstone about his neck.

THE LORD'S COMMANDMENTS REGARDING TEACHERS

> . . . and if ye receive not the Spirit ye shall not teach. (D&C 42:14)

If this is the law of the Church, why is it? Everything you teach is either true or false. Without the spirit you cannot tell the difference. If you teach falsehoods, whether false facts or false laws you are promoting the work of the devil. That you are teaching falsehood in ignorance will not save you. If you are doing this you are teaching the false traditions and creeds of men which is the mainspring of all corruption. If you teach falsehood for hire you are subjecting yourself to the influence of Satan as have so many other groups throughout history. Brigham Young said we were not to even teach the ABC's without the spirit. Nephi said,

> Cursed is he that putteth his trust in man, or maketh flesh his arm, or shall hearken unto the precepts of men, save their precepts shall be given by the power of the Holy Ghost. (2 Ne. 28:31)

Jacob described the cunning plan of the evil one.

> O that cunning plan of the evil one! O the vainness, and the frailties, and the foolishness of men! When they are learned they think they are wise, and they hearken not unto the counsel of God, for they set it aside, supposing they know of themselves, wherefore, their wisdom is foolishness and it profiteth them not. And they shall perish. (2 Ne. 9:28)

> Woe unto the world because of offenses! for it must needs be that offenses come; but woe to that man by whom the offence cometh. (Matt. 18:7)

Can those who desire to use force to prevent parents from having freedom to rear their children expect to be parents in the eternities or even to live in a society where there are children?

Would you call it evil if a person or a group of persons set up a private school outside of government and used force and the threat thereof to compel people to send their children to their school and compel the parents to pay the cost thereof? What is the difference? Not only that, but suppose they compel neighbors to help pay their expenses whether or not they sent children into the system. Nehor, Amlici, the Zoramites, the Priests of King Noah, etc. did this with adults. They had a religion they wanted to establish. We don't know much about it except its doctrine that religious freedom would be abolished. There would be only one type of doctrine taught which of course was false because the Lord's doctrine is that there should be freedom of worship.

But the type of religion being taught in our public school system is far worse than any type known because instead of teaching freedom of worship, it teaches that everyone must support a religion the worst feature of which is the use of force to compel attendance and compel every taxpayer whether a believer in socialism, atheism, enforced priestcraft, etc. to support the system and impose it on little children. It teaches only the precepts of men, evolution, a false interpretation of history, and no faith in God, all of which destroy faith. Is there any scheme more evil than this cunning socialist scheme?

MODERN DAY PROPHETS HAVE IDENTIFIED SATAN'S CUNNING PLAN

The last of the ten points of the Communist Manifesto contains this provision:

> Free education for all children in public schools. (See Appendix III)

In a general conference address given to the Priesthood of the Church in the General Conference of April, 1966, the late President David O. McKay gave the following warning:

> The entire concept and philosophy of Communism is diametrically opposed to everything for which the Church stands.
>
> No member of this Church can be true to his faith . . . while lending aid, encouragement or sympathy to any of these false philosophies; for if he does, they will prove snares to his feet. (See Appendix I)

After comparing Satan's cunning plan of free education today with the plan of enforced priestcraft described so often in the Book of Mormon, can it be doubted but that the Lord has placed those many stories in there to warn us against a danger we have succumbed to? Both plans provide for government control of education. Both plans force taxpayers to pay the cost of implementing them. Both prohibit the teaching of the gospel.

When we compare the two plans, we see that the principle differences between them are that Satan's plan today is aimed primarily against little children rather than adults, and that in countries like the United States and Russia, the falsehoods being taught are the precepts of men, including organic evolution, rather than the teachings of a corrupted religion. Both plans are specifically prohibited by the Lord, and for the same reasons as are indicated by the Book of Mormon definition of priestcraft:

> He commandeth that there shall be no priestcrafts; for, behold, priestcrafts are that men preach and set themselves up for a light unto the world, that they may get gain and praise of the world; but they seek not the welfare of Zion. Behold, the Lord hath forbidden this thing . . . (2 Ne. 26:29, 30)

It is not at all unlikely that the massive destruction of faith in God, and the acceptance of false beliefs in the world today is largely attributable to the massive substitution of public education for that of the parents. D&C Section 123 attributes the very mainspring of all corruption to:

> . . . the influence of that spirit which hath so strongly riveted the creeds of the fathers, who have inherited lies, upon the hearts of the children, and filled the world with confusion . . . (v. 7)

Then in D&C Sec. 93 we find this:

> And that wicked one cometh and taketh away light and truth, through disobedience, from the children of men, and because of the tradition of their fathers. (v. 39)

MODERN DAY PROPHETS HAVE CONDEMNED SOCIALIZED EDUCATION

It may come as a surprise to some that in the early days of the Church when the concept of public schools was being demanded by the Federal Congress as one of the prices for statehood, Church leaders vigorously condemned the entire concept of public education. One can see many examples of this by studying the discourses of the brethren during this period. We provide the following statement by President Brigham Young as an example of that opposition:

> Many of you may have heard what certain journalists have had to say about Brigham Young being opposed to free schools. I am opposed to free education as much as I am opposed to taking property from one man and giving it to another who knows not how to take care of it. . .
>
> But when you come to the fact, I will venture to say that I school ten children to every one that those do who complain so much of me. I now pay the school fee of a number of children who are either orphans or sons and daughters of poor people. But in aiding and blessing the poor I do not believe in allowing my charities to go through the hands of a set of robbers who pocket nine-tenths themselves, and give one-tenth to the poor. Therein is the difference between us. I am for the real act of doing and not saying. Would I encourage free schools by taxation? No! (JD 18:357; see also JD 19:248; 20:48, 60, 107-8; 22:222, 315; 24:168, 352; 26:97, 112; CR Oct. 1915:4)

Since the people of the State of Utah were forced to accept the concept of free education as a price of statehood, and since it has for many years been the law of the land, Church leaders have largely remained silent about the matter. It may also be of interest to many to know that when the idea of a national university was proposed in the Constitutional Convention of 1787, it was turned down by the delegates.

Said Karl G. Maeser, "I would rather have my child exposed to smallpox, typhus fever, cholera, or other malignant and deadly diseases than to the degrading influence of a corrupt teacher. It is infinitely better to take chances with an ignorant but pure-minded teacher than with the greatest philosopher who is impure."

Vocational education, correspondence courses, establishment in a family business are being considered for their children by an increasing number of parents.

The tenth plank in Karl Marx's Manifesto for destroying our kind civilization advocates the establishment of "free education for all children in public schools." There were several reasons why Marx wanted government to run the schools. Dr. A.A. Hodge pointed out one of them when he said:

> It is capable of exact demonstration that if every part in the State has the right of excluding from public schools whatever he does not believe to be true, then he that believes most must give way to him that believes least, and then he that believes least must give way to him that believes absolutely nothing, no matter in how small a minority the atheists or agnostics may be. It is self-evident that on this scheme, if it is consistently and persistently carried out in all parts of the country, the United States system of national popular education will be the most efficient and widespread instrument for the propagation of atheism which the world has ever seen.

After the tragic prayer decision was made by the U.S. Supreme Court, President David O. McKay stated, "The Supreme Court of the United States severs the connecting cord between the public schools of the United States and the source of divine intelligence, the Creator, himself." (*Relief Society Magazine*, December 1962, p. 878)

Does that make any difference to you? Can't you see why the demands of conscientious parents is increasing the number of private Christian- and Americanist-oriented schools? (Ezra Taft Benson, *God, Family, Country,* p. 225-226

XXVI

THE LORD'S PLAN VERSUS ENFORCED PRIESTCRAFT

THE CENTRAL POSITION OF THE FAMILY IN THE GOSPEL PLAN

To accomplish His purposes here on earth, the Lord has established three organizations: The family, the Church and government. However it is the family which is the important one of the three. The other two exist mainly for the purpose of enabling it to function properly. It is the only one of the three which will survive death.

As it is the Lord's work and glory to bring to pass the immortality and eternal life of His children, even so this should be the work and glory of parents here on earth. The scriptures declare that eternal life is the greatest of all the gifts of God. (D&C 14:7) But this gift is a continuation of the family relationship into the eternities.

Earth life is a proving ground during which we demonstrate our worthiness for parenthood hereafter. What greater power could the Lord confer than that of parenthood? To possess within ourselves the well-springs of life, and to be entrusted with the molding of the lives of pure, innocent children seems to be the ultimate stewardship. This privilege is most desireable above all others because it enables us to obtain the greatest happiness possible. The family relationship is the source of true joy, and joy is the transcendent object of existence. (2 Ne. 2:25)

THE RESPONSIBILITY OF PARENTS FOR TRAINING CHILDREN

The conduct of parents is of infinite importance to their children because in large measure it determines whether or not those children will obey the Lord's commandments. In the book of Proverbs we find this:

> Train up a child in the way he should go: and when he is old, he will not depart from it. (Prov. 22:6)

The Book of Mormon confirms the above statement and adds the infinitely important truth that if, due to parental neglect, children commit sins, responsibility for those sins rests upon the parents. Just before his death, Father Lehi pronounced a blessing upon the heads of the children of Laman and Lemuel in which he said:

> But behold, my sons and my daughters, I cannot go down to my grave save I should leave a blessing upon you; for behold, I know that if ye are brought up in the way ye should go ye will not depart from it.
>
> Wherefore, if ye are cursed, behold, I leave my blessing upon you, that the cursing may be taken from you and be answered upon the heads of your parents. (2 Ne. 4:5, 6)

Similar statements have been made by modern prophets. The late President Joseph F. Smith said this:

> Not one child in a hundred would go astray, if the home environment, example and training, were in harmony with the truth in the Gospel of Christ, as revealed and taught to the Latter-day Saints.
>
> Fathers and mothers, you are largely to blame for the infidelity and indifference of your children. You can remedy the evil by earnest worship, example, training and discipline, in the home. (*Gospel Doctrine*, P. 301)

The following scripture which imposes upon delinquent parents the sins of their children is especially interesting because it indicates the critical period during which the teaching should be done:

> And again, inasmuch as parents have children in Zion . . . that teach them not to understand the doctrine of repentance, faith in Christ the Son of the living God, and of baptism and the gift of the Holy Ghost by laying on of the hands, *when eight years old,* the sin be upon the heads of the parents. (D&C 68:25; *emphasis added*)

This scripture appears to state that parents must prepare their children for baptism and the reception of the gift of the Holy Ghost, teaching them to understand the first four principles and ordinances of the Gospel prior to the age of accountability. In this connection let us remember that the Lord has said:

> . . . little children . . . cannot sin, for power is not given unto Satan to tempt little children, until they begin to become accountable before me: (D&C 29:46, 47)

Thus during this early age, the Lord, by controlling Satan, gives parents a special advantage in guiding and training their children without interference from the evil one.

CAN ANY OBLIGATION BE MORE IMPORTANT THAN THE TRAINING OF CHILDREN?

If it be true that the righteousness or wickedness of children is largely a consequence of how parents perform their duties; and if delinquent parents must bear responsibility for the sins of their children, does the Lord consider the parental duty to train children more important than any other? The following revelation given to the prophet Joseph Smith, Frederick G. Williams and Sidney Rigdon who, at the time the revelation was given constituted the First Presidency of the Church, appears to indicate that He does:

> And that wicked one cometh and taketh away light and truth through disobedience, from the children of men, and because of the tradition of their fathers.
>
> But I have commanded you to bring up your children in light and truth.
>
> And verily I say unto you, my servant Frederick G. Williams, you have continued under this condemnation;
>
> You have not taught your children light and truth, according to the commandments; and that wicked one hath power, as yet, over you, and this is the cause of your affliction.
>
> And now a commandment I give unto you—if you will be delivered you shall set in order your own house, for there are many things that are not right in your house.
>
> Verily, I say unto my servant Sidney Rigdon, that in some things he hath not kept the commandments concerning his children; therefore, first set in order thy house. Verily, I say unto my servant Joseph Smith, Jun., . . . you have not kept the commandments, and must needs stand rebuked before the Lord;
>
> Your family must needs repent and forsake some things, and give more earnest heed unto your sayings, or be removed out of their place.
>
> What I say unto one I say unto all . . . (D&C 93:39-49)

Let us first note that according to the verse last quoted, these instructions given to the First Presidency are applicable to everyone. Then let us note that among these admonitions is this: therefore, first set in order thy house. This appears to state that regardless of the position we hold in the Church or in society, our first duty is our family. This agrees with President McKay's well known dictum that:

> No other success can compensate for failure in the home.

Another point which seems of particular importance is this: because of Frederick G. William's failure to teach his children light and truth, he was being afflicted and subject to the power of Satan. He was admonished that if he would be delivered, he must set in order the things of his house.

How many Church members are suffering afflictions for the same reason as did Frederick G. Williams? How many have considered the possibility that we can be afflicted and subjected to the power of Satan for failure to bring up our children in light and truth? When things go well at home, no problem on the outside seems too great to overcome. But when we are failing to discharge our primary and most important responsibility properly, our resolve is weakened, we have feelings of guilt, our ability to help others solve their problems is diminished and our courage is sapped. The wisdom of obeying the Lord's admonition to, first set in order thy house, and to bring up your children in light and truth, is most important.

INHERITED LIES ARE THE MAINSPRING OF ALL CORRUPTION

The Lord has stated that in these last days,

> . . . darkness covereth the earth, and gross darkness the minds of the people, and all flesh has become corrupted before my face. (D&C 112:23; see also D&C 38:11; 82:5; 84:49)

We are given an indication of the primary reason for this darkness by the following scripture which speaks of:

> . . . the influence of that spirit which hath so strongly riveted the creeds of the fathers, who have inherited lies, upon the hearts of the

children, and filled the world with confusion, and has been growing stronger and stronger, and is now the very mainspring of all corruption, and the whole earth groans under the weight of its iniquity. (D&C 123:7)

In another modern day revelation the Lord says:

And that wicked one cometh and taketh away light and truth through disobedience and because of the tradition of their fathers. (D&C 93:39)

How Can This Chain Of Inherited Lies Be Broken?

If inherited lies and false traditions which are being handed down from generation to generation constitute the mainspring of all corruption, how can this chain of falsehood and deception be broken? In Section 123 of the Doctrine and Covenants part of which is quoted above, the Lord gives the following as the way in which this may be done:

For there are many yet on the earth among all sects, parties, and denominations, who are blinded by the subtle craftiness of men, whereby they lie in wait to deceive, and who are only kept from the truth because they know not where to find it—

Therefore, that we should waste and wear out our lives in bringing to light all the hidden things of darkness, wherein we know them; and they are truly manifest from heaven—

These should then be attended to with great earnestness.

Let no man count them as small things; for there is much which lieth in futurity, pertaining to the saints, which depend upon these things.

You know, brethren, that a very large ship is benefited very much by a very small helm in the time of storm, by being kept workways with the wind and the waves.

Therefore, dearly beloved brethren, let us cheerfully do all things that lie in our power; and then may we stand still, with the utmost assurance, to see the salvation of God, and for his arm to be revealed. (D&C 123:12-17)

This is just one of many scriptures which teach that those who have the gospel have an obligation to share its teachings with those who are in darkness. Church members are called to be the very small helm, the salt of the earth, and the light of the world. From the scriptures quoted above it would appear that one of the most important of all truths which could be taught to a world in darkness is that parents have a responsibility to bring up their children in light and truth. Or as the late President Kimball once expressed the matter, the home truly is the place to save society.

SCRIPTURAL TRUTHS REGARDING THE TRAINING OF CHILDREN

A. WHAT SHOULD CHILDREN BE TAUGHT?

Reference has already been made to D&C 68:25 wherein the Lord commanded parents in Zion to teach their children concerning the first four principles and ordinances of the gospel. After giving that instruction He goes on to admonish parents to "teach their children to pray, and to walk uprightly before the Lord;" to observe the Sabbath day, to avoid idleness, to seek for the riches of eternity and avoid greediness. Let us consider some other scriptural instructions regarding what children should be taught.

After the Lord had explained to Adam such things as the fall, the atonement, free agency, faith and repentance He told him:

> Therefore I give unto you a commandment, to teach these things freely unto your children . . . (Moses 6:58)

Concerning the Ten Commandments with their related statutes and judgments, the Children of Israel were told this:

> And these words, which I command thee this day, shall be in thine heart:
>
> And thou shalt teach them diligently unto thy children, and shalt talk of them when thou sittest in thine house, and when thou walkest by the way, and when thou liest down, and when thou risest up.
>
> And thou shalt bind them for a sign upon thine hand, and they shall be as frontlets between thine eyes.
>
> And thou shalt write them upon the posts of thy house, and on thy gates. (Deut. 6:6-9)

Finally we mention again the Lord's commandment to bring up your children in light and truth. (D&C 93:40)

B. WHAT SHOULD CHILDREN NOT BE TAUGHT?

To destroy the faith of a child by teaching him false doctrines seems to be one of the worst sins one can commit. Such is severely condemned by the Lord in the following passage:

> But whoso shall offend one of these little ones which believe in me, it were better for him that a millstone were hanged about his neck, and that he were drowned in the depth of the sea. (Matt. 18:6)

How can one be certain that he is not teaching falsehood? The prophet Mormon sternly warns us against making a mistake in distinguishing between beliefs which come from Christ and those which come from the devil and gives the following advice on how to avoid doing so:

> Wherefore, take heed, my beloved brethren, that ye do not judge that which is evil to be of God, or that which is good and of God to be of the devil.
>
> For behold, my brethren, it is given unto you to judge, that ye may know good from evil; and the way to judge is as plain, that ye may know with a perfect knowledge, as the daylight is from the dark night.
>
> For behold, the Spirit of Christ is given to every man, that he may know good from evil; wherefore, I show unto you the way to judge; for every thing which inviteth to do good, and to persuade to believe in Christ, is sent forth by the power and gift of Christ; wherefore ye may know with a perfect knowledge it is of God.
>
> But whatsoever thing persuadeth men to do evil, and believe not in Christ, and deny him, and serve not God, then ye may know with a perfect knowledge it is of the devil; for after this manner doth the devil work, for he persuadeth no man to do good, no, not one; neither do his angels; neither do they who subject themselves unto him. (Moro. 7:14-17)

The Lord gave us another method for distinguishing between truth and falsehood, and that is by examining the fruits of those from whom the teaching comes. Said he:

> Beware of false prophets, which come to you in sheep's clothing, but inwardly they are ravening wolves.
>
> Ye shall know them by their fruits. Do men gather grapes of thorns, or figs of thistles?
>
> Even so every good tree bringeth forth good fruit; but a corrupt tree bringeth forth evil fruit.
>
> A good tree cannot bring forth evil fruit, neither can a corrupt tree bring forth good fruit.
>
> Every tree that bringeth not forth good fruit is hewn down, and cast into the fire.
>
> Wherefore by their fruits ye shall know them. (Matt. 7:15-20; 3 Ne. 14:15-20)

C. Should Children Be Taught The Precepts Of Men?

The Book of Mormon prophets warn latter-day Gentiles repeatedly against accepting the "precepts of men." While there is no specific definition given of the term, it appears safe to conclude that by the term "precepts of God" they meant to include the scriptures and the teachings of the prophets, while by the term "precepts of men" they meant to include all other teachings.

While there does not seem to be any outright prohibition against teaching the precepts of men, the following scriptures condemns such unless they are taught by the power of the Holy Ghost:

> Cursed is he that . . . shall hearken unto the precepts of men, save their precepts shall be given by the power of the Holy Ghost. (2 Ne. 28:31)

The terrible danger of learning the precepts of men and the wisdom of the world without being firmly grounded in the gospel is explained in the following passage:

> O that cunning plan of the evil one! O the vainness, and the frailties, and the foolishness of men! When they are learned they think they are wise, and they hearken not unto the counsel of God, for they set it aside, supposing they know of themselves, wherefore, their wisdom is foolishness and it profiteth them not. And they shall perish. (2 Ne. 9:28)

A case history is provided by the Book of Mormon in which the Lamanites were taught the Nephite language and also to read and write. However they were not taught the commandments of God along with this learning, and the result was disastrous. (Mosiah 24:4-7) Nephi foresaw that in these latter days, even the humble followers would err in many instances because they are taught by "the precepts of men." (2 Ne. 28:14) Modern day scripture states that even though the fulness of the gospel is given to the Gentiles in these latter days, "they turn their hearts from me because of the precepts of men." (D&C 45:28, 29)

D. WHO IS QUALIFIED TO TEACH CHILDREN?

We have already noted that the Lord has given parents the responsibility for teaching their own children. Some parents may feel themselves unqualified or incapable of teaching their children that which they need to know. Should they feel so? What does the Lord require that children be taught? The following words of the prophet, Nephi should help answer this question:

> . . . feast upon the words of Christ; for behold, the words of Christ will tell you all things what ye should do.
>
> For behold, again I say unto you that if ye will enter in by the way, and receive the Holy Ghost, it will show unto you all things what ye should do. (2 Ne. 32:3, 5)

This quotation appears to state that all of the knowledge essential to our eternal welfare is contained in the words of Christ. The Lord has included within the scriptures all of the directions necessary to guide our actions. Is it not true then that if we teach our children to understand the words of Christ, we have fulfilled our obligation to bring them up in light and truth? Is this beyond the capacity of parents? Certainly not. The Lord never requires anything of us which is beyond our ability. Since the sin is upon their heads if children are not taught properly, they will want to be extremely cautious before delegating this duty to others. To whom may they safely turn for help if such appears necessary?

The prophet, Alma who had seen the awful consequences of allowing corrupt priests to teach, specified that teachers possess these qualifications:

> And also trust no one to be your teacher nor your minister, except he be a man of God, walking in his ways and keeping his commandments. (Mosiah 23:14)

Modern revelation requires the same qualification in these words:

> . . . and if ye receive not the spirit ye shall not teach. (D&C 42:14)

In choosing teachers, parents should beware of those who practice priestcraft. According to the Book of Mormon, those guilty of this sin are to be feared more than any others and should be avoided at all costs.

Their character and motives are described thus:

> He (the Lord) commandeth that there shall be no priestcrafts; for, behold priestcrafts are that men preach and set themselves up for a light unto the world, that they may get gain and praise of the world; but they seek not the welfare of Zion. (2 Ne. 26:29)

THE PLAN OF THE ADVERSARY FOR REARING CHILDREN

In accordance with the doctrine which declares there must be an opposition in all things, and that men must be given the opportunity to choose between good and evil, the Lord has permitted the adversary to present to us his plan for training children. It is expressed in the tenth point of the Communist Manifesto in these words:

> Free education for all children in public schools.

If we use the test the Savior gave for distinguishing between good and evil, i.e., that an evil tree cannot bring forth good fruit, we know that public schools are wrong. They are wrong because communism and all of its programs are evil.

The late President David O. McKay in stating the position of the Church on communism, said this:

> The entire concept and philosophy of Communism is diametrically opposed to everything for which the Church stands . . . No member of this Church can be true to his faith, nor can any American be loyal to his trust, while lending aid, encouragement, or sympathy to any of these false philosophies, for if he does, they will prove snares to his feet. (See Appendix I)

If we use the test proposed by Mormon to judge public schools, they must again be condemned because instead of teaching students to believe in Christ, they teach doctrines like evolution which deny that He created the world.

By implementing this tenth provision of the Manifesto, Satan proposes to rob parents of that stewardship by which they may gain eternal life. At the same time he would accomplish certain other goals which are diametrically contrary to the scriptures. As noted in Chapter XI, placing education under the control of the state, and using the police power to compel people to finance and support it, constitutes the practice of enforced priestcraft. This is specifically forbidden by the Lord and will cause the destruction of that nation which engages in it. (Alma 1:12)

Since in nations like the United States and Russia, the public schools teach only the precepts of men and are forbidden to teach the scriptures and the commandments of God, this is contrary to the scriptures. And finally the public school system denies parents the right to select teachers who meet the qualifications required of them by the scriptures.

The Problem Of Those Who Oppose Enforced Priestcraft

Public education in the United States today is a huge government enterprise. It spends more money and hires more people than any other enterprise. Approximately one half of all taxes collected at the state and local level are used for its support. Other billions of dollars are spent on it each year by the federal government.

There are many fine people who not only send their children to public schools, but are employed by the system. For those who believe or suspect that it constitutes the sin of enforced priestcraft which is condemned so often and so severely in the Book of Mormon, this presents a most serious practical problem.

If government did not compel parents to keep their children in some regularly organized school, and if they were not compelled to financially support the public system even while paying the cost of a private education, their problem would be less difficult. Or if parents had the option of sending their children to a public school wherein they could have their children taught faith in God along with the precepts of men, certainly this would alleviate the difficulty of the problem they face.

It should be remembered that public education laws in some areas permit parents to school their children in their own homes, provided of course, that the children are taught in those subjects dictated by the state. This may prove to be a workable alternative for some. Also those righteous souls who make their living in the system may find some solace in the thought that since public schools are mandated by law, and since the system needs good moral people as teachers, they are making it better than it otherwise would be.

Nevertheless, if public education constitutes enforced priestcraft as has been concluded herein, we should remember that it is considered a serious sin in the eyes of the Lord and that if we do not abolish it voluntarily, He will do so when He comes. (3 Ne. 21:19)

Furthermore if the chain of inherited lies is to be broken so that coming generations can know the truth, the responsibility of doing so rests upon those who have the knowledge regarding enforced priestcraft contained in the Book of Mormon.

XXVII

Unenforced Priestcraft

The Book Of Mormon Contains Information Regarding Unenforced Priestcraft

In our discussion of priestcraft in prior chapters, we have been concerned almost exclusively with the type which was enforced by governments. We gave particular attention to this issue not only because it is treated so extensively in the Book of Mormon, but also because of the possibility that it might cause the destruction of our nation today. Alma stated that if priestcraft were enforced among his people it would cause their entire destruction. Our concern is that our public school system might constitute the practice of enforced priestcraft which if not halted, will cause our destruction. But the Book of Mormon also provides information regarding the sin of unenforced priestcraft which may be of value to those who are desirous of knowing under what circumstances it is proper in the eyes of the Lord to receive pay when rendering service to the Church. While modern day scriptures give some guidance on this matter, the Book of Mormon may help to answer questions not specifically dealt with therein. Information on this topic would not have been included in the Book of Mormon were it not for our edification. It would be most unwise to ignore it, especially when the penalty for the sin of priestcraft is so severe.

Righteous Nephite Kings Served Their People Without Pay

Since under our constitutional system of government in the United States today church and state are divided, that information in the Nephite record regarding unenforced priestcraft which should be most helpful to us would be that given regarding their practices during the time when their church and state were divided. During that period, employees of the government received pay for their services as judges, but those who rendered services for the Church were strictly forbidden to receive contributions unless their economic situation was such that without help they would perish.

Nevertheless the practices followed by their kings concerning the receipt of pay during that period when the Church and state were united should be instructive because they served simultaneously as monarchs, judges, prophets and religious teachers. The information included in the record, although brief, was surely placed there for our benefit. When, just a few years prior to his death, king Benjamin called his people together and appointed his son as king, he reminded them in these words of the fact that he had received no pay:

> And even I, myself, have labored with mine own hands that I might serve you, and that ye should not be laden with taxes, and that there should nothing come upon you which was grievous to be borne—and of all these things which I have spoken, ye yourselves are witnesses this day. (Mosiah 2:14)

Then when Benjamin's son, king Mosiah voluntarily resigned his position as king and established a government subject to the voice of the people, the record says this about him:

> And they did wax strong in love towards Mosiah; yea, they did esteem him more than any other man; for they did not look upon him as a tyrant who was seeking for gain, yea, for that lucre which doth corrupt the soul; for he had not exacted riches of them, . . . (Mosiah 29:40)

The one exception to the rule that the Nephite kings supported themselves with the labor of their own hands was that of the wicked king Noah. He imposed a twenty per cent income tax upon the people to support himself, his priests and their wives and concubines. Doubtless this account was placed in the record so that the practices of wicked and righteous monarchs could be contrasted.

Priests And Teachers Were Forbidden To Accept Economic Pay

Alma who had been one of the wicked priests of king Noah, listened to the words of Abinadi, repented, and then converted a group whom he led away from under the tyranny of king Noah to establish a society of their own. The following scripture tells us he was given power from God to establish a true Church among his people and to ordain priests to serve them:

> And it came to pass that Alma, having authority from God, ordained priests; even one priest to every fifty of their number did he ordain to preach unto them, and to teach them pertaining to the kingdom of God. (Mosiah 18:18)

However the record explains that the priests who were appointed, were not to receive pay for their services:

> And he (Alma) also commanded them that the priests whom he had ordained should labor with their own hands for their support.
>
> And the priests were not to depend upon the people for their support; but for their labor they were to receive the grace of God that they might wax strong in the Spirit, having the knowledge of God, that they might teach with power and authority from God. (Mosiah 18:24, 26)

There was an exception to the rule against priests and teachers receiving financial help. It is explained in the following quotation:

> And there was a strict command throughout all the churches that there should be no persecutions among them, that there should be an equality among all men;
>
> That they should let no pride nor haughtiness disturb their peace; that every man should esteem his neighbor as himself, laboring with their own hands for their support.
>
> Yea, and all their priests and teachers should labor with their own hands for their support, in all cases save it were in sickness, or in much want; and doing these things, they did abound in the grace of God. (Mosiah 27:3-5)

This scripture justifies the priests and teachers receiving help from others only in cases of sickness or much want. But the following scripture appears to indicate that this same rule pertained to every worthy member of the Church.

> And again Alma commanded that the people of the church should impart of their substance, every one according to that which he had; if he have more abundantly he should impart more abundantly; and of him that had but little, but little should be required; and to him that had not should be given.
>
> And thus they should impart of their substance of their own free will and good desires towards God, and to those priests that stood in need, yea, and to every needy, naked soul. (Mosiah 18:27, 28)

The foregoing scriptures indicate that when a Nephite served the Church as a teacher or a priest, he did so without pay. Any financial help came not because of his services, but because his economic situation qualified him to be treated as a welfare case. Only when his own resources and those of his family were insufficient to sustain him was he entitled to relief. Of course this is the rule followed in the Church today with respect to those called to serve in such positions as bishops, stake presidents and missionaries.

The above scriptures also state that those who taught the gospel without pay, received "the grace of God," waxed strong in the Spirit, and taught "with power and authority from God." On the other hand the consequences of rendering Church service for gain are as follows:

> But the laborer in Zion shall labor for Zion; for if they labor for money they shall perish. (2 Ne. 26:31)

Another point of transcendent importance which is made by the foregoing scriptures is that the teacher who fails to labor with his own hands for his support is subjected to the terrible temptation to become proud. The following scripture emphasizes this same point:

> And when the priests left their labor to impart the word of God unto the people, the people also left their labors to hear the word of God. And when the priest had imparted unto them the word of God they all returned again diligently unto their labors; and the priest, not esteeming himself above his hearers, for the preacher was no better than the hearer, neither was the teacher any better than the learner; and thus they were all equal, and they did all labor, every man according to his strength. (Alma 1:26)

The rule against the payment of teachers had for its purpose the prevention of priestcraft:

> He commandeth that there shall be no priestcrafts; for, behold, priestcrafts are that men preach and set themselves up for a light unto the world, that they may get gain and praise of the world; but they seek not for the welfare of Zion. (2 Ne. 26:29)

When a paid teacher reflects upon the fact that the reason many are called but few are chosen is that the many "set their hearts so much upon the things of this world and aspire to the honors of men," he can see the awful risk of his profession.

Pride is the great curse of the teaching profession and it would appear from the foregoing that the only way to escape it is for teachers to render their services without pay. This was the issue which caused the great division among the Nephites. When the church was separated from the government and when the rule was adopted prohibiting Church leaders from receiving pay for their services, a great schism developed which led to much bloodshed.

Separation Of Church And State

When Alma led his small group of people back to the land of Zarahemla to join the people there, king Mosiah gave up his position as leader of the Church, and conferred this right upon Alma. The record says this of the change:

> Now king Mosiah had given Alma the authority over the church. (Mosiah 26:8)
>
> And it came to pass that king Mosiah granted unto Alma that he might establish churches throughout all the land of Zarahemla; and gave him power to ordain priests and teachers over every church. (Mosiah 25:19)

(Note: This chapter was never completed, and I wish it was, as I hesitated to put it in, incomplete as it is. The only additional comment I would make, to avoid leaving the wrong impression, is that Daddy told me the General Authorities were not well paid and he knew there were many others who did not need what they received, and simply turned it back to the Church also.)

Words of Ezra Taft Benson

I have faith that the Constitution will be saved as prophesied by Joseph Smith. But it will not be saved in Washington. It will be saved by the citizens of this nation who love and cherish freedom. It will be saved be enlightened members of this Church—men and women who will subscribe to and abide the principles of the Constitution. (Ezra Taft Benson, *The Constitution, A Heavenly Banner,* 1986)

XXVIII

PROPHECIES REGARDING FATE OF GENTILES

DOES NEPHITE HISTORY FORESHADOW THAT OF THE GENTILES?

In this work we have undertaken to use the Nephite experience with self-government to help us understand the problems faced by those living under the united states constitutional system today. We commenced our treatment of this theme by noting that our living prophet is calling for repentance and pointing out that pride is one of our greatest sins. In a conference address he discussed this sin at some length noting those scriptures which state that, (1) it was pride which destroyed the Nephites and that, (2) the Lord has in modern revelation warned us to beware of pride lest we become as the Nephites of old.

He reminded us of the scourge and a judgment which will fall upon the children of Zion unless we repent and do as the Lord has said in the Book of Mormon. (D&C 84:54-59) We tried to identify the particular sins the Lord has reference to by examining admonitions therein directed to the Gentiles. We found statements by Him, Nephi, Mormon and Moroni which indicated that the Gentiles would become so wicked that unless we repented we would be destroyed. We gave particular attention to predictions that secret combinations would be among us and would destroy us if we allowed them to get above us.

With this in mind we examined the Nephite history of the reign of the judges. We saw that during the first sixty years there were continuing attempts by Nephite apostates to capture control of the Nephite government so they could use it to practice enforced priestcraft.

During the second sixty years it was the secret combinations who were continually seeking to gain political control. They succeeded the first time they tried and did so by seducing even the more part of the righteous Nephites to join with them in corrupting the laws and using government as an instrument of plunder.

The prophet Nephi called them to repentance but they rejected him. Thereupon they were afflicted, first with civil war, and then with a famine which finally caused them to cleanse their government. A few years thereafter the band formed again and from that point on until the coming of Christ there was a great division among the people with those Nephites and Lamanites who believed in communism, constantly waging aggressive warfare against those who did not. This situation ended only when Christ came and destroyed all of the wicked.

Since we have reached that point in our own history when we have turned our own government into an instrument of plunder, we may well wonder if that which happened to the Nephites after they reached this point, foreshadows what will happen to us. Let us contrast our situation with theirs.

A Comparison Between Corruption Of Nephite And Gentile Governments

The Book of Mormon states that the first time the Nephites adopted communism, it was because even the more part of the righteous had been seduced into doing so. (Hela. 6:38) We are also told that their prophet Nephi, who had been governor and chief judge, had pointed out the nature of their wickedness, called them to repentance, and warned of great destruction if they failed to heed. (Hela. Ch. 6-10) Let us compare that situation with our own today.

It is assumed that virtually all will agree that the corruptions of our own laws described in preceding chapters would be evil if performed outside the framework of government. As we discussed laws pertaining to licensing, regulatory, welfare state, currency and socialized education, we pointed out that in each case they would constitute violations of the Golden Rule and the Ten Commandments if done by the individual.

It is submitted that if we do not realize that by legalizing these evils we do nothing to change their immoral nature, then we are allowing ourselves to be seduced as were the Nephites. Let those who doubt this compare the conditions in our own country with those of the Nephites when they completely corrupted their government. It is described as follows:

> And seeing the people in a state of such awful wickedness, and those Gadianton robbers filling the judgment-seats—having usurped the power and the authority of the land; laying aside the commandments of God, and not in the lease aright before him; doing no justice unto the children of men;
>
> Condemning the righteous because of their righteousness; letting the guilty and the wicked go unpunished because of their money; and moreover to be held in office at the head of government, to rule and do according to their wills, that they might get gain and glory of the world, and, moreover, that they might the more easily commit adultery, and steal, and kill, and do according to their own wills—(Hela. 7:4, 5)

It will be admitted that the tragedy which has occurred in our nation can be traced directly to our own judiciary as was the case with theirs. Judges have largely destroyed the right of self government and this is especially true of federal judges. On the one hand they have so extensively interfered with the administration of criminal justice by the states, that evil cannot be properly punished at the local level.

On the other hand, by denying the right to a jury trial in administrative law cases, they have prevented the people from defending themselves against the crimes of a bloated bureaucracy which asserts the power to punish everything except evil. The corruption of the currency has enabled the federal government to nourish this bureaucratic monster with such an immense amount of irredeemable paper, that it is now recognizable as the fearsome threat Nephi describes. (See below) Nevertheless the Lord never would have allowed this situation to develop had not the people become so wicked as to deserve it.

That we have been warned by our prophets about our political sins as were the Nephites, is also indisputable. President McKay's statement regarding the official position of the Church on communism delivered in the priesthood session of general conference in April, 1966, is adequate evidence of this. But in addition to this, there have been numerous discourses given, admonitions issued and books written by our leaders on these dangers since the beginning of the Church. Our living prophet has been in the forefront of this cause. (See Appendix II)

THE FATE OF GENTILES WHO DO NOT REPENT

In D&C Section 84:59, the Lord asks this question:

> For shall the children of the kingdom pollute my holy land? (He answers it thus.) Verily, I say unto you, Nay.

How does He propose to put an end to the pollutions? Perhaps He will remove us from the land and give it to the seed of Lehi to whom it has been covenanted forever. (2 Ne. 1:5) This may be what He meant by those statements found in Third Nephi where He says on three different occasions that if we do not repent, the seed of Lehi will come among us like a lion among a flock of sheep and tread us down and there will be none to deliver. (3 Ne. 16:10-15; 20:14-16; 21:11-12; See also Mormon's statement to this same effect, Mor. 5:22-24) Perhaps this is what He meant when He said:

> For thou shalt break forth on the right hand and on the left, and thy seed shall inherit the Gentiles and make the desolate cities to be inhabited. (3 Ne. 22:3)

HOPE GIVEN TO GENTILES WHO REPENT?

The scriptures indicate that in these last days there will come a great division between the righteous and the wicked. There are two scriptures in the Doctrine and Covenants which mention the separation between the wise and the foolish virgins. One of them reads thus:

> And until that hour (the day of the coming of the Son of Man) there will be foolish virgins among the wise; and at that hour cometh an entire separation of the righteous and the wicked; and in that day will I send mine angels to pluck out the wicked and cast them into unquenchable fire. (D&C 63:54; see also 45:56, 57)

Other scriptures in the Doctrine and Covenants describe it as a separation of the wheat from the tares. (D&C 86; 88:94) In Joseph Smith's translation of Matthew Chapter 24, the Lord speaks of the elect who are of the covenant who will be deceived, (v. 22) and the elect who treasure up His word who are not deceived. (v. 37)

These scriptures indicate that Gentiles who stop polluting this holy land, may be preserved. As we discussed the prophecies regarding Gentile destruction, we noticed that they always left open the possibility of repentance. It has been our thesis herein that one aspect of repentance must consist of obeying the Golden Rule and the Ten Commandments when we act in the name of government. Let us undertake to confirm this conclusion by noting what Nephi has to say about the basis upon which the separation of the righteous from the wicked will be made in these latter days.

THE GREAT AND ABOMINABLE CHURCH OF THE DEVIL

Perhaps Nephi provides the clearest and most complete information available regarding how the Lord will divide the righteous from the wicked at the time of His second coming. He was given a vision, only a part of which he was permitted to record, in which he saw battle lines drawn between the members of the Church of the Lamb and those of the church of the devil. Here is a part of what he was shown:

> And he (the angel) said unto me: Behold there are save two churches only; the one is the church of the Lamb of God, and the other is the church of the devil; wherefore, whoso belongeth not to the church of the Lamb of God belongeth to that great church, which is the mother of abominations; and she is the whore of all the earth.
>
> And it came to pass that I beheld that the great mother of abominations did gather together multitudes upon the face of all the earth, among all the nations of the Gentiles, to fight against the Lamb of God. (1 Ne. 14:10, 13)

To understand this division, it will not be sufficient merely to identify those who are members of the Church of the Lamb. We must also be able to identify those who belong to the church of the devil. This is so because the scriptures regarding the ten virgins, the tares, and the elect, indicate that many members of the Church of the Lamb will also belong to the devil's church. Let us then note what Nephi says regarding those who are members of the latter group.

Like John the Revelator who also saw this satanic organization in vision, Nephi used a number of names to describe it. Not only did he call it "the great and abominable church of the devil," but also "the mother of abominations," and "the whore of all the earth." Also like John, Nephi was always careful to state that it was the greatest wickedness on the earth, and that it was a single, identifiable organization, separate and distinct from all others. He saw that it was built up by the devil; that it sheds the blood of the saints and brings them down into captivity; and that in these latter days it would have

> . . . dominion over all the earth, among all nations, kindreds, tongues and people. (1 Ne. 14:11)

But these sins, attributes, and objectives are the same as those of the secret combinations as described by Mormon and Moroni. They too are: (1) built up by the devil, (2) to kill and enslave the prophets, (3) are the most abominable above all in the sight of God, (4) seek to overthrow the freedom of all lands, nations, and countries, and (5) bring to pass the destruction of all people. (Ether Ch. 8; Hela. Ch. 2)

Is it not apparent that Nephi was describing the same world-wide movement as Mormon and Moroni? Can there be two satanic organizations which are the ultimate in wickedness? Obviously not, but we need not speculate about the matter because a modern prophet has identified communism as "the greatest satanical threat on the earth today." (See Appendix I)

Identifying Satan's church as the socialist-communist conspiracy, clarifies many scriptural statements which otherwise would be difficult to explain. What other organization can claim world-wide membership and dominion as Nephi foresaw would be the case? What other movement or organization do members of the Church of the Lamb also belong to? In describing its activities in these latter days Nephi saw that,

> . . . there began to be wars and rumors of wars among all the nations which belonged to the mother of abominations, . . . (1 Ne. 14:16)

Does not this confirm that he is describing a political combination? Also when we reflect upon the fact that it is corrupted government through which men commit countless abominations, we understand why it is called the mother of abominations. Through what organization other than government can this be done? And when we further recognize that Satan and his forces prostitute the Lord's government, and use it to destroy freedom rather than preserve it, we understand better why the prophets would call it the whore of all the earth.

Will The Gentiles Be Given A "Space For Repentance?"

We noticed in studying the Nephite record that when they were seduced into prostituting their government, the Lord sent a "repentance famine" which caused them to cleanse their government of its abominations. We also noted that for a forty-year period following this, a great division occurred between the people based entirely upon differences in political philosophy. Those who favored Satan's plan of communism, joined the Gadianton band and sought through constant aggressive warfare to conquer those who opposed it.

As noted above, the Lord has promised that in these last days, He

> . . . shall cause a great division among the people, and the wicked will he destroy; and he will spare his people, yea, even if it so be that he must destroy the wicked by fire. (2 Ne. 30:10)

Just how He will bring about the division, the scriptures do not say. Obviously it could be done with a famine. Those who have stored provisions could subsist in a famine-stricken area while others could not. But regardless of how it happens, we can rest assured that the division will come and from the conclusions drawn herein, it will occur along political lines as was the case with the Nephites.

The Laws Of Man In The Light Of The Laws Of God

It is rather sobering to reflect that under a government subject to the voice of the people we can, with no more risk, effort or inconvenience than that required to mark a ballot, destroy our freedom and jeopardize our eternal welfare. Merely by yielding to the common disposition to "cover our sins" by legalizing them; "gratifying our pride, our vain ambition" by voting for laws which unjustly provide us with the things of this world and "the honors of men;" and succumbing to the almost universal disposition to exercise unrighteous dominion, we can forfeit those blessings we prize above all others. (D&C 121)

At the opening of the J. Reuben Clark Law School in Provo, Utah, Marion G. Romney, then a member of the first presidency of the Church, delivered an address in which he stated:

> The board of trustees, in establishing this school of law, did so, that there may be an institution in which you, the members of this class, and all those who shall follow you, may 'obtain a knowledge of ...(The) laws of ... Man' in the light of the 'laws of God. (Speech dated August 27, 1973)

It would seem that this should be an objective of every member of the Church and indeed, of every person who desires to preserve freedom by reestablishing the Ten Commandments and the Golden Rule as the law of the land.

WORDS OF PRESIDENT BENSON

I testify that wickedness is rapidly expanding in every segment of our society. (See D&C 1:14-16; 84:49-53.) It is more higly organized, more cleverly disquised, and more powerfully promoted than ever before. Secret combinations lusting for power, gain, and glory are flourishing. A secret combination that seeks to overthrow the freedom of all lands, nations, and countries is increasing its evil influence and control over America and the entire world. [See Ether 8:18-25] (Ezra Taft Benson, *Ensign,* November 1988, p. 87)

XXIX

If Ye Are Not One Ye Are Not Mine

The Responsibilities Of The Salt Of The Earth

It should be a point of the most intense interest to members of the Lord's Church that they are so few in number and yet bear responsibilities of such enormous magnitude. Strange though it may seem, the scriptures indicate that it is common for the Lord to select a small number and place upon them the vital duty of bearing the message of His gospel to the many. He told His disciples among the Jews that they were called to be "the salt of the earth," (Matt. 5:13) and made a similar statement to those He addressed among the Nephites. (3 Ne. 12:13)

The Lord has identified those He has called to be the salt of the earth in this last dispensation as follows:

> When men are called unto mine everlasting gospel, and covenant with an everlasting covenant, they are accounted as the salt of the earth and the savor of men;
>
> They are called to be the savor of men; therefore, if that salt of the earth lose its savor, behold, it is thenceforth good for nothing only to be cast out and trodden under the feet of men. (D&C 101:39-40)

To be counted among that small number who are the covenant people is, of course, a high privilege. But as the foregoing scripture indicates, the penalty for failing to carry out the duties connected therewith is extremely severe. To hold a position and calling so high and important, and then to be accounted so worthless and good for nothing that we are cast out and trodden under foot seems to be the ultimate disgrace. And yet the Lord told the Nephites and Lamanites that this is exactly what would happen to Gentile Church members of this dispensation who failed to repent of the sins He enumerated. (3 Ne. 16:10-15)

THE NEED TO AWAKEN

The first thing which is necessary for Church members to do in discharging their duties as the salt of the earth, is to recognize what those duties are, which, according to the Lord and our modern prophets seems to be particularly urgent.

In his keynote address to Church members in the general conference of April, 1986, President Benson referred to some "awake" passages in the Book of Mormon as he urged us to study that book. One such scripture is found in Ether 8:24 wherein the Lord commands us to "awake to a sense of your awful situation because of this secret combination which shall be among you."

In his statement on communism given in the priesthood session of general conference in April, 1966, President David O. McKay expressed the desire that all Church members would become informed regarding this movement and awaken to the alarming conditions which are rapidly advancing about us.

As Church members we are the only people on the face of the earth who are aware of these warning messages and the predicted tragedy which will come upon this nation if we fail to heed them. This should give us some idea of the responsibility we bear as the salt of the earth. Surely we are good for nothing if we do nothing about them.

UNITY NECESSARY AMONG THOSE CALLED TO BE THE SALT OF THE EARTH

It should be most apparent that the salt of the earth will largely fail in their responsibilities unless they are united. Working separately and alone we can do but little. On the other hand if we join together, miracles are possible. The following scripture should provide much encouragement to those who fear defeat because those called to be the salt of the earth are so few in number:

> Therefore, that we should waste and wear out our lives in bringing to light all the hidden things of darkness, wherein we know them; and they are truly manifest from heaven—
>
> These should then be attended to with great earnestness.
>
> Let no man count them as small things; for there is much which lieth

> in futurity, pertaining to the saints, which depends upon these things.
>
> You know, brethren, that a very large ship is benefited very much by a very small helm in the time of a storm, by being kept workways with the wind and the waves. (D&C 123:13-16)

The following quote from our late prophet, Spencer W. Kimball, seems appropriate here:

> I come to realize more and more as my experience broadens, the vast influence and power that a small minority may wield in this work, in politics, in religion, in social activities, everywhere you go. A small group, united in purpose, with definite goals may greatly influence the great majorities. (*Teachings*, p. 178)

Unity Is Possible Only On The Basis Of Truth

Only by using the word of the Lord as our guide can we ever hope to reach agreement on the goals we should seek and the procedure which should be followed in reaching them. This means that we must cast aside the misleading precepts of men and the wisdom of the world and accept the Lord as our guide, our king, and our lawgiver.

This may be difficult because some are not accustomed to looking to the scriptures for guidance in political matters. However as we have heretofore seen, our political convictions constitute our most deeply held moral and religious convictions. Therefore those scriptures which caution us against hearkening to the precepts of men are especially applicable to our beliefs about the laws of the land. When the following scriptures are read with this thought in mind they may take on new meaning. (2 Ne. 9:28; 28:14; D&C 45:28, 29)

Unity Of Belief Demands Humility

By going to the Lord for guidance on political matters, we thereby demonstrate that humility we must have to become united. However since the sin of pride is so pervasive, and since it is the primary cause of disunity, let us note what the scriptures say must be done to overcome it.

First let us remind ourselves that according to the following oft-quoted scripture, almost all men are afflicted with this sin:

> Behold, there are many called, but few are chosen. And why are they not chosen?
>
> Because their hearts are set so much upon the things of this world, and aspire to the honors of men . . . (D&C 121:4-5)

The first step in overcoming the sin of pride is to recognize that in all probability, we are guilty. We can know for certain that we have not overcome it if we have a spirit of contention. The Lord told the Nephites this:

> . . . And there shall be no disputations among you, as there have hitherto been; neither shall there be disputations among you concerning the points of my doctrine, as there have hitherto been.
>
> For verily, verily I say unto you, he that hath the spirit of contention is not of me, but is of the devil, who is the father of contention, and he stirreth up the hearts of men to contend with anger, one with another. (3 Ne. 11:28-29)

The following scripture gives some specific rules regarding what must be done to overcome pride:

> And whoso knocketh, to him will he open; and the wise, and the learned, and they that are rich, who are puffed up because of their learning, and their wisdom, and their riches—yea, they are they whom he despiseth; and save they shall cast these things away, and consider themselves fools before God, and come down in the depths of humility, he will not open unto them. (2 Ne. 9:42)

The Necessity Of Implicit Faith In God And His Justice

If we have complete faith in the omnipotence, the omniscience and the justice of God, we will realize that when the Lord gives a commandment, we need have no fear regarding the consequences which will flow from obedience thereto. The Lord knows the end from the beginning. He anticipates and makes provision for every event which will occur.

> . . . all things have been done in the wisdom of him who knoweth all things,
>
> . . . men are free according to the flesh; and all things are given them which are expedient unto man. (2 Ne. 2:24, 27)

A failure to exercise faith in God and His justice is a sin as the following scripture indicates:

> And in nothing doth man offend God, or against none is his wrath kindled, save those who confess not his hand in all things, and obey not his commandments. (D&C 59:21)

To obey not the Lord's commandments because we fear that by so doing we might cause injustice or harm to others, would appear to be contrary to this scripture. What we should really concern ourselves with is the justice which will be meted out to us if we fail to follow His commandments. But in deciding what should be done, we should always remember that the Lord has His prophets here on earth and that we should follow their counsel implicitly. The scriptures are most plain that those who do not follow the Lord and His prophets and apostles, will be "cut off from among the people." (D&C 1:14; Joseph Smith 2:40)

WORDS OF EZRA TAFT BENSON

This is a most important lesson for all of us to learn, namely, that the communists use the socialists to pave the way for them wherever possible. This is why communists and socialists are often found supporting each other, collaborating together and fighting for the same goals.

The paramount issue today is freedom against creeping socialism. The well-known British writer, John Strachey, who for many years was an openly avowed communist and who served as Minister of War in the Socialist government in 1950, made this very plain in his book, "The Theory and Practice of Socialism." Said he:

> It is impossible to establish communism as the immediate successor to capitalism. It is accordingly proposed to establish socialism as something which we can put in place of our present decaying capitalism. Hence, communists work for the establishment of socialism as a necessary transition stage on the road to communism.

Now obviously, the worst thing that can happen to a socialist is to have himself openly identified with the work of the communists who are generally feared and despised.

The socialists know they cannot seize property and power by "due process of law" unless they are politically popular, therefore, they try desperately to avoid the taint of the communists and present their program so that it appears "moral," "democratic," "peaceful," and so gradual that the people will not resist it. (Ezra Taft Benson, *The Red Carpet, Socialism, The Royal Road to Communism,* pp. 69-70)

APPENDIX I

Statement concerning the position of the Church on Communism, made by President David O. McKay at the general priesthood session of the 136th Annual Conference of the Church held in the Salt Lake Tabernacle, Saturday, April 9, 1966, at 7:00 pm, read by Robert R. McKay.

In order that there may be no misunderstanding by bishops, stake presidents, and others regarding members of the Church participating in nonchurch meetings to study and become informed on the Constitution of the United States, Communism, etc., I wish to make the following statements that I have been sending out from my office for some time and that have come under question by some stake authorities, bishoprics, and others.

Church members are at perfect liberty to act according to their own consciences in the matter of safeguarding our way of life. They are, of course, encouraged to honor the highest standards of the gospel and to work to preserve their own freedoms. They are free to participate in nonchurch meetings that are held to warn people of the threat of Communism or any other theory or principle that will deprive us of our free agency or individual liberties vouchsafed by the Constitution of the United States.

The Church, out of respect for the rights of all its members to have their political views and loyalties, must maintain the strictest possible neutrality. We have no intention of trying to interfere with the fullest and freest exercise of the political franchise of our members under and within our Constitution, which the Lord declared he established 'by the hands of wise men whom [he] raised up unto this very purpose' (D&C 101:80) and which, as to the principles thereof, the Prophet Joseph Smith, dedicating the Kirtland Temple, prayed should be 'established forever.' (D&C 109:54) The Church does not yield any of its devotion to or convictions about safeguarding the American principles and the establishments of government under federal and state constitutions and the civil rights of men safeguarded by these.

The position of this Church on the subject of Communism has never changed. We consider it the greatest satanical threat to peace, prosperity, and the spread of God's work among men that exists on the face of the earth.

In this connection, we are continually being asked to give our opinion concerning various patriotic groups or individuals who are fighting Communism and speaking up for freedom. Our immediate concern, however, is not with parties, groups, or persons, but with principles. We therefore commend and encourage every person and every group who is sincerely seeking to study Constitutional principles and awaken a sleeping and apathetic people to the alarming conditions that are rapidly advancing about us. We wish all of our citizens throughout the land were participating in some type of organized self-education in order that they could better appreciate what is happening and know what they can do about it.

Supporting the FBI, the police, the congressional committees investigating Communism, and various organizations that are attempting to awaken the people through educational means is a policy we warmly endorse for all our people.

The entire concept and philosophy of Communism is diametrically opposed to everything for which the Church stands—belief in Deity, belief in the dignity and eternal nature of man, and the application of the gospel to efforts for peace in the world. Communism is militantly atheistic and is committed to the destruction of faith wherever it may be found.

The Russian Commissar of Education wrote: 'We must hate Christians and Christianity. Even the best of them must be considered our worst enemies. Christian love is an obstacle to the development of the revolution. Down with love for one's neighbor. What we want is hate. Only then shall we conquer the universe.'

On the other hand, the gospel teaches the existence of God as our Eternal and Heavenly Father and declares: '. . . him only shalt thou serve.' Matt. 4:10)

Communism debases the individual and makes him the enslaved tool of the state, to which he must look for sustenance and religion. Communism destroys man's God-given free agency.

No member of this Church can be true to his faith, nor can any American be loyal to his trust, while lending aid, encouragement, or sympathy to any of these false philosophies; for if he does, they will prove snares to his feet.

Appendix II

Statements By Ezra Taft Benson

We must keep the people informed that collectivism, another word for socialism, is a part of the communist strategy. Communism is essentially socialism. (*This Nation Shall Endure*, p. 90)

We should all be opposed to socialistic-communism, for it is our mortal and spiritual enemy—the greatest evil in the world today. But the reason many liberals don't want the American people to form study groups to really understand and then fight socialistic-communism is that once the American people get the facts, they will begin to realize that much of what these liberals advocate is actually helping the enemy.

The liberals hope you'll believe them when they tell you how anti-communist they are. But they become alarmed if you really inform yourself on the subject of socialistic-communism. For after you inform yourself you might begin to study the liberal voting record. And this study would show you how much the liberals are actually leading America toward socialism itself.

For communism is just another form of socialism, as is fascism. So now you can see the picture. These liberals want you to know how much they are doing for you—with your tax money of course. But they don't want you to realize that the path they are pursuing is socialistic and that socialism is the same as communism in its ultimate effect on our liberties. When you point this out they want to shut you up; they accuse you of maligning them, of casting aspersions, of being political. No matter whether they label their bottle as liberalism, progressivism, or social reform, I know the contents of the bottle is poison to this Republic and I'm going to call it poison.

We do not need to question the motive of these liberals. They could be most sincere. But sincerity or supposed benevolence or even cleverness is not the question. The question is: "Are we going to save this country from the hands of the enemy and the deceived?" (*An Enemy Hath Done This*, p. 43)

Our nation will continue to degenerate unless we read and heed the words of the God of this land, Jesus Christ, and quit building up and upholding secret combinations, . . . (*Ensign*, July 1988, p. 80)

I testify that wickedness is rapidly expanding in every segment of our society. (See D&C 1:14-16; 84:49-53.) It is more highly organized, more cleverly disguised, and more powerfully promoted than ever before. Secret combinations lusting for power, gain, and glory are flourishing. A secret combination that seeks to overthrow the freedom of all lands, nations, and countries is increasing its evil influence and control over America and the entire world. [See Ether 8:18-25] (*Ensign*, November 1988, p. 87)

Now, we have not been using the Book of Mormon as we should. Our homes are not as strong unless we are using it to bring our children to Christ. Our families may be corrupted by worldly trends and teachings unless we know how to use the book to expose and combat falsehoods in socialism, rationalism, etc. . . . The situation in the world will continue to degenerate unless we read and heed the words of God and quit building up and upholding secret combinations, which the Book of Mormon tells us proved the downfall of ancient civilizations. (*Ensign*, January 1988, p. 5)

We cannot afford to minimize the threat of socialism in America. We must be on guard against unsound theories and programs which strike at the very root of all we hold dear. . . Today's Socialists . . . are using the federal government to redistribute wealth in our society—not as a matter of voluntary charity, but as a so-called matter of right. . . Yes, we have traveled a long way down the soul-destroying road of socialism. . . Men . . . ascended to high political offices by promising what was not theirs to give, and citizens voted them into office in hopes of receiving what they had not earned.

I fear for the future when I realize that our once-free institutions—political, economic, educational, and social—have been drifting into the hands of those who favor the welfare state, and who would "centralize all power in the hands of the political apparatus in Washington. This enhancement of political power at the expense of individual rights, so often disguised as 'democracy' or 'freedom' or 'civil rights,' is 'socialism, no matter what name tag it bears." (*Teachings*, 1988, p. 692-693)

I have noted within the Church a difference in discernment, insight, conviction, and spirit between those who know and love the Book of Mormon and those who do not. That Book is a great sifter. (*Ensign*, December 1988, p. 4)

The Book of Mormon brings men to Christ through two basic means. First, it tells in a plain manner of Christ and His gospel. It testifies of His divinity and of the necessity for a Redeemer and the need of our putting trust in Him. . . . Second, the Book of Mormon exposes the enemies of Christ. It confounds false doctrines and lays down contention. (See 2 Ne. 3:12.) It fortifies the humble followers of Christ against the evil designs, strategies, and doctrines of the devil in our day. The type of apostates in the Book of Mormon are similar to the type we have today. God, with his infinite foreknowledge, so molded the Book of Mormon that we might see the error and know how to combat false educational, political, religious, and philosophical concepts of our time. (*Ensign*, January 1988, p. 3)

Two great American Christian civilizations—the Jaredites and the

Nephites—were swept off this land because they did not 'serve the God the land, who is Jesus Christ' (Ether 2:12.) What will become of our civilization? (*Ensign,* November 1987, p. 7)

. . . we as a nation have apostatized in various degrees from different Constitutional principles as proclaimed by the inspired founders. We are fast approaching that moment prophesied by Joseph Smith when he said: 'Even this nation will be on the verge of crumbling to pieces and tumbling to the ground, and when the Constitution is upon the brink of ruin, this people will be the staff upon which the nation shall lean, and they shall bear the Constitution away from the very verge of destruction.' . . . How then can we best befriend the Constitution in this critical hour and secure the blessings of liberty and ensure the protection and guidance of our Father in heaven? First and foremost, we must be righteous. (*Ensign*, November 1987, p. 6)

. . . basic to our understanding of the Constitution is that governments should have only limited power. . . . It cannot claim the power to redistribute money or property nor to force reluctant citizens to perform acts of charity against their will. (*Ensign*, September 1987, p. 8)

The record of the Nephite history just prior to the Savior's visit reveals many parallels to our own day as we anticipate the Savior's second coming. The Nephite civilization had reached great heights. They were prosperous and industrious. They had built many cities with great highways connecting them. They engaged in shipping and trade. They built temples and palaces. But, as so often happens, the people rejected the Lord. Pride became commonplace. Dishonesty and immorality were widespread. Secret combinations flourished because, as Helaman tells us, the Gadianton robbers 'had seduced the more part of the righteous until they had come down to believe in their works and partake of their spoils' (Hel. 6:38) 'The people began to be distinguished by ranks, according to their riches and their chances for learning' (3 Nephi 6:12) And 'Satan had great power, unto the stirring up of the people to do all manner of iniquity, and to the puffing them up with pride, tempting them to seek for power, and authority, and riches and the vain things of the world,' even as today (v. 15).

Mormon noted that the Nephites 'did not sin ignorantly, for they knew the will of God concerning them' (v. 18). (*Ensign*, May 1987, p. 4)

THE CHURCH OF JESUS CHRIST OF LATTER-DAY SAINTS
47 EAST SOUTH TEMPLE STREET
SALT LAKE CITY, UTAH

EZRA TAFT BENSON

April 24, 1967

H. Verlan Andersen
1155 East 930 North
Provo, Utah

Dear Brother Andersen:

I have just read your letter of April 22nd and leave in an hour for Europe, to be gone about four weeks. I am asking my secretary to sign this letter and get it off to you.

May I suggest two things. One, why don't you try preparing a twenty-minute draft of what you think might appropriately be presented to a General Conference. I would then discuss this with the President and also raise the question regarding the Prophet issuing a statement. Meantime, it will be a pleasure to discuss with you a draft which you may have ready when I return and before you submit it to the Era. Why don't you give me a ring sometime after the 24th of May.

I appreciate very much, your scholarship, your spirit, and your desire to be helpful in saving our freedom through alerting the Priesthood to their responsibilities.

Sincerely your friend and brother,

Ezra Taft Benson per SD

Ezra Taft Benson

ETB:sd

Appendix III

Excerpts From The Communist Manifesto

. . . But Communism abolishes eternal truths, it abolishes all religion, and all morality, instead of constituting them on a new basis; it therefore acts in contradiction to all past historical experience. . . .

We have seen above that the first step in the revolution by the working class is to raise the proletariat to the position of ruling class, to win the battle of democracy. . . . These measures will of course be different in different countries.

Nevertheless, in the most advanced countries the following will be pretty generally applicable:

1. Abolition of property in land and application of all rents of land to public purposes.
2. A heavy progressive or graduated income tax.
3. Abolition of all right of inheritance.
4. Confiscation of the property of all emigrants and rebels.
5. Centralization of credit in the hands of the State, by means of a national bank with State capital and an exclusive monopoly.
6. Centralization of the means of communication and transport in the hands of the State.
7. Extension of factories and instruments of production owned by the State, the bringing into cultivation of waste lands, and the improvement of soil generally in accordance with a common plan.
8. Equal liability of all to labor. Establishment of industrial armies, especially for agriculture.
9. Combination of agriculture with manufacturing industries; gradual abolition of the distinction between town and country by a more equable distribution of population over the country.
10. Free education for all children in public schools. Abolition of children's factory labor in its present form. Combination of education with industrial production, etc., etc.

But behold, I say unto you, that little children are redeemed from the foundation of the world through mine Only Begotten;

Wherefore, they cannot sin, for power is not given Satan to tempt little children, until they begin to become accountable before me;

For it is given unto them even as I will, according to mine own pleasure, that great things may be required at the hand of their fathers. (D&C 29:46-48)

APPENDIX IV

TURN THE HEARTS OF THE FATHERS

The purpose of our Father in Heaven in creating His children is that we might become as He is. To become as He is means that we will have eternal life which is eternal joy. The Lord, Jesus Christ told us that we can become as our Eternal Father when He said:

> Be ye therefore perfect, even as your Father which is in heaven is perfect. (Matt. 5:48; see also 3 Ne 12:48)

From this we know that it is possible for us to become as our Heavenly parent because surely the Lord would never give us a commandment which we could not obey. To become as God is means that we will have eternal increase or eternal families, and so our great purpose in life is to prepare ourselves for eternal parenthood. We may do this by obeying God's commandments regarding family duties and obligations. Among these duties is that of going to the temple and being sealed together as husbands and wives and as parents and children. What a blessing it is to live in an age when we have the gospel to teach us what we must do to have eternal life and when temples and the sealing power is on the earth to join us together as eternal families.

In the last chapter of the Old Testament, the Lord speaking through His prophet, Malachi, states this:

> For behold, the day cometh, that shall burn as an oven; and all the proud, yea, and all that do wickedly, shall be stubble: and the day that cometh shall burn them up, saith the Lord of hosts, that it shall leave them neither root nor branch.
>
> Behold, I will send you Elijah the prophet before the coming of the great and dreadful day of the Lord:
>
> And he shall turn the heart of the fathers to the children, and the heart of the children to their fathers, lest I come and smite the earth with a curse. (Mal. 4:1, 5, 6)

On April 3, 1836 the Lord fulfilled this promise when Elijah appeared to Joseph Smith and Oliver Cowdery who related the event in these words:

> After this vision had closed, another great and glorious vision burst upon us; for Elijah the prophet, who was taken to heaven without tasting death, stood before us, and said:
>
> Behold, the time has fully come, which was spoken of by the mouth of Malachi—testifying that he [Elijah] should be sent, before the great and dreadful day of the Lord come—
>
> To turn the hearts of the fathers to the children, and the children to the fathers, lest the whole earth be smitten with a curse—
>
> Therefore, the keys of this dispensation are committed into your hands; and by this ye may know that the great and dreadful day of the Lord is near, even at the doors. (D&C 110:13-16)

Reference to this event appears several times in the scriptures, one of which contains the following commandment:

> Therefore . . . seek diligently to turn the hearts of the children to their fathers, and the hearts of the fathers to the children; . . . lest I come and smite the whole earth with a curse, and all flesh be consumed before me. (D&C 98:16, 17)

We have two compelling reasons then for performing our family duties. One is that we will have eternal families and eternal joy, the other is that we will escape the Lord's punishment which would otherwise come upon us.

Many Church members have turned their hearts to their fathers and performed much vicarious work for them. But herein we desire to discuss the commandment to fathers to turn their hearts to their children. Surely the commandment to turn our hearts to our children deserves as much attention and effort as does the obligation to our ancestors. In what follows, a possible meaning of this requirement is discussed.

The scriptures teach both by precept and example, that when the Lord brings a people to the promised land of the Americas, gives them the gospel and then they fail to bring up their children in light and truth, they are destroyed. Four different times in as many verses, the Lord promises destruction to those who inhabit His promised land and then fail to serve Him. (Ether 2:8-11)

The scriptures provide three dramatic examples that the Lord's decrees of destruction are fulfilled. Only eight adults survived the Noachian flood; two were spared when the Jaredite civilization disappeared, and only one righteous man escaped when the Nephites became extinct. Could these disasters have been avoided had parents turned their hearts to their children and taught them the gospel?

President Ezra Taft Benson, the living prophet of God, has, since assuming this position in late 1985, warned against the sin of pride. He dwelt on this topic in his first general conference address as the prophet in April, 1986, and returned to it again in another conference address delivered in April, 1989. In the latter address he labelled pride as the universal sin, the great vice and the great stumbling block of the Church.

Assuming that pride is now universal as our prophet has stated, we are in terrible danger because unless adults change their ways, their children will grow up to be proud like their parents and our society will disappear as did the Nephites. It appears that there is only one way to prevent this from happening and that is for the fathers to turn their hearts to their children, teach them to retain their humility as they grow to maturity, and become equally as humble as their children in the process. The scriptures are unequivocal in stating that only those who are as humble as a little child can enter the Celestial Kingdom.

In this last dispensation, the Lord has given to parents in Zion a law concerning the teaching of their children, which if not obeyed, will cause them to be moved out of their place. On the other hand, if that law is obeyed, eternal life seems to be assured for both children and their parents.

In what follows an attempt is made to explain some of the scriptures which require parents to turn their hearts to their children.

TURN YOUR HEARTS TO YOUR CHILDREN

In these latter days the Lord has exhorted us to:

> . . . seek diligently to turn the hearts of the children to their fathers, and the hearts of the fathers to the children . . . lest I come and smite the whole earth with a curse, and all flesh be consumed before me. (D&C 98:16, 17; see also Malachi 4:5, 6; 3 Ne. 25:5, 6)

Why would the Lord consume all flesh if we fail to follow this instruction? The Lord's purpose is to bring to pass the immortality and eternal life of man, (Moses 1:39) and this is His greatest gift to man. (D&C 14:7) But eternal life means eternal families, and to have the blessing of an eternal family means we must obey those laws upon which that blessing is predicated. (D&C 130:21, 22; 132:21-25; 88:22)

Therefore when parents cease to perform their family duties and cease to teach their children to do so, the possibility of eternal life ceases and the civilization is destroyed. This is what happened to the antediluvian's, the Jaredites and Nephites.

Among the family laws which must be obeyed to gain eternal life are the following:

1. Marry, multiply and replenish the earth. (Gen. 2:24; D&C 131:2-4)
2. Since no unclean thing can enter heaven, the Lord's laws forbidding adultery and lustful desires must be obeyed. (Ex. 20:14; Matt. 5:27, 28; D&C 42:22, 23)
3. Fathers must support their families. (D&C 75:28; 83:4; 1 Tim. 5:8)
4. Children must respect and obey parents. (Exo. 20:12; Eph. 6:1, 2)
5. Parents must teach their children the gospel. (Moses 6:57-59; D&C 68:25-32)

Parents have been commanded to teach their children to understand the basic doctrines and principles of the gospel when eight years old and if they do not, they have committed a sin which may cause them to be removed out of their place unless they repent. (D&C 68:25-32; 93:38-50) To be removed out of one's place may mean a loss of the right of eternal parenthood.

While we may not know the Lord's reasons for requiring that children be taught to understand the doctrines of the gospel before eight years of age, we do know that during these early years:

1. Satan cannot tempt them and this is the only time in their lives when the Lord provides this opportunity; when lost, it never returns. (D&C 29:39, 46-47)
2. Little children are so humble and pure that if they die prior to the age of accountability, they are saved in the Celestial Kingdom. (D&C 137:10) Being humble, they are more teachable at this age than any other.
3. Being clean and pure, little children can understand spiritual truths better than their parents. (3 Ne. 26:14-16)
4. If children are brought up properly, they will not depart from the right path. (2 Ne. 4:5, 6; Prov. 22:6; 4 Ne. 1:2-18; D&C 45:58)
5. Little children are so completely subject to the control and direction of their parents, that their minds and souls may be trained and molded as the parents determine. This also is a condition which when lost, never returns.

Almost all parents have a personal problem which must be overcome before they can bring up their children in light and truth as the Lord has commanded, and that problem is pride. (D&C 121:34-46; see also 2 Ne. 28:14; Mor. 8:34-38; Ether 4:13-15; D&C 84:54-59) Our living prophet, President Ezra Taft Benson has declared that today the sin of pride is universal, that it is the great vice, and the stumbling block to the Church. (CR, April, 1989)

The situation we face then is this: While little children are humble and ready to enter the Celestial Kingdom, pride among adults is universal. Therefore unless parents repent of their sin and set a proper example, their children will grow up and become proud like other adults. On the other hand the scriptures are unequivocal in stating that parents must become as humble as little children or they cannot enter the kingdom of God. (Matt. 18:1-6; 3 Ne. 11:37-38) Our question then is this: What must we do as parents to become as humble as our little children while at the same time preventing them from becoming as proud as their parents?

THE SCRIPTURES OFFER A PLAIN AND CERTAIN SOLUTION TO THE PROBLEM OF PRIDE

The following scripture states the way by which parents can conquer their own pride while at the same time preventing their little children from falling victim to this universal sin:

> And again, behold I say unto you that he (a man) cannot have faith and hope, save he shall be meek, and lowly of heart.
>
> If so, his faith and hope is vain, for none is acceptable before God, save the meek and lowly in heart; and if a man be meek and lowly in heart, and confesses by the power of the Holy Ghost that Jesus is the Christ, he must needs have charity; for if he have not charity he is nothing; wherefore he must needs have charity. (Moro. 7:43-44)

This statement indicates that without humility, faith is impossible, and without charity, which is the pure love of Christ, humility is not possible. The solution then is to develop a pure love of Christ within ourselves and our little children. The following verse also from Moroni 7, states one way in which this may be done:

> Wherefore, my beloved brethren, pray unto the Father with all the

> energy of heart, that ye may be filled with this love, which he hath bestowed upon all who are true followers of his Son, Jesus Christ; . . . (Moro. 7:48)

If parents and their little children were to earnestly plead with the Father to fill their souls with a love for His Son, and if they were to pray always as commanded, (3 Ne. 18:15, 18) the promise is made that the request will be granted if made with sufficient faith. (3 Ne. 18:20)

A second method of reaching the tree of life and partaking of its fruit which is the pure love of Christ, is by clinging constantly to the iron rod. (1 Ne. Ch. 8, 11, 15) In His great intercessory prayer the Lord said:

> And this is life eternal, that they might know thee the only true God, and Jesus Christ, whom thou has sent. (John 17:3)

It would be difficult if not impossible to love the Lord without knowing Him. But the way to know Him is to study the scriptures which testify of Him. (John 5:39) We are promised that if we will press forward to the end, feasting upon the words of Christ, we will have eternal life. (2 Ne. 31:20; Alma 32:40-43; 37:43-47) Parents who believe, and who teach their children to believe, that the scriptures contain the answers to all of their questions, (2 Ne. 32:3) should have no difficulty clinging to the iron rod. They will go to the word of God to test every belief and to solve every problem.

A Third Way To Learn To Love The Lord Is By Serving Him

The Lord has stated that:

> If ye love me, keep my commandments.

He has also stated that He will separate the sheep from the goats on the basis of the service performed to our fellow men. (Matt. 25:31-46)

The Lord has provided a particular method by which we can serve Him by feeding His sheep and doing so by carrying out a specific stewardship in His Church. This method also keeps us in constant remembrance of our family duties by helping others to do the same. It is through the programs of home and visiting teaching.

INDEX

—D—

—E—

—F—

—G—

—L—

—M—

—N—